Total English

ADVANCED

Teacher's Book with Resource Disc

Will Moreton

Contents

Resource Disc

     Photocopiable class activities and teaching notes

     Photocopiable video activities and answer key

     Progress tests with answer key and audio

     Achievement tests with answer key, audio and audioscripts

     Printable version of Class CD audioscripts and videoscripts

What's new about *New Total English*?

What makes *New Total English* different from – and better than – the first edition? Firstly, don't worry – we haven't thrown the baby out with the bathwater! We haven't changed everything. We've listened to what you said you liked about the first edition and have kept the most popular features. You'll certainly recognise the look, the format and some integral features from the first edition: the Lead-in pages, the easy-to-use lessons, the comprehensive Reference and Review and practice sections, the popular video clips. Changing to the new edition won't mean that you have to get to grips with a completely new course.

Real solutions to real needs

Some things <u>are</u> different, however. We've looked at every aspect of the course and tried to find solutions for some of your real needs. We've improved the flow of many of the lessons in the Students' Book, integrating more Can do statements and making sure that they all have clear 'outcomes'. We've also given more space to important aspects of language learning such as vocabulary, writing and listening. There's a free online Vocabulary Trainer with each level to help learners memorise new words and phrases; a complete Writing bank at the back of the Students' Book, covering different text types and writing sub-skills, as well as new semi-authentic listening extracts to help students gain confidence in dealing with features such as redundancy, hesitation and ungrammatical speech. And, as you'd expect with a new edition, we've given the grammar, vocabulary and pronunciation syllabus a complete overhaul as well as updating much of the content.

New digital components

We've also included new digital components in the course package. The ActiveBook component features the Students' Book pages in digital format and includes integrated audio and video as well as interactive exercises for students to do in class or at home. The ActiveTeach component will help you get the most out of the course with its range of interactive whiteboard software tools and *MyEnglishLab* (Elementary – Upper Intermediate levels) will help students get better results with its range of interactive practice exercises, progress tests and automatic gradebook.

To sum up, we've kept all the best ingredients of the first edition, improved other features and added exciting new digital components to make *New Total English* an even better package. We hope you and your students will continue to enjoy using it.

The *New Total English* author team

Course package

Students' Book with ActiveBook and DVD

The *New Total English* Students' Books with ActiveBook and DVD are divided into 10–12 units that contain approximately 80–120 hours of teaching material. Each unit contains a balanced mix of grammar, vocabulary, pronunciation and skills:

- clear aims and objectives linked to the CEFR (Common European Framework of Reference)
- revised grammar, vocabulary and pronunciation syllabus
- new reading, listening and video material
- new Writing bank with model texts and focus on sub-skills
- revised and extended Pronunciation bank

ActiveBook:

- digital version of Students' Book with interactive activities and integrated audio and video
- video clips can be selected when you use the ActiveBook in your computer, or play it in a DVD player

Students' Book with ActiveBook, DVD and MyEnglishLab

Packaged with the *New Total English* Students' Book with ActiveBook and DVD, *MyEnglishLab* (Elementary–Upper Intermediate levels) provides students with everything they need to make real progress both in class and at home:

MyEnglishLab:

- interactive exercises with feedback
- regular progress and achievement tests
- automatic marking and gradebook

Class CDs

The *New Total English* Class CDs contain all the recorded material from the Students' Books.

Workbook and Audio CD

The *New Total English* Workbooks contain further practice of language areas covered in the corresponding units of the Students' Books:

- extra grammar, vocabulary, skills and pronunciation exercises
- regular Review and Consolidation sections
- audioscripts and accompanying Audio CD
- with and without key versions available

Teacher's Book with Resource Disc

The *New Total English* Teacher's Books provide all the support teachers need to get the most out of the course:

- background notes and instructions on how to exploit each unit
- suggestions for warm-up and extension activities

Resource Disc:

- extensive bank of photocopiable and printable classroom activities
- editable and printable progress and achievement tests
- audio and video scripts

ActiveTeach and DVD

The *New Total English* Teacher's Books will be further enhanced by the ActiveTeach component which features:

- Students' Book in digital format with all the material from the ActiveBook
- all the material from the Resource Disc
- interactive whiteboard software tools
- video clips can be selected when you use the ActiveTeach in your computer, or play it in a DVD player

Vocabulary Trainer

The *New Total English* Vocabulary Trainer is a new online learning tool designed to help students revise and memorise key vocabulary from the course.
Check this exciting new component out on
www.newtotalenglish.vocabtrainer.net

Website

New Total English has its own dedicated website. In addition to background information about the course and authors, the website features teaching tips, downloadable worksheets and links to other useful websites as well as special offers and competitions. Join us online at
www.pearsonELT.com/newtotalenglish

Structure of a Students' Book unit

Each unit of the *New Total English* Students' Books has the same structure:

- **Lead-in page**
  - acts as a springboard into the topic of the unit and engages learners' interest.
  - introduces essential vocabulary related to the topic so that learners start with the same basic grounding.

- **Input lessons**
  - three input lessons, thematically linked, offering interesting angles on the unit topic. Lessons are double-page at lower levels and triple-page at Intermediate and above.
  - each input lesson leads towards a Can do learning objective in line with the CEFR Can do statements.
  - each 90-minute lesson focuses on a specific grammar area and includes vocabulary and skills work.
  - each unit usually contains at least two reading texts, a substantial listening element (including semi-authentic listenings) and pronunciation work.
  - How to... boxes develop students' competence in using language, in line with the CEFR.
  - Lifelong learning boxes offer tips and strategies for developing learners' study skills.

- **Communication page**
  - revises language taught in the previous three lessons in a freer, more communicative context.
  - each communication task practises a range of skills and has a measurable goal or outcome.

- **Vocabulary page (Intermediate and above)**
  - focuses on vocabulary systems and word-building.
  - helps learners to expand and develop their vocabulary.

- **Reference page**
  - summarises the main grammar points covered in each unit and provides a list of key vocabulary.
  - helps learners to catch up if they miss lessons and is an essential revision tool.

- **Review and practice page**
  - provides a range of exercises to consolidate key grammar and vocabulary covered in the unit.
  - can be used to check progress, enabling teachers to identify areas that need further practice.

- **Writing bank**
  - provides models and tips on how to deal with different types of writing (articles, essays and so on).
  - provides guidance on different writing sub-skills such as formality, writing styles and organisation.

- **Pronunciation bank**
  - provides a list of English phonemes, guidance on stress, connected speech and intonation.
  - summarises the pronunciation points covered in each unit of the Students' Book.

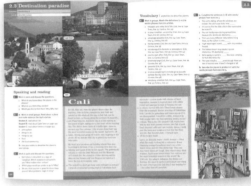

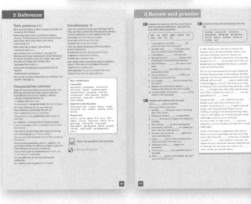

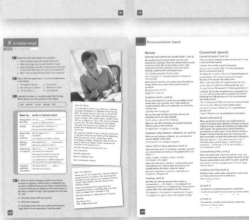

A range of support components help you get the most out of each unit:

- **Students' Book with ActiveBook and DVD**
  - digital version of Students' Book with interactive activites.
  - integrated audio for Students' Book listening activities (including Reference pages and pronunciation activities).
  - wide variety of video clips (including drama, documentary and comedy) which can be selected when you use the ActiveBook in your computer, or play it in a DVD player.
  - interactive video activities.

- **Workbook with Audio CD**
  - consolidation of work covered in the Students' Book.
  - extensive practice of grammar, vocabulary and skills, including pronunciation.
  - regular Review and consolidation sections.
  - can be used in class or for self-study.

- **Students' Book with ActiveBook and MyEnglishLab (Elementary–Upper Intermediate levels)**
  - interactive Workbook with instant feedback and automatic marking.
  - progress and achievement tests with automatic marking and gradebook.

- **Teacher's Book with Resource Disc**
  - provides step-by-step teaching notes including ideas for warmers and extension activities.
  - includes background notes and tips for dealing with particularly difficult language points.
  - Resource Disc features an extensive bank of photocopiable and printable classroom activities as well as editable and printable progress and achievement tests.

- **ActiveTeach**
  - digital version of the Students' Book to be used in class.
  - video clips that can be selected when you use the ActiveTeach in your computer, or play it in a DVD player.
  - all the material from the Teacher's Book Resource Disc.
  - a range of interactive whiteboard software tools.

- **Vocabulary Trainer**
  www.newtotalenglish.vocabtrainer.net
  - new online learning tool designed to help students revise and memorise key vocabulary from each unit of the course.

- **Website**
  www.pearsonELT.com/newtotalenglish
  - features background information about the course and authors as well as teaching tips, downloadable worksheets and links to other useful websites.

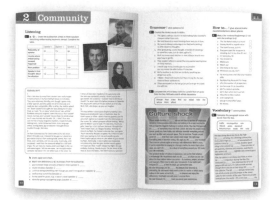

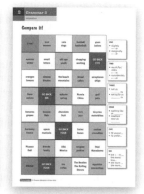

Grammar

New Total English places a lot of emphasis on providing learners with the grammar 'building blocks' they need to communicate confidently. It aims to give learners a thorough foundation in grammar and, at the same time, provides plenty of structured and free practice. Each unit deals with grammar in a broadly similar way:

• Clear presentation and analysis

Each lesson has a clear grammar aim which is stated at the top of the page. Lessons are double-page at lower levels and triple-page at Intermediate and above. New language items are presented in context via reading and/or listening texts and grammar rules are then analysed and explained via the Active grammar boxes, which are a key feature of each lesson. *New Total English* takes a 'guided discovery' approach to grammar and learners are actively invited to think about grammar and work out the rules for themselves.

Active grammar

When using comparatives, if we want to be specific about the degree of difference between two people/things, we use modifiers, e.g. *far*, *nowhere near*, *slightly*.

*I'm **slightly** taller than my brother.*
*The green house is **nowhere near** as beautiful as the red one.*

We can use combined comparisons to describe how a change in one thing causes a change in another.

***The longer** you wait, **the worse** it will be.*

1 A big difference	
2 A little difference	
3 *the* + comparative + *the* + comparative	

• Varied, regular practice

Once learners have grasped the important rules, all new language is then practised in a variety of different ways so that learners are able to use the grammar with confidence. Practice activities include form-based exercises designed to help learners manipulate the new structures as well as more meaningful, personalised practice. Additional grammar practice exercises can be found in the Review and practice sections at the end of each unit as well as in the Workbooks and *MyTotalEnglishLab*. This component, which features the Workbook exercises in digital format, also provides learners with extra guidance, tips and feedback. The Teacher's Book provides a lot of guidance on how to deal with tricky grammar points. It also contains a Resource Disc with an extensive bank of printable and photocopiable classroom grammar activities which are designed to practise the language in freer, more communicative contexts.

• Easily accessible reference material

In addition to the explanations contained in the Active grammar boxes, there is a Reference section at the end of each unit which provides a summary of the grammar rules as well as extra language notes and examples. Audio recordings of the rules and examples are available on the ActiveBook and ActiveTeach components.

Vocabulary

New Total English recognises the central role that vocabulary plays in successful communication. The emphasis is on providing learners with high-frequency, useful vocabulary which is regularly practised and revised. New vocabulary is presented and practised in a variety of different ways.

• Lead-in pages

Each unit starts with a Lead-in page which provides a springboard into the topic of each unit. Featuring a variety of attractive picture prompts and related exercises, the Lead-in pages are designed to help teachers elicit vocabulary that learners already know as well as pre-teach essential vocabulary for the rest of the unit.

• Topic-based vocabulary

Each unit focuses on useful vocabulary relating to the topic of the lessons as well as vocabulary arising from the listening and reading texts. Items are generally presented in context and practised through a variety of exercises.

Vocabulary | achievement

 a Work in pairs. Find the words/expressions (1–8) in the articles and try to work out the meaning.

1 head (straight for the top)
2 pursue (a dream)
3 deal with (chauvinism)
4 face (barriers)
5 believe in (what you can achieve)
6 have the potential (to do something)
7 persevere (with something)
8 keep pushing someone (to do something)

Additional vocabulary practice is provided in the Review and practice sections of the Students' Book and in the practice exercises in the Workbook. Photocopiable vocabulary activities are also available on the ActiveTeach and on the Resource Disc which accompanies the Teacher's Book.

• Vocabulary pages (Intermediate and above)

At the lower levels there is a lot of emphasis on building learners' knowledge of high-frequency words and phrases as well as common lexical sets. Learners are introduced to collocation work at a very early stage and from Intermediate level onwards, there is a greater emphasis on vocabulary systems and word-building.

• Vocabulary Trainer

Each level of *New Total English* is accompanied by a Vocabulary Trainer. This unique online learning tool focuses on the key vocabulary in each unit and helps learners memorise new words and phrases.

Speaking

The key aim for most learners is spoken fluency. However, most learners find it difficult to talk about topics which hold no interest for them and many cannot express themselves easily without support. *New Total English* develops spoken fluency in a number of ways – by giving learners discussion topics they want to talk about; by setting up situations where they are motivated to communicate in order to complete a specific task; by providing clear models and examples of how to structure discourse and by encouraging them, wherever possible, to express their own ideas and opinions.

• Fresh angles on familiar topics

Topics in *New Total English* have been chosen for their intrinsic interest and relevance. Obscure topics, i.e. those which are only likely to appeal to a minority audience, have been avoided and discussion questions have been deliberately chosen to encourage learners to draw on their own lives and experience. Inevitably, many of the topics have been covered in other ELT coursebooks but wherever possible, we have tried to find a fresh angle on them.

• Structured speaking activities

Many of the lessons in *New Total English* culminate in a structured final speaking activity in the form of a survey, roleplay, etc. Learners are given time to prepare what they are going to say and prompts to help them. The activities often involve pair and group work to maximise learners' opportunities to speak in class. Many of the structured speaking activities are linked to the CEFR Can do statements.

• How to... boxes

There are regular How to... boxes throughout the course which focus on the words and expressions learners need to carry out specific functions, e.g. how to express priorities.

How to... express priorities

Saying it's very important	My (1) _____ priority is ... The essential thing for me is ... This is (2) _____ vital! I couldn't (3) _____ without ...
Saying it's not important	I'm not (4) _____ bothered/concerned (5) _____ this. This isn't a major priority. I (6) _____ do without ...

• Communication pages

Communication pages feature at the end of each unit and engage learners in a variety of problem-solving tasks and activities. These give learners practice in a number of different skills including speaking.

• Photocopiable class activities

The photocopiable activities on the ActiveTeach and on the Resource Disc are also specifically designed to promote speaking practice.

Pronunciation

New Total English pays particular attention to pronunciation, which is integrated into lessons which present new language. The pronunciation syllabus includes word and sentence stress, intonation and connected speech. The Pronunciation bank at the back of the Students' Books provides a summary of all pronunciation points in the book as well as a list of English phonemes, guidance on intonation and weak forms. The ActiveTeach includes audio to accompany the Pronunciation bank. There is additional pronunciation practice in the Workbooks and Workbook Audio CD.

Listening

Listening is one of the most difficult skills to master and *New Total English* places particular emphasis on developing learners' confidence in this area. Listening texts include short scripted dialogues as well as longer, unscripted semi-authentic listenings. There is additional listening practice in the Workbooks and the video clips on the ActiveBook and ActiveTeach components further enhance learners' confidence in understanding the spoken word.

• Scripted listening activities

Scripted listening activities include short dialogues as well as longer extracts including conversations, interviews and stories. There are lots of simple 'Listen and check your answer' exercises as well as longer, more challenging extracts where learners have to listen for specific information.

• Semi-authentic listening activities

As well as the more traditional scripted listening activities, *New Total English* also includes a range of semi-authentic listening texts, i.e. recordings of one or more people speaking in an unprepared, unscripted way, although they are aware of the relevant level and therefore have adapted their own language to a certain extent accordingly. Learners benefit from listening to a semi-authentic recording because the spontaneity of spoken English means that it is full of false starts, hesitations, redundancy and 'ungrammatical' sentences. Learners need to be aware of these features and they need to develop confidence in dealing with them in order to cope with listening in the 'real world'.

• Video clips

New Total English provides a video clip to accompany each unit of the Students' Book. The videos feature a range of authentic material from a variety of different sources including short films and clips from TV documentaries and drama. The video clips expose learners to real English and are designed to motivate learners to 'raise their game' in terms of developing their listening skills.

To make the material more accessible to learners, photocopiable activities for each video clip are available on the ActiveTeach and on the Resource Disc. There are additional interactive video exercises on the ActiveBook and ActiveTeach which students can complete in class or at home.

The video clips are available on the ActiveBook which accompanies each Students' Book and on the ActiveTeach. You can select the video clips when you use the discs in your computer, or you can play them in a DVD player.

Teaching approaches

Reading

Many learners need to be able to read texts in English – for their studies, for work or simply for pleasure – and *New Total English* recognises that reading is an extremely important skill that can have a beneficial effect on all aspects of language learning including vocabulary, spelling and writing.

New Total English encourages learners to read as much as possible – in most units there are at least two substantial reading texts – and care has been taken to introduce students to as wide a range of text types as possible, from simple forms and advertisements to short texts from newspapers and magazines.

Reading texts are accompanied by a range of activities that are designed to check comprehension as well as develop key reading skills such as reading for gist, reading for specific information, guessing the meaning of words from the context and so on.

• Choice of texts

As with the listening material in *New Total English*, texts have been chosen for their intrinsic interest as well as for their usefulness in providing a vehicle for the particular grammar and vocabulary points in focus. Many of the texts have been adapted from authentic, real-life sources such as magazines and websites, and where texts have been adapted or graded, every effort has been made to remain faithful to the orignal text type in terms of content and style.

• Exploitation of texts

Each reading text in *New Total English* is accompanied by a number of exploitation exercises that have been carefully selected to develop learners' reading skills. Activities include comprehension and vocabulary work as well as practice in dealing with different reading sub-skills such as reading for gist. There are also a number of jigsaw readings where learners work together and share information.

Speaking and reading

1 Work in pairs and discuss the questions.

1 What do you know about the places in the photos?

2 What do you think they are like?

3 Would you like to visit them? Why/Why not?

2 a Work in small groups. Read about a place and make notes on the topics below.

Student A: read about Cali.

Student B: read about Cape Town on page 149.

Student C: read about Corsica on page 153.

- atmosphere
- things to do
- things to see
- food
- the local community

b Use your notes to describe the place to your group.

• Length and complexity

The length and complexity of the reading texts in *New Total English* get more challenging as the course progresses. At lower levels, the texts are very short and the emphasis is on training learners to read for specific information. At higher levels, learners are introduced to a a greater range and variety text types and more emphasis is placed on textual analysis.

Writing

In these days of electronic media, it is easy to forget that writing is not simply speech written down – effective writing has all sorts of conventions that differ from speech and that are necessary to learn in one's own language as well as in a foreign language.

New Total English pays particular attention to the important skill of writing. One of the most important new features of the revised edition is the Writing bank at the back of each Students' Book which contains 10–12 lessons that focus on different types of writing – emails, blogs, formal and informal letters and so on. Each lesson also provides additional advice and guidance on different writing sub-skills such as formality, connotation and paragraph construction.

• Model text types

Each Writing bank lesson has a Can do statement which refers to the written output that students complete at the end of the lesson. The lesson usually starts with a warmer that engages students in the topic. Learners then go on to focus on a model of the text type and in most cases, there is some comprehension work to ensure that students are familiar with the content before they start working on the format and related sub-skills. The lesson always finishes with a contextualised written output.

• Writing sub-skills

One of the most important aspects of the Writing bank is that it examines the sub-skills of writing in detail. This is important as it helps learners to build on and develop their writing skills, rather than simply providing practice in writing. Among the sub-skills covered are punctuation, grammatical cohesion, paragraphing and features such as varying the vocabulary used to both enhance interest and ensure lexical cohesion.

• How to... boxes

How to... boxes are a particular feature of the Writing bank. They usually focus on a particular sub-skill of writing and in some cases on written conventions, such as email or letter layout, appropriate formality of language for the text type or order of presentation of the content (such as in a review).

How to... write persuasively

State your position	*I will here argue that ..., the key question is ..., in essence, ... the fact is ...*
give examples or use lists to illustrate a point	*for example, ...; one example of this is ...*
anticipate counter-arguments	*some might say... , the counter-argument is..., it has been argued that ... (but ...)*
use hedging devices (cautious language to sound less direct)	*perhaps, it can be argued, apparently, tend to, may/ might/could, generally*

Learner training

New Total English places a strong emphasis on learner training and good study habits are encouraged and developed via the Lifelong learning boxes which are featured in many lessons. The Lifelong learning boxes provide useful tips and suggestions on how to continue learning outside the classroom.

In your own words

! When learning new words it can be useful to keep a note of synonyms.

Using synonyms can help us to:

1 avoid repeating a word we have just used.
2 make what we say and write more interesting and memorable.
3 be more specific about the things we are describing.

Lifelong learning

Revision and testing

There are plenty of opportunities for revision in *New Total English* and language is constantly recycled throughout the course. At the end of every unit, there are special Review and practice pages which take the form of mini-progress checks, enabling learners to identify areas where they might need further practice. Interactive versions of the activities on these pages are available on the ActiveBook and ActiveTeach. The Workbook and accompanying Audio CD provide further practice in grammar, vocabulary and skills covered in the corresponding Students' Book. The Workbook is available in with key and without key versions.

For learners at Elementary–Upper Intermediate levels who are really serious about making rapid progress in English, *MyEnglishLab* provides the perfect solution. This exciting component features the Workbook exercises in digital format as well as tips and feedback on common errors.

Regular progress and achievement tests are provided on the ActiveTeach, Resource Disc and *MyEnglishLab*. *MyEnglishLab* also includes automatic marking and a gradebook.

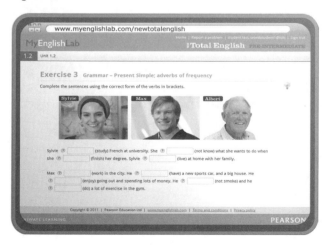

New Total English and exams

The table below shows how the different levels of *New Total English* relate to the University of Cambridge ESOL main suite examinations in terms of the language taught and the topics covered.

Starter	Builds foundation for KET
Elementary	Useful for KET
Pre-Intermediate	Useful for PET
Intermediate	Useful for FCE
Upper Intermediate	Useful for FCE
Advanced	**Useful for CAE**

While *New Total English* is not an examination preparation course, a student who has, for example, completed the Advanced level would have sufficient language to attempt the Cambridge ESOL CAE (Advanced Certificate in English) examination. Many of the exercises in the *New Total English* Students' Books and other components are similar in format to those found in the Cambridge ESOL main suite examinations, but specific training is required for all EFL examinations and we would strongly recommend this.

New Total English and the CEFR

New Total English is correlated to the CEFR (Common European Framework of Reference). Please see the *New Total English* website: **www.pearsonELT.com/newtotalenglish** for details of CEFR Can do statements for each level of the course.

CEFR	
A1	Starter
A2	Elementary
B1	Pre-intermediate
B1+	Intermediate
B2	Upper Intermediate
C1	**Advanced**

Students' Book contents

UNIT		Can do	Grammar
Do you know ...? p 6			
1 **Challenges** p 7–20	1.1 Polyglots	discuss your language-learning experiences	verbs/adjectives/nouns with prepositions
	1.2 Famous firsts	say how much you know/don't know about things	passives: distancing
	1.3 Burning ambitions	talk about your achievements	perfect aspect
	Vocabulary p 17 Communication p 18 Writing bank p 155	prefixes respond in detail to a questionnaire write a promotional leaflet	
2 **Communities** p 21–34	2.1 My community	give advice/make recommendations about places	verb patterns (1)
	2.2 It's a wiki wiki world	distinguish between, and use, features of formal and informal language	comparatives (review)
	2.3 Destination paradise	describe a place	introductory *it*
	Vocabulary p 31 Communication p 32 Writing bank p 156	phrasal verbs present ideas clearly in an informal context write a formal email	
3 **Tales** p 35–48	3.1 Famous hoaxes	tell an anecdote	narrative tenses review
	3.2 A good read	describe a person in detail	
	3.3 Jokers	tell a humorous story	participle clauses
	Vocabulary p 45 Communication p 46 Writing bank p 157	metaphors tell an extended story write a detailed narrative	
4 **Progress** p 49–62	4.1 Superpowers	describe the chances of something happening	future probability
	4.2 Thinking ahead	talk about plans and arrangements	future forms (review)
	4.3 Great expectations	take detailed and accurate notes	inversion
	Vocabulary p 59 Communication p 60 Writing bank p 158	two-part expressions present and argue a case for something write a detailed article	
5 **Fortunes** p 63–76	5.1 A new leaf	talk about professional relationships	emphasis
	5.2 Rags and riches	discuss financial decisions/regrets	conditional sentences
	5.3 In good company	express priorities	sentence adverbials
	Vocabulary p 73 Communication p 74 Writing bank p 159	idioms (1) negotiate write a persuasive piece	

Students' Book contents

UNIT		Can do	Grammar
6 **Power** p 77–90	6.1 Images of power	describe an important building/structure	articles
	6.2 Kid power	take detailed notes from fluent connected speech	*whatever, whoever, whenever,* etc.
	6.3 Charisma	write an autobiographical statement	link words of time and contrast
	Vocabulary p 87 **Communication** p 88 **Writing bank** p 160	idioms (2) argue your case write about your personal history	
7 **Nature** p 91–104	7.1 Animal instinct	explain procedures	relative clauses
	7.2 Going to extremes	make inferences based on extended prose	verb patterns (2)
	7.3 Perfect pets?	write an advert for an object	*as ... as* and describing quantity
	Vocabulary p 101 **Communication** p 102 **Writing bank** p 161	suffixes develop and justify your ideas write an advertisement	
8 **Issues** p 105–118	8.1 A better future	stall for time when asked a difficult question	reported speech
	8.2 Idlers and strivers	discuss lifestyle in detail	the continuous form
	8.3 Everyday issues	explain everyday problems	fronting
	Vocabulary p 115 **Communication** p 116 **Writing bank** p 162	academic English present different points of view write an essay that describes cause and effect	
9 **Vision** p 119–132	9.1 Ahead of their time	express a degree of certainty	dependent prepositions
	9.2 I know what I like	use colloquial expressions to explain your tastes	discourse markers
	9.3 The bigger picture	respond to hypothetical questions	unreal past
	Vocabulary p 129 **Communication** p 130 **Writing bank** p 163	commonly confused words present a proposal write a detailed proposal	
10 **Feelings** p 133–146	10.1 Feeling lucky?	discuss how feelings affect you	modals (and verbs with similar meanings)
	10.2 What does it feel like?	make guesses about imaginary situations	modal verbs of deduction (present and past)
	10.3 Looking back	describe a childhood memory	uses of *would*
	Vocabulary p 143 **Communication** p 144 **Writing bank** p 164	phrasal verbs and particles express strong feelings write a personal anecdote	

Communication activities p 147–154   **Writing bank** p 155–164   **Pronunciation bank** p 165–166

14

15

1 Challenges

Overview

Lead-in	**Vocabulary:** Challenges
1.1	**Can do:** Discuss your language-learning experiences **Grammar:** Verbs/adjectives/nouns with prepositions **Vocabulary:** Learning languages **Reading:** Great language learners **Listening:** Language learning
1.2	**Can do:** Say how much you know/don't know about things **Grammar:** Passives: distancing **Vocabulary:** Knowledge **Speaking and pronunciation:** **How to...** say how much you know/don't know Word stress (1) **Listening:** Who did it first? **Reading:** News headlines
1.3	**Can do:** Talk about your achievements **Grammar:** Perfect aspect **Vocabulary:** Achievement **Speaking and pronunciation:** **How to...** talk about an achievement **Reading:** Ambitious people **Listening:** Challenging activities
Vocabulary	Prefixes
Communication	Respond in detail to a questionnaire
Writing bank	Write a promotional leaflet **How to...** write a promotional leaflet/promote something
Extra resources	ActiveTeach and ActiveBook

CEFR Can do objectives
1.1 Discuss your language-learning experiences
1.2 Say how much you know/don't know about things
1.3 Talk about your achievements
Communication Respond in detail to a questionnaire
Writing bank Write a promotional leaflet

CEFR Portfolio ideas
a) Think about your best and worst experiences of learning English or another foreign language. Discuss your experiences with others.
b) How has your life changed because you can speak English well? Write about your achievements in a short article.
c) Write ten quiz questions about different topics. Try the quiz with other people.
d) Prepare a website for a business which you know well. Explain the services offered by the business or the items they sell. Think about the questions that customers will ask. Make them feel confident about using the business.

Lead-in

OPTIONAL WARMER

Write the word *challenge* on the board. In pairs, Ss write a definition of the word. Ss read out their definitions to the rest of the class. Ss then decide, as a class, which of the definitions is the best. Write the following questions on the board for the Ss to discuss in pairs:
1 *What challenges did you face as a child/teenager?*
2 *What challenges do you face now as an adult?*
3 *What was the last challenge you faced? Were you successful?*
Get feedback from different pairs.

1 ▶ Focus Ss' attention on the photos. In pairs, Ss discuss the different challenges illustrated in each one. Ss can then tell their partners if they have ever faced challenges like the ones shown and if these are the types of challenges they are likely to face in the future. Get feedback from the whole class.

2 ▶ Ss match sentence beginnings 1–8 to endings a–h. Let them compare with a partner. Check Ss' answers as a class and make sure that Ss understand the meaning of the underlined phrases.

Answers					
1	c	4	e	7	d
2	f	5	a	8	b
3	g	6	h		

3 ▶ Ask Ss to discuss the questions in groups of three or four. Encourage Ss to use the phrases from exercise 2 where possible. Monitor the conversations carefully for errors. Get feedback from the whole class and write any errors the Ss have made on the board. Ask different Ss to correct the errors. Finally, focus Ss' attention on any interesting language they used in the conversation, and congratulate them on its use.

EXTEND THE LEAD-IN

Focus Ss' attention on the four photos again. In pairs, Ss rank the challenges that the photos illustrate in order of difficulty. Ask Ss to work with a different student so that they are working with a new partner. Ss explain the order they have chosen to their new partners, giving reasons. Get feedback from various Ss, then get the whole class to try and decide on an order. This may start a debate between Ss as to whether a physical, mental or emotional challenge is the most difficult. If such a discussion starts, do not push for all Ss to agree on an order.

1.1 Polyglots

In this lesson, Ss read a text about famous polyglots. They go on to look at vocabulary from a text about learning languages. They listen to a person talking about his experiences as a language learner. Ss then look at prepositions which collocate with different verbs, nouns and adjectives.

OPTIONAL WARMER

In the previous lesson, or for homework prior to the lesson, ask Ss to do some research either using the Internet or an encyclopaedia. The topic is languages around the world. Ss find interesting facts about, for example, which language is spoken by the most/least people, the language spoken in an obscure country, etc. Ss bring their facts to the next class, and in pairs, create a quiz from their facts. Ss ask another pair their quiz questions and note the score. Get feedback from the whole class by asking which pair got the highest score and which quiz was the most difficult.

Reading

A polyglot is a person who has a high degree of proficiency in several languages. For different reasons, it can be very difficult to calculate accurately how many languages a person speaks. Perhaps most importantly, it is very difficult to define what it actually means to speak a language. For example, a four-year-old Spanish girl would usually be considered able to speak Spanish fluently, but may not have as accurate a command of the subjunctive as a foreign student of the language. There have been many famous people who have been credited with being polyglots. James Joyce, the author of *Ulysses*, reputedly spoke 13 languages, including Danish, Dutch, French and Irish. J.R.R. Tolkien, the author of *The Lord of the Rings*, apparently also knew 13 languages. Pope John Paul II learned as many as 11 languages in his lifetime.

---

1 ▶ Ask Ss to discuss questions 1–4 in pairs or small groups. Get feedback and discuss Ss' ideas as a class.

2a ▶ Focus Ss' attention on questions 1–6. Ss read through the questions first, then read the article and answer the questions. Tell Ss not to worry about any words or expressions they don't know, as you will deal with any difficult vocabulary later.

b ▶ Ss compare their answers with a partner. Check the answers, and the paragraphs they are found in, with the class.

Suggested answers
1   He mingled with the international community on a trip to Russia.
2   He came from a multilingual family. His father was also a linguist.
3   They have a talent similar to that of a musician.

---

4   It can be easy if you already know related language.
5   'Garbling' languages (getting them confused). They may start speaking in one language and accidentally drift into another language.
6   Bonuses: he has appeared on television, and was able to help the police to identify the nationality of a man. Problems: he was suspected of being a terrorist because he spoke Chinese and Russian.

▶ Ask Ss if there are any words or phrases from the text that they don't understand. Encourage Ss to answer each others' questions or consult a dictionary before you explain the vocabulary to the class.

3 ▶ Focus Ss' attention on the questions. Ss discuss the questions in pairs or small groups. Get feedback from various Ss and discuss the Ss' ideas with the whole class. Finally, write any errors from the Ss' discussions in exercises 1 and 2 on the board. Look at the errors with the class and encourage different Ss to correct them. Focus Ss' attention to any interesting language that they have used and praise them on its use.

Vocabulary | learning languages

4 ▶ Ss cover definitions a–h. In pairs, Ss discuss the meaning of words and expressions 1–8. They can look back at the article if necessary and try to work out the meaning from the context. Ss then uncover definitions a–h and match them to the words and expressions. Get Ss to compare their answers with another pair. Check the answers with the whole class.

Answers

1	e	4	h	7	a
2	b	5	f	8	c
3	g	6	d		

5a ▶ Ss use the words and expressions from exercise 4 to complete sentences 1–8. Check the answers with the whole class.

Answers
1   It's easy to <u>let</u> foreign languages <u>slide</u> if you don't use them regularly.
2   In many countries, people can understand the standard form of their language and also a local <u>dialect</u>.
3   The best way to <u>pick up</u> new vocabulary is by reading a lot.
4   It may be impossible to <u>master</u> a foreign language completely.
5   For most students, more than ten new words per lesson equals <u>information overload</u>.
6   Many language learners find that native speakers speak <u>unintelligibly</u> – they use lots of idioms and colloquial expressions.
7   When babies <u>babble</u>, they are imitating adult language.
8   If you know three or more languages, you're more likely to <u>garble</u> your words.

---

b ▶ Ss tick the sentences that they agree with. Ss compare their ideas with a partner. Get feedback from the different pairs and discuss the sentences with the whole class.

Listening

6a ▶ 🔵 1.02 Focus Ss on questions 1–5. Now play the recording. Ss listen to Mark Spina talking about his experiences as a language learner, and make notes on each of the questions.

b ▶ Play the recording again. Ss compare their answers with a partner.

Answers
1 seven
2 classes, travel (for example, he spent a lot of time in Russia) and private study
3 memory training, watching films in their original language, sticking lists of words around the house
4 He loves languages.
5 Occasionally it gets confusing. He's speaking in one language and suddenly a word from another language slips out.

7 ▶ Ss discuss if they have any similar experiences of language learning to Mark Spina.

Grammar | verbs/adjectives/nouns with prepositions

8a ▶ Focus Ss on the Active grammar box. Ss underline the preposition in examples 1–5. Ss then decide what type of word each preposition follows (a verb, an adjective or a noun). Point out that there is sometimes more than one preposition in each example.

Active grammar
1 succeeded <u>in</u> (verb)
2 stems <u>from</u> (verb); joy <u>of</u> (noun)
3 benefited <u>from</u> (verb)
4 nervous <u>about</u> (adjective)
5 difficult <u>to</u> (adjective); distinguish <u>between</u> (verb)

b ▶ Focus Ss on rules A and B in the Active grammar box. Ss answer the questions and then compare their answers with a partner. Check answers with the whole class. Then draw Ss' attention to the Reference on page 19. Give Ss time to read through the section relating to this language point. Answer any questions that might arise. Alternatively, Ss could read this for homework.

Active grammar

A
1 learning Swedish, Sanskrit and Persian
2 the joy of solving the puzzle
3 the fact that he came from a multilingual family
4 garbling their languages
5 distinguish between related languages

B
sentences 1 and 4

9a ▶ Organise Ss into groups of three or four. In their groups, Ss complete sentences 1–10 with the correct prepositions from the box. Tell Ss that if there are any expressions they haven't seen before they can check them in their dictionaries. Check answers with the whole class.

Answers
1	in	6	from
2	for	7	to
3	from	8	about
4	in	9	about
5	with	10	from

b ▶ In pairs, Ss match questions 1–10 from exercise 9a to possible answers a–j. Ss compare their answers with another pair. Check answers with the whole class.

Answers
1	c	6	a
2	f	7	d
3	i	8	b
4	h	9	j
5	e	10	g

Speaking

10a ▶ Ss work in pairs to discuss questions 1–10 from exercise 9a and the suggested answers from exercise 9b. They decide if the answers are true for them or not, explaining why/why not. Monitor the conversations and take note of any important errors.

b ▶ Get feedback and ask various Ss to tell the class what they have found out about their partners. Write any important errors you have heard on the board and ask different Ss to correct them.

> **OPTIONAL EXTENSION**
>
> Ask Ss to suggest five methods they think are the best to improve their level of English. Ss compare their ideas with a partner and explain why they think the methods they have chosen are the best. Ss then compare ideas with another pair. Get feedback from different pairs and discuss as a class which of the methods are the most practical and why.

1.2 Famous firsts

In this lesson, Ss look at expressions for saying how much they know/don't know about things. Ss do a quiz about the first people to do important things, and look at the grammar of passives. They listen to some news headlines before going on to write a news bulletin.

> **OPTIONAL WARMER**
>
> Make sure that Ss are familiar with the concept of a 'famous first', giving examples if necessary. Ss decide what they consider to be the most important 'famous first' in history. Ask Ss to work in groups of four to share their ideas and justify their choices. Each group should try to reach agreement about what the most important 'famous first' is. Re-group Ss into new groups of four to share their ideas with three Ss from different groups. Get feedback and ask the class to try to agree on the three most important 'famous firsts' in history.

Vocabulary | knowledge

1 ▶ Ss choose the correct words in sentences 1–12. Ss compare answers with a partner. Check answers with the class.

Answers			
1	a clue	7	by
2	head	8	out
3	I don't know	9	next
4	heard	10	idea
5	hand	11	certain
6	sure	12	positive

2a ▶ Ss put the underlined expressions from exercise 1 into the correct section of the How to... box. Ss compare their answers with a partner. Check answers with the whole class.

Answers	
I know	**I don't know**
I'm pretty sure	I haven't a clue
I know it like the back of my hand	I don't know off the top of my head
I know it by heart	I don't know offhand
I know it inside out	I've never heard of him
I'm fairly certain it is	I know next to nothing about it
I'm positive it is	I haven't the faintest idea

b ▶ In pairs Ss discuss the questions. Get feedback from the whole class.

> **Suggested answers**
> *I'm pretty sure* means 'I'm quite certain'.
> *I don't know off the top of my head* and *I don't know offhand* are similar. They mean 'I can't tell you the answer now (without looking for the relevant information)'.
> We use *I've never heard of ...* when we don't recognise the name of the thing mentioned (it could be a person, an object, a place, etc.).
> We use *next to nothing* when we recognise the name of the subject, but know almost nothing about it/him/her. We use this expression in response to a 'What do you know about ...?' question, or in the expression 'I know next to nothing about it.'
> *I know it like the back of my hand* is often used to talk about a place, while *I know it inside out* is often used to talk about a subject. *I know it by heart* is used for something we have memorised, perhaps a poem or a speech.
> The strongest are: *I know it like the back of my hand, I know it by heart, I know it inside out, I haven't a clue, I haven't the faintest idea.*
> The expressions with a similar meaning are: *I know it like the back of my hand, I know it by heart* and *I know it inside out*. They mean 'I know it extremely well'.

Speaking

3 ▶ Ss ask a partner how much they know or don't know about the quiz questions. To encourage Ss to use the language in the How to... box, tell Ss that each time they use an expression, they should put a tick next to it. Monitor the conversations for use of the expressions. Get feedback from the whole class and discuss which of the expressions they used when answering the quiz. Don't confirm any answers about the quiz at this point.

> **OPTIONAL EXTENSION**
> Ask Ss to think about what they know or don't know about other Ss in the class. Ss write down one thing they think they know and one thing they don't know about five other Ss in the class. Ss then mingle and tell these Ss how much they know or don't know using the expressions from the How to... box.

Listening

4a ▶ 🌐 1.03 Explain to Ss that they are going to listen to extracts from a radio programme to check their answers to the quiz. Play the recording. Ss listen and check.

> The first woman to sail solo around the world was Krystyna Chojnowska-Liskiewicz, in 1976. She completed the journey in 401 days. Three years later, Naomi James sailed around the world in 272 days via Cape Horn.

> **Answers**
> 1a) Alberto Santos Dumont or b) the Wright brothers
> 2b) Alexander Graham Bell or c) Antonio Meucci
> 3a) Robert Peary or perhaps b) Frederick Cook
> 4a) Edison
> 5b) Uruguay
> 6b) New Zealand
> 7c) Naomi James
> 8c) Greece

b ▶ Ss discuss the questions in pairs. Monitor conversations and take note of errors. Get feedback and discuss Ss' ideas with the whole class. Finally, write errors you took note of earlier on the board. Ask different Ss to correct the errors.

> **Answers**
> Photo 1: the first person to reach the North Pole
> Photo 2: the first woman to sail solo around the world via Cape Horn
> Photo 3: the first country which allowed women to vote
> Photo 4: the first football World Cup

Grammar | passives: distancing

> **OPTIONAL GRAMMAR LEAD-IN**
> Ask Ss to share with a partner what they can remember about Ziad Fazah from the article on pages 8–9. Get feedback from various Ss, then write the following sentence on the board. *People from different countries tested his linguistic abilities on TV programmes.* Under this sentence write: *His linguistic abilities ...* Ask the class to complete the second sentence so that it has the same meaning as the first sentence. If Ss cannot produce the correct answer, write it on the board: *His linguistic abilities were tested by people from different countries.* Ask Ss what the difference between the two sentences is (sentence 1 is active, sentence 2 is passive). In pairs, Ss discuss how the passive is formed and why it is used in English. Focus Ss' attention on the use of *by* to include the agent, or 'doer', in a passive sentence.

5a ▶ Focus Ss on the Active grammar box and give them time to read through and underline the passives.

> **Active grammar**
> 1 Santos Dumont was widely believed to have flown the first plane.
> 2 He's said to be the first person to have owned a flying machine.
> 3 It's commonly assumed that Bell invented the telephone.
> 4 In 2003, files were discovered which suggest that Philipp Reis had invented the phone.
> 5 The cheering of the crowd is said to have been the loudest noise ever heard in Uruguay.
> 6 It is often thought that rugby and sheep are the main claims to fame for New Zealand.

b ▶ Focus Ss on rules A–C in the Active grammar box and ask them to decide whether each is true or false.

> **Active grammar**
> A   T
> B   F
> C   T

c ▶ In pairs, Ss discuss the question in relation to examples 1–6 in the Active grammar box. Then, refer Ss to the Reference on page 19. Give Ss time to read through the notes.

> **Active grammar**
>
> The passive is used in these examples to distance the speaker from the statements made. They are not the speaker's own opinion, and in some cases, it is not 100% certain that the information is correct.

6 ▶ In pairs, Ss complete sentences 1–8. Make sure that students use the verbs in brackets. Ss compare answers with another pair. Check answers with the whole class and write the correct sentences on the board.

> **Answers**
> 1   seems as
> 2   is thought to have
> 3   is asserted
> 4   was assumed
> 5   was claimed
> 6   are believed to have
> 7   was reported
> 8   is (now) believed

Listening

> **OPTIONAL WARMER**
>
> With a monolingual class, ask Ss to tell you what is happening in the news in their country at the moment. With a multilingual class, Ss can tell a partner what is happening in the news in their countries. Get feedback from different pairs.

7a ▶ 🔘 1.04 Tell Ss they are going to hear some radio news headlines about different achievements. Play the recording and ask Ss to take notes about the achievements mentioned. Ss compare their ideas with a partner.

> **Answers**
> the breeding of cloned wild animals
> American millionaire circumnavigates the world in a balloon
> Don Gorske has entered the record books for having eaten over 15,000 Big Macs

b ▶ 🔘 1.05 Play the recording. Ss listen to the headlines and write down exactly what they hear.

c ▶ Ss compare what they have written with a partner. Refer Ss to audioscript 1.04 on page 167 so they can compare what they have written with the actual headlines. Discuss with Ss what problems they had and why they think they had these problems. Common issues may include weak forms, other features of connected speech, or the speed of the speaker.

Pronunciation | word stress (1)

8a ▶ Focus Ss again on the headlines in bold in audioscript 1.04 on page 167. In pairs, they identify which are the content words, and which are the function words.

> **Suggested answers**
>
> **Content words**
> conservation, institute, United States, produced, wild kittens, cross-breeding cloned adult cats
> American millionaire, succeeded, long-held ambition, circumnavigate, world, balloon
> finally, story, man, entered, record books, world's most renowned eater, burgers
>
> **Function words**
> A, in the, has, by
> An, has, in his, to, the, in a
> And, the, of a, who has, the, as the, of

b ▶ 🔘 1.05 Play the recording again. Ss listen to the headlines and underline the stressed words. Point out to Ss that we usually stress content words. We do not usually stress function words.

c ▶ Ss repeat the headlines, stressing the sentences naturally.

Writing and speaking

9 ▶ In pairs, Ss discuss questions 1–3. Monitor conversations for errors. Get feedback from different pairs. Write errors you have heard on the board and ask Ss to correct them.

10a ▶ Ask Ss to work in pairs to choose one of the cartoons. Tell Ss that they are going to write a news bulletin based on the cartoon they have chosen. Before Ss start writing, review the passive constructions for distancing facts and write them on the board. Monitor what Ss are writing, helping where necessary. Make sure that Ss include passive constructions in their bulletins.

b ▶ Give Ss time to practise reading their news bulletins with their partners. As you monitor, encourage Ss to concentrate on stress patterns.

c ▶ Ss read their bulletins to the rest of the class. Give praise for attempts to use correct stress patterns. These could be recorded on audio or video for later evaluation.

11 ▶ Focus Ss' attention on the Lifelong learning box. Ask Ss to work with a partner to think about watching or listening to the news in English. Get feedback from various Ss.

1.3 Burning ambitions

In this lesson, Ss look at different activities and discuss if they are generally done better by men or by women. Ss read different texts about people and swap information about what they have read. Ss listen to people who have achieved difficult things and through this context look at the grammar of the perfect aspect. Ss also prepare a talk about their greatest achievement.

OPTIONAL WARMER

Ss make a list of four activities that they do well and four activities that they do badly. In pairs, Ss compare their lists and explain why they are good or bad at the activities.

Reading

1 ▶ In pairs, Ss discuss the questions. Monitor conversations for errors. Get feedback from the class and write any important errors you have heard on the board. Try and elicit the correct forms from Ss before correcting them yourself. Discuss the danger of stereotyping with the whole class.

2 ▶ Put Ss in two groups, A and B. Ss A read the text on page 15. Ss B read the text on page 147. While reading, Ss make notes on questions 1–5. If Ss have any questions about vocabulary, explain that this will be addressed later in the lesson.

▶ When Ss have finished, they can check what they have written in their groups.

Suggested answers
B = Bia Figueiredo
C = Carlos Acosta
What is/was their ambition?
B: to be a Formula One driver
C: to reach the final of the Prix de Lausanne
To what extent have they achieved it?
B: She is competing in the Brazilian Formula Renault Championship.
C: He won the Grand Prix and the Gold Medal at the Paris Ballet.
What challenges have they faced?
B: chauvinism, money problems, time constraints when she was studying
C: prejudice (boys don't do ballet), fighting and teasing from boys at school. He was brought up in a rough suburb in Havana.
Who has helped them achieve their ambitions? How?
B: her father – he has both encouraged and financed her ambition; her mechanic and mentor. He has coached other great drivers.
C: his father – enrolled him in the National Ballet School. When the school threw Carlos out, his father went to speak for him, and pushed him to stay with ballet as a good career. His teacher, Ramona – she 'persevered' with him.

Other information
B: She has a forceful personality, and believes in herself. She was very young when she fell in love with motor racing. Her father told her to wait until she was seven to learn to drive. Naylor believes Bia is comparable to his other protégés, such as Rubens Barrichello.
C: At ten, he was mixing with delinquents – his father thought he might end up shooting someone. His father would have liked to take up ballet, but didn't have the opportunity. Carlos didn't understand ballet at first, but later realised he was very good at it – in spite of missing classes. He says ballet was his 'destiny'.

3 ▶ Pair Ss so that Ss A are working with Ss B. Ss swap information about their texts (from looking at their notes, not the texts), and complete the table with any missing information. Ss then decide with their partners if there are similarities between the two stories and then discuss the similarities as a class.

4 ▶ Put Ss in pairs. Ss discuss questions 1–4. Re-group Ss so that they are working in new pairs with different Ss. Ss report what they have discussed. Monitor the conversations for important errors and interesting language Ss use. Get feedback from the whole class. Write important errors you have heard on the board and encourage Ss to correct them. Finally, write up examples of interesting language Ss have used.

Vocabulary | achievement

5a ▶ Focus Ss' attention on words and expressions 1–8. Ask Ss to discuss in pairs the meaning of the vocabulary. Encourage Ss to use the context of the articles on page 15 and page 147 to help work out the meaning of the vocabulary. Get feedback by asking various Ss to explain the meaning of the words and expressions to the whole class.

OPTIONAL VARIATION

Write the headwords from exercise 5a (*head*, *pursue*, *deal with*, etc.) in a column on the left-hand side of the board. Write the expressions in brackets (*straight for the top*, etc.) in a separate column on the right-hand side of the board in a different order. Get Ss to work in pairs to match the headwords with the expressions in the right-hand column. Get feedback, and ask one student from each pair to come to the board and connect the words and expressions. Then ask Ss to write an example sentence for each word/expression. Ss compare sentences with a partner. Monitor and note any good examples. Write these on the board and give praise to Ss who wrote them.

b ▶ Ss complete sentences 1–8 using the words and expressions from exercise 5a. Ss compare their answers with a partner. Check the answers with the whole class.

Answers
1	potential	4	facing	7	heading
2	deal	5	believe in	8	push
3	pursued	6	persevered		

Listening

6 ▶ Put Ss in pairs to discuss the questions. Monitor conversations and take note of errors and interesting language Ss use.

▶ Get feedback from various groups and discuss with the whole class how difficult it would be achieve the different things. Write errors you have heard in the conversations on the board. In pairs, Ss correct the errors. Get feedback from various pairs and write the correct forms on the board. Focus Ss' attention on any interesting language they used in the conversations.

> **OPTIONAL VARIATION**
>
> Put Ss in groups of three. Tell Ss to rank the activities in order of difficulty but that they should not agree with the other Ss in their group. They should try to convince the other Ss of their point of view. Give Ss a few minutes to think about what they are going to say, then let them start the discussion. Monitor the different groups closely, listening especially for any expressions for disagreeing that the Ss use. Get feedback from the whole class.

7 ▶ ● 1.06 Tell Ss that they are going to listen to different people talking about the things they have achieved. Ss read the questions. Play the recording. Ss answer the questions.

▶ Give Ss time to compare their answers with a partner. Play the recording again. Check answers with the whole class.

> **Answers**
> 1 Speaker 1: raised money for a good cause by helping to organise and taking part in a long-distance cycle ride.
> Speaker 2: is doing volunteer work abroad teaching English to children in a remote village.
> Speaker 3: ran a marathon.
> 2 Speaker 1: It was a fantastic learning experience, and they were pleased they'd accomplished something important and raised lots of money.
> Speaker 2: It's been an amazing experience and he's learnt a lot.
> Speaker 3: It was great and felt like a major achievement; a fantastic run and a good atmosphere.
> 3 Speaker 1: It was very tough cycling, especially in Spain against the heat.
> Speaker 2: He'd never left Europe or done any teaching before. It was a real culture shock initially.
> Speaker 3: She had to train really hard; she'd never done any training like that before.

Grammar | perfect aspect

8 ▶ Focus Ss' attention on the Active grammar box. Give Ss time to read through the notes in the box. Ss underline the perfect tense in each sentence (1–3) and identify each tense. Ss compare their answers with another student. Check answers with the class.

> **Active grammar**
> 1 I've always run, but just for myself. (Present Perfect)
> 2 Next week I'll have been here for three months. (Future Perfect)
> 3 I'd always thought it would be great to cycle across a whole country. (Past Perfect)

▶ Focus Ss' attention on the Reference on page 19. Give Ss time to read through the notes.

9a ▶ Focus Ss' attention on sentences 1–8. In pairs, Ss correct the sentences. Check answers with the whole class.

> **Answers**
> 1 Jake, this is my friend Amy, who I've **known** for absolutely ages. (*I've been knowing* is incorrect – we don't use the continuous form with a state verb)
> 2 I asked what had **happened**, but nobody could tell me. (*had been happened* is incorrect – we need the active, not the passive form here)
> 3 I chose this school because I'd **heard** it was the best. (need to use a past participle to form the Past Perfect tense)
> 4 He should have **finished** by the time we get back. (*should have finish* is incorrect – the Future Perfect requires the past participle)
> 5 Before I came to the US, I **had** never been abroad. (*never been abroad* is incorrect – it needs an auxiliary verb)
> 6 I'm so exhausted. **I've** been working hard all week. (*I'm so ... I'd been* is incorrect – we can only use the Past Perfect with another past tense)
> 7 By the time she retires, she'll have **been** working there for more than 50 years. (*she'll have be working* is incorrect – the Future Perfect Continuous requires *been + ing*)
> 8 I'll phone you as soon as we **have** arrived. (*we will have arrived* is incorrect – we do not use *will* in time clauses)

b ▶ ● 1.07 Play the recording. Ss check their answers.

c ▶ In pairs, Ss practise saying the sentences in pairs. Ask different Ss to say the sentences for the rest of the class.

Speaking

10 ► Focus Ss' attention on the How to... box. In pairs, Ss complete the sentences with the words from the box. Check answers with the whole class.

> **Answers**
> 1 We <u>decided</u> to organise ...
> 2 I didn't know what to <u>expect</u>
> 3 The whole thing was quite a <u>challenge</u>.
> 4 It exceeded my <u>expectations.</u>

11a ► Give Ss time to think about what they consider to be their greatest achievement. Ss make notes using the language from the How to... box.

b ► Ss tell the whole class about their achievement. Monitor the language used by Ss and take note of errors. When all the Ss have finished talking about their achievements, write important errors on the board. In pairs, Ss correct the errors. Focus Ss' attention on any interesting language used and correct use of language from the How to... box, and congratulate them on its use.

1 Vocabulary | Prefixes

In this lesson, Ss look at different prefixes and the effect they have on root words.

> **OPTIONAL WARMER**
> Put Ss in two groups, A and B. Tell group A that they love football and group B that they are totally anti-football. Give the groups five minutes to think of reasons to support their points of view. Put Ss in pairs, so that Ss A are working with Ss B. Ss then try and convince their partner of their point of view. Get feedback from the whole class and discuss if football receives too much attention nowadays.

1a ► Ss read through the story and underline the 12 prefixes. Ss compare their answers with a partner. Check answers with the whole class and write the words with the prefixes on the board.

> **Answers**
> <u>multi</u>-talented, <u>semi</u>-professional, <u>sub</u>-standard, <u>un</u>impressive, <u>super</u>human, <u>arch</u>-rivals, <u>over</u>cautious, <u>under</u>-prepared, <u>single</u>-handedly, <u>out</u>played, <u>mis</u>fired, <u>ir</u>relevant

b ► Ss read the story again and answer questions 1–4.

> **Answers**
> 1 multi, super, over, out
> 2 sub, under
> 3 semi
> 4 sub, un, over, under, out, mis, ir

c ► Ss compare their answers with a partner. Check answers with the whole class.

> **Answers**
> 1 not (not decisive)
> 2 not (not possible)
> 3 single (single-syllabic)
> 4 not (not motivated)

2 ► Ask Ss to work in pairs to complete the sentences with the root words in brackets and a prefix. Tell Ss that they may have to change the form of the root word to fit the context of the sentence. Ss compare their answers with another pair. Check answers with the whole class.

> **Answers**
> 1 misunderstood
> 2 unaware
> 3 semi-retired
> 4 outnumbered
> 5 overweight
> 6 underestimated

3a ▶ Focus Ss' attention on the opposites in 1–5. In pairs, Ss discuss the meaning of the words and the effect the prefixes have on the root word. Ss mark on scales 1–5 where they think they fit best.

b ▶ Ss compare their position on the scales with other Ss and explain why they have completed the scales in this way. Get feedback from the whole class.

1 Communication

In this lesson, Ss do a questionnaire to see if they are the type of person who likes challenges or not.

OPTIONAL WARMER

Write the following questions on the board:
1 *What type of magazine can you find questionnaires in?*
2 *Do you ever answer questionnaires in magazines? Why/Why not?* Ss discuss the questions with their partners and whether they believe the results of questionnaires in magazines. Get feedback from different pairs and tell Ss they are going to answer a questionnaire.

1a ▶ Individually, Ss do the questionnaire by choosing answers a, b or c for each question. Monitor to check that Ss understand the vocabulary in the questionnaire. If there are any unknown words, encourage them to answer each others' questions before you explain the words to them.

▶ When the Ss have finished answering the questions, they can share their answers with a partner and explain why they have chosen them. Get feedback from different pairs.

▶ Ss then work with a partner to add another question to the questionnaire. Help Ss as necessary and check the questions Ss are writing. Ss can decide what each of the answers would say about the personality of a person doing the questionnaire.

▶ Ss ask other Ss in the class the extra question they have written and tell them what their answers mean about their personality.

b ▶ ● 1.08 Play the recording. Ss check their answers.

c ▶ Ss then discuss with a partner if they agree/disagree with the information in the recording.

2 ▶ Put Ss in different groups so that they are working with new partners. In their groups, Ss discuss questions 1–4. Monitor the conversations for important errors and any interesting language Ss use.

▶ Get feedback from various groups. Finally, write any important errors on the board. In pairs, Ss correct the errors. Get feedback from different pairs and write the correct forms on the board.

1 Review and practice

1 ▶

Answers

1	(c) faced	6	(b) distinguished from
2	(a) daunting	7	(c) lacking in
3	(a) babbling	8	(a) benefited from
4	(b) pick up	9	(c) succeeded in
5	(c) relied on	10	(a) intelligible

2 ▶

Answers

1 Giant multinational research centre Sci-Corps seems to **have abandoned** its research into cloning after pressure from the government.
2 Ex-President Michael Nkrumah is said **to** be recovering well from the stroke he suffered last Thursday
3 Michaela Kritzkoff, the explorer who disappeared for a month while canoeing along the Amazon, has been found in a village in Brazil. It **is** believed that she had drowned during a storm.
4 British Commonwealth boxing champion Roderick Bland appears to **have** finally retired, at the age of 46.
5 And finally, it seems **as** if summer really is coming. Sarah Smith reports on tomorrow's weather.

3 ▶

Answers

1 By the time she finishes her degree, she will have been at the university ten years.
2 correct
3 I feel healthier now that I have taken up kickboxing.
4 Where were you? I've been waiting here for an hour.
5 It was a shock when I saw him. I would have expected to see a big man, but he was tiny.
6 When she got to work, she found out she had been fired. Her desk was empty, everything gone.
7 Hi, John! We've just been talking about you!
8 It's 9 o'clock. Mandy will have landed at the airport by now.
9 I'd been running for years before I entered my first competition.
10 We'll have used up all the world's oil long before 2100.

4 ▶

Answers

1 A: Have you ever been to Prague?
   B: Yes, I know it like the back of my hand.
2 A: How many women have succeeded in Formula 1 racing?
   B: I don't know offhand, but not many.
3 A: Can you help me? I need some information about space travel.
   B: I know next to nothing about it.
4 A: When's the best time to go there?
   B: As far as I'm concerned, never.
5 A: Who's Michael Vaughan?
   B: I've never heard of him.
6 A: Who's the President of Colombia?
   B: I can't tell you off the top of my head.

1 Writing bank

1 ▶ Focus Ss' attention on the leaflet. Ss answer the questions. Get feedback from the whole class.

Answers

1 language courses
2 all over Europe, courses begin on the first Monday of each month
3 over 20 years
4 dedicated teachers, lecturers and historians, with an average of 15 years' experience in the classroom

2 ▶ In pairs, Ss answer the questions. Get feedback from the whole class.

Answer
e

3 ▶ Focus Ss' attention on the How to... box. Ss find more expressions from the leaflet.

Suggested answers
Use a clear layout with subheadings for the key points: About us; Dates; Staff; Prices; What they say about us; Contact
Write clearly and concisely and use lists: You can learn Italian language and culture in Rome; Spanish language and culture in Madrid; Russian language and culture in Moscow and many more
Use positive language: outstanding staff; dedicated teachers
Include a slogan: Courses that change your life!
Include recommendations/testimonials: An excellent service to students all over Europe; Simply the best value for money in language and culture courses
Give reasons why the product/service/event is special: ... we have branches in 18 major cities in Europe; with an average of 15 years' experience in the classroom
Include contact details: email: languageculture@LL.org

4a ▶ Individually, Ss plan and then write a leaflet for a course or event. Encourage Ss to use the topics from the How to... box. Go round and monitor Ss who need any help with the planning or writing stages.

b ▶ In pairs, Ss read each others' leaflets. Encourage them to make positive comments on their partner's work, and to give constructive criticism if the leaflet does not make them interested in the course or event.

Overview

CEFR Can do objectives

2.1 Give advice/make recommendations about places
2.2 Distinguish between, and use, features of formal and informal language
2.3 Describe a place
Communication Present ideas clearly in an informal context
Writing bank Write a formal email

CEFR Portfolio ideas

a) Imagine you have won a prize for one of your achievements. The prize will be presented by a Very Important Person, (VIP). Describe what you will wear at the presentation. Write the short dialogue between the VIP and yourself at the presentation.

b) Your friend runs a shop, business, restaurant, hotel or club. Your friend asks you to write a promotional leaflet in English for tourists.

c) An English-speaking friend will be coming for a first visit to your country for two weeks. Unfortunately, you will be busy. Write a phone conversation with your friend. Suggest places that your friend should visit and explain what your friend might do in these places.

d) You receive an email offering you the chance to go on a two-week cruise in the Caribbean. Write a formal email thanking for the offer and explaining why you cannot accept.

Lead-in

OPTIONAL WARMER

Ask Ss to think back to when they were children and to write notes about the community in which they lived. To help, you could write the following prompts on the board: *house/flat*, *family*, *area*, *school*. Ss share what they have written with a partner and discuss the positive and negative aspects of the community in which they lived. Get feedback from the whole class.

---

1 ▶ Focus Ss' attention on the photos of the different communities. In pairs, Ss discuss what type of community is shown in each of the photos. Ss then decide on the positive and negative aspects of each of the communities. Get feedback from the whole class and write Ss' ideas on the board.

▶ Put Ss in pairs with a different partner. Ss discuss which of the communities they would like to be a part of and which they would not like to be a part of and why/why not. Get feedback from different pairs.

2a ▶ In pairs, Ss discuss whether each word or phrase is positive or negative. Get feedback from the whole class and discuss why they think the sentences are positive or negative.

Suggested answers

1	+	9	−
2	+	10	−
3	+	11	−
4	+	12	−
5	+	13	−
6	+	14	−
7	+	15	−
8	+	16	+

---

b ▶ In pairs, Ss discuss which four of the positive or negative things are the most important to them and why.

EXTEND THE LEAD-IN

Ask Ss to think about the place where they live or where they are from. Ss describe the place they live to their partners, using as much of the vocabulary from exercise 2a as possible. Get feedback from the whole class to compare the different places that Ss live in or are from.

2.1 My community

It is becoming more common for people to work or study in other countries for a period of time. This is especially true within the European Community, where it is increasingly easy to work or to travel in different member countries. European students are finding it easier to study in other countries because of exchange programmes such as the Erasmus programme, where students study in a university in another European country, normally for an academic year. Students who participate in these programmes often find studying in a different country to be enriching as they learn about a different culture and meet people from all over Europe.

In this lesson, Ss listen to different people discussing their experiences of living abroad. They look at the grammar of verb patterns. Ss also focus on language for giving and making recommendations.

OPTIONAL LEAD-IN

Ss make a list of all the things they think a foreign person might find difficult if they came to live in their country. In a monolingual class, Ss make the list in pairs. Get feedback from different pairs. In a multilingual class, Ss make the list then share it with a partner from a different country. Get feedback from different Ss.

Reading

1 ▸ Focus Ss' attention on the four photos. In pairs, they discuss the questions. Get feedback from the whole class.

2 ▸ Ss read the comments (A–D). In pairs, Ss decide which writers are more negative or more positive about their communities. Get feedback from the whole class.

Suggested answers
community is changing for the worse: A, C
positive things to say: B, D

---

3 ▸ In pairs, Ss answer the questions. Get feedback from the whole class.

Suggested answers
1   The area used to be full of shops selling Italian food, where the Italian dialect could be heard.
2   youngsters visit the elderly; people look after each other's children; everybody knows everybody else
3   local shops have been replaced by big supermarkets; local schools are closing
4   perhaps because Greece is made up of several islands, with people living in close proximity to one another

---

4 ▸ Put Ss in groups to discuss the questions. Get feedback from the whole class.

Grammar | verb patterns (1)

OPTIONAL LEAD-IN

Write the following gapped sentences on the board:
You can take a bus and go _____ in the mountains 40 minutes later.
I was studying German so I wanted _____ a year there.
Ss discuss what words could go in the gaps and what form the words should be in. Write the words Ss suggest in the spaces. Ask Ss why the verbs are in these forms. Elicit that when a verb is followed by another verb, the second verb is either in the infinitive or the *-ing* form.

5a ▸ In pairs, Ss identify the verb + verb patterns in the extract.

Answers
afford to buy
thinking of going
advised him to do it

---

b ▸ In pairs, Ss find six more patterns in the comments on page 22. Check the answers with the whole class.

Answers
don't mind helping	can't stand shopping
can't imagine living	don't want to go
avoid going out	object to sending

---

6 ▸ In pairs, Ss identify and correct the grammatical mistakes in sentences 1–15. Ss compare their answers with another pair. Check answers with the whole class.

Answers
1   I'm thinking **of visiting** the community where I used to live.
2   If you can't afford **to eat** in expensive restaurants, there are lots of cheaper *trattorias*.
3   I can't imagine **living** in a different community.
4   We look forward to **seeing** you.
5   You can avoid **to** offending people by learning the host country's customs.
6   I don't mind **looking** after my niece and nephew.
7   I don't fancy **eating** Greek food tonight.
8   She doesn't want **to live** far away from her family.
9   I can't stand **shopping** in big supermarkets.
10 If you object to **paying** lots of money for clothes, don't go shopping in Ginza, Tokyo.
11 I advise you **to go** to the Antipodes festival.
12 I'd encourage all foreigners **to try** some *baklava*.
13 I'd urge you **to visit** the different communities in New York.
14 I'd recommend **going** to the local restaurant.
15 She persuaded us **to visit** Cork in the spring.

---

7 ▶ Ss answer questions 1–3 in pairs. Check answers with the whole class.

Answers
1   C – recommendations; B – likes/dislikes
2   *Fancy* and *want* have a similar meaning. *Want* is stronger in meaning than *fancy*. *Can't stand* and *object* are similar in meaning. *Can't stand* is stronger than *object*.
3   *Encourage* and *urge* are similar in meaning. *Urge* is stronger than *encourage* in meaning. *Recommend* and *advise* are similar in meaning. *Advise* is stronger than *recommend* in meaning.

8 ▶ Ss write the underlined words from exercise 6 in the Active grammar box. Check answers with the whole class.

Active grammar

verb + *ing*: imagine, avoid, don't mind, fancy, can't stand, recommend
verb + infinitive: can afford, want
verb + object + infinitive without *to*: advise, encourage, urge, persuade
verb + preposition + *ing*: think of, look forward to, object to

▶ Refer Ss to the Reference on page 33. Ss read through the notes.

9 ▶ In pairs, Ss rewrite sentences 1–8, using *I*, *I'd* or *I'm*. Point out to Ss that they may need to change the form of the verb. Check answers with the whole class.

Answers
1   I can't **afford** to go to the theatre.
2   I'd **advise** you to go to Brixton Market on Sunday.
3   I'd **encourage** people to use the parks more.
4   I **look forward** to seeing you next weekend.
5   I'd **recommend** buying tickets early for Buckingham Palace.
6   I **avoid** taking Intercity trains because they're more expensive.
7   I **fancy** taking a short trip to Paris.
8   **I'm thinking** of going to Thailand in February.

Speaking

10 ▶ In pairs, Ss discuss if they know any expressions which use the words in the box. Get feedback from various Ss. Then, Ss write the words from the box in the correct places in the How to... box. Check answers with the whole class.

Answers
1   value
2   all
3   found
4   were
5   sure
6   out
7   wary

11a ▶ Put Ss in groups of four. Ss choose a place they know and write notes. Encourage Ss to think about expressions from the How to... box.

b ▶ Put Ss in groups. Ss take turns to describe their place.

Listening

12 ▶ Get Ss to discuss questions 1–3 in pairs. Ss studying English abroad will be able to discuss their current experiences and any problems they might have encountered. Monitor conversations for errors. Get feedback from various Ss and discuss the questions. Write errors you have heard on the board and ask Ss to correct them.

13a ▶ 🔘 1.09 Focus Ss' attention on the table and give Ss time to read through the questions. Play the recording. Ss complete the table with the information about the three speakers.

▶ Ss compare their answers with a partner. Play the recording again for Ss to check their answers. Check answers with the whole class.

Answers
Where did he/she live?
Speaker 1:   Canada
Speaker 2:   Austria
Speaker 3:   Japan
What was he/she doing there?
Speaker 1:   starting a packaging business in the publishing industry
Speaker 2:   gap year from university, work as a teaching assistant
Speaker 3:   English-language teacher
What did he/she like about the host country?
Speaker 1:   beautiful city, beaches, mountains, etc, food, friendly people
Speaker 2:   long weekends, skiing, ice skating, scenery, people
Speaker 3:   the people
Is there anything he/she didn't like, or that was difficult?
Speaker 1:   starting a business when Canada's economy wasn't doing well was difficult
Speaker 2:   the food – Austrians tend to eat a lot of meat, which was difficult as she is vegetarian
Speaker 3:   she couldn't read Japanese so everyday things (like shopping) were an adventure for her
What are his/her favourite memories of the country?
Speaker 1:   the open spaces, vastness and the friendly people
Speaker 2:   scenery, going off into the mountains after school, skiing or swimming in the lakes
Speaker 3:   the people and learning about Japanese customs and culture

b ▶ In pairs, Ss discuss which of the speakers (1, 2 or 3) said each thing. Get feedback from the whole class.

c ▶ Play the recording again for Ss to check their answers. Check answers with the whole class.

Answers					
a	2	e	2	i	3
b	3	f	3	j	1
c	1	g	1		
d	3	h	2		

14 ▶ Focus Ss' attention on questions 1–3. In pairs, Ss discuss the questions. Monitor conversations for errors and interesting language Ss use. Get feedback from various Ss.

> **OPTIONAL EXTENSION**
>
> In a monolingual class, Ss talk in pairs and decide on the five things they would miss the most about their country if they went to live abroad. Ss share their ideas with another pair. In a multilingual class, Ss write a list of the five things they would miss most, then share it with a partner from another country, explaining why they would miss it. Get feedback from the whole class.

2.2 It's a wiki wiki world

In this lesson, Ss listen to two people talking about the Internet. Through this context, Ss review ways of making comparisons. Ss then read an article about Wikipedia before looking at features of formal and informal writing styles.

> **OPTIONAL WARMER**
>
> Write *Internet* on the board. Give Ss two minutes to write down as many words as they can think of connected to the Internet. In pairs, Ss compare their words and explain why they are connected to the Internet. Get feedback from the class and write the words on the board to check the spelling.

Listening

1 ▶ In pairs, Ss discuss questions 1–4. Monitor for interesting language Ss use. Get feedback and discuss the questions with the whole class.

> **OPTIONAL VARIATION**
>
> After getting feedback to question number 4, put Ss in two groups, A and B. Tell group A that they think the Internet is a good thing. Tell group B that they think the Internet is a bad thing. Give Ss five minutes in their groups to think of reasons to support their view. Put Ss in pairs so that Ss A are working with Ss B. Ss try and convince their partners of their point of view. Get feedback from the whole class.

2 ▶ 🔘 1.10 Explain to Ss that they are going to hear two people discussing the questions from exercise 1. Play the recording. Ss decide which issues the people are discussing and whether their ideas are similar to the ideas of the people on the recording.

▶ Ss compare their ideas with a partner. Check answers with the whole class.

Answer
They discuss 2, 3 and 4.

3 ▶ Give Ss time to read through phrases 1–12. Tell Ss that they are going to listen to the discussion again and that this time they should tick the phrases they hear. Play the recording again and Ss tick the phrases.

▶ Ss compare the phrases they have ticked with a partner. Check answers with the whole class.

Answers
1, 3, 4, 6, 7, 9, 10, 12

Grammar | comparatives (review)

4a ▶ Focus Ss on the Active grammar box. In pairs, Ss write the phrases from exercise 3 in the correct place in the box. They then add the words/phrases at the bottom of the box to the correct column. Ss compare answers with another pair. Check answers with the whole class.

Active grammar

1 (it's) miles easier; (it's) far easier; (it's) nowhere near as ... as; (it's) nothing like as good as; it's definitely not as ... as; it's considerably + comparative (formal); (it's) much + superlative

2 (it's) not quite as ... as ...; it's marginally + comparative (formal); (it's) much the same

3 the less we ..., the less we ...; the more we ..., the more we ...

▶ Refer Ss to the Reference on page 33. Make sure that Ss have time to read through the notes.

5 ▶ Focus Ss' attention on sentences 1–6. Ss cross out the incorrect alternatives in each sentence, then compare their answers with a partner. Check answers with the whole class.

Answers
1 not like
2 It's best
3 easier
4 extremely
5 a mile
6 As much as we use

Speaking

6a ▶ Ss look at the sentences in exercise 5 again. Ss decide how much they agree or disagree with each statement.

b ▶ Ss compare their answers in small groups. Monitor the conversations for important errors. Get feedback from various Ss. Finally, write errors you have heard on the board and encourage Ss to correct them.

Reading

Wikipedia is a free web-based encyclopaedia created in 2001. It allows any visitor to the site to freely edit its content. It has several million articles in more than 270 languages. There has been some controversy about how reliable the contents of Wikipedia are. As it is possible for anyone to edit the content of the encyclopaedia, some think it is liable to vandalism and that it can be inconsistent. To consult Wikipedia, see www.wikipedia.org.

7 ▶ Write *Wikipedia* on the board. In pairs, Ss discuss if they know what it is or have ever used it, and if so why they have used it and why it is special. If the Ss haven't heard of it, ask them to predict what it might be. Get feedback from the whole class and discuss Ss' ideas and experiences.

8 ▶ Ss read the article and match the headings to the paragraphs. Ss should not worry about any difficult vocabulary at this stage. Ss compare answers with a partner. Check answers with the whole class.

Answers
a 2
b 5
c 7
d 3
e 6
f 4
g 1

9 ▶ Ss read the article again and answer the questions.

Answers
1 a pooling of knowledge
2 because the editors care more than the vandals
3 the founder of Wikipedia; he is described as a 'regular' (or normal) 'guy'
4 the wiki

10a ▶ Write *Formal* and *Informal* on the board at the top of two columns. Put Ss in two groups. Each group takes one of the styles and makes a list of features of that style of writing. Elicit and write Ss' ideas on the board in the correct column and discuss them with the whole class.

▶ Ss read the article again quickly and decide if it is formal or informal in style. Get feedback from the whole class.

Answer
The article is informal. It contains colloquialisms, spoken English, humour, etc.

b ▶ Focus Ss' attention on the headings in the box. Ask Ss to complete the How to... box.

Answers
1 Informal vocabulary
2 Style (spoken English)
3 Ellipsis (omitting words)
4 Humour

c ▶ Ss answer questions 1–3. Check answers with the whole class.

Suggested answers

1 *savvy* = clever, smart; *guy* = person, man
2 informal vocabulary: *how come?*; *breezed through*
   spoken English: *It's amateurs; But is it the most reliable?*
   humour: *For the vandals, it's about as worthwhile as a graffiti artist using invisible ink.*
3 *And what about the future?*

OPTIONAL EXTENSION

In pairs, Ss compare an entry from Wikipedia with an a entry from a traditional encyclopaedia. While doing so, encourage Ss to use the expressions for comparing things from exercise 3.

---

11 ▶ Ss look at the techniques and decide whether they are generally used more in formal or informal texts. Ss compare answers with a partner.

Answers

1 formal   3 informal
2 informal   4 formal

---

12 ▶ Ss read through the two formal emails. Ss replace language which is too informal with a word or phrase from the box. Ss compare answers with a partner. Check answers with the whole class.

Answers

Dear Mr Fry,

Following our telephone conversation, ...

... **Could you please confirm your attendance** by 4 November? **We would be grateful if you could** bring copies of the sample contract. Don't hesitate to get in touch if you have any **queries.**

Regards

Mary Johnson

Dear Ms Johnson,

Thank you very much for the invitation to **attend** the meeting on 15 November, **concerning** the plan to start a new website, and thank you also for the agenda. **I will be very happy to attend.**

As requested, I will bring copies of the sample contract. Unfortunately, **I will be unable to attend** the dinner because of **a previous arrangement.**

I look forward to seeing you there.

Yours sincerely,

Peter Fry

---

13 ▶ In pairs, Ss discuss the questions in the Lifelong learning box in relation to the article and the emails they have just read. Get feedback from various Ss. Encourage Ss to think about these questions when writing their own texts.

2.3 Destination paradise

> Cali in Colombia is situated some 1,000 metres above sea level and because it is close to the equator, it doesn't experience major climate changes. It is the third largest city in Colombia with over two million inhabitants, many of them recent immigrants from poor rural areas. It can be a dangerous city because of drug-related violence.
>
> Cape Town is the third biggest city in South Africa and is a very popular destination with tourists who go there in part for its Mediterranean-style climate. It was home to many leaders of the anti-apartheid movement and Nelson Mandela made his first public speech there after being released from prison. It can be a dangerous city as it has one of the world's highest homicide rates.
>
> Corsica is the fourth largest island in the Mediterranean and is located to the south-east of France. It has a Mediterranean climate, with hot, dry summers and mild, rainy winters. Corsica is famous for being the birthplace of Napoleon Bonaparte.

In this lesson, Ss read about three places then swap information about them. Ss then go on to focus on adjectives to describe places.

OPTIONAL WARMER

Write the following countries on the board: *Colombia*, *South Africa* and *France*. Organise Ss into three groups. Each group takes one of the countries and lists everything they know about it. You could write the following prompts on the board to help Ss: *weather, food, customs, people*. Organise the Ss into new groups of three so that each group contains one student from the previous groups. Ss then share the information about the country with their new group. Get feedback from the different groups.

Speaking and reading

1 ▶ Focus Ss on the three photos. In pairs, Ss discuss the questions. Monitor the conversations and take note of any important errors.

▶ Get feedback from various and discuss the questions as a class. Finally, write any important errors you have heard on the board and get Ss to correct them with a partner. Check the correct forms with the whole class and write them on the board.

2a ▶ Put Ss in groups of three, A, B and C. Ss A read the text about Cali, Ss B reads the text about Cape Town and Ss C read the text about Corsica. While reading Ss make notes. Tell Ss not to worry about any words and expressions they don't understand at this stage, as you will be dealing with them later.

b ▶ When Ss have finished taking notes, they describe the places they have read about to the other Ss in their group. Get feedback from various Ss to check the information. Ask Ss if there are any words or phrases that they do not know the meaning of. Encourage Ss to explain the meanings to each other or consult an English–English dictionary before explaining the words and expressions yourself.

3 ▶ Put Ss in pairs so that they are working with new partners. In their pairs, Ss discuss questions 1–3. Monitor the conversations for errors and any interesting language the Ss use.

▶ Get feedback and discuss the questions with the whole class. Write any errors you have heard on the board. Encourage Ss to give you the correct forms and write them on the board. Finally, draw Ss' attention to any interesting language they have used and congratulate them on its use.

OPTIONAL EXTENSION

Tell Ss that for homework, you want them to find out as much as possible about one of the places they have read about on the Internet or using any other resources they can think of. In the following class, the Ss can then give a presentation on the place they chose to the rest of the group. Encourage Ss to be aware of engaging their audience, maintaining eye contact, the use of visuals and varying their tone of voice.

Vocabulary | adjectives to describe places

OPTIONAL WARMER

In a monolingual class, give Ss a few minutes to think of a place in their country, and adjectives they would use to describe it. Ss describe the place to a partner who tries to guess the place which is being described. In a multilingual class, Ss can describe famous cities or places in the world for their partners to guess.

4 ▶ Put Ss in groups of three or four. In their groups, Ss look through the three articles to find the words described in 1–10. Monitor carefully to check that the Ss have found the correct words. Check answers with the whole class.

Answers			
1	bustling	6	side-by-side
2	run-down	7	vast
3	stunning	8	tranquil
4	diverse	9	off the beaten track
5	unspoilt	10	packed

5a ▶ Focus Ss' attention on sentences 1–8. In pairs, Ss complete the spaces with words from exercise 4. Ss compare their answers with another pair.

Answers			
1	run-down	5	side-by-side
2	off the beaten track	6	vast
3	packed	7	tranquil
4	diverse	8	unspoilt

b ▶ Put Ss in groups of three or four. Ss look at the three photos and describe the places. While describing the photos, encourage Ss to use the vocabulary from exercise 4. Monitor the conversations carefully for errors and to help the Ss where necessary.

▶ Get feedback from each group. Congratulate Ss on their correct use of the adjectives. Write any errors you have heard on the board and ask various Ss to correct them for you.

OPTIONAL EXTENSION

Put Ss in groups of three. Each student chooses one of the photos. Tell Ss that they have to try and 'sell' the place shown in their photo as a holiday destination. Give Ss a few minutes to think about what they are going to say. Ss then tell the other Ss in their group about their destination, trying to convince them that it is a great place to go to on holiday. When the Ss have finished describing their destinations, each group decides who was best at 'selling' their destination. Get feedback from various groups.

Speaking

6a ▶ In pairs, Ss think of different places which fit the topics. Ss can then compare their ideas with their partners.

▶ Put Ss in different pairs. Ss share their ideas with their new partners. Get feedback and discuss the places the Ss have chosen to fit the descriptions.

Grammar | introductory *it*

7a ▶ Give one minute for Ss to skim the paragraph.

Answer
Cali

b ▶ Focus Ss on the underlined phrases from the paragraph. In pairs, Ss discuss the question and find a further example from exercise 2.

Suggested answers
They all use *it* to introduce an idea.
It's no wonder this city is adored by everyone who visits.

c ▶ Focus Ss on rule A in the Active grammar box. In pairs, Ss complete examples 2–4. Get feedback from the whole class.

Active grammar

2   it's a pity
3   it appears
4   it cannot be denied

d ▶ Focus Ss on rule B in the Active grammar box. In pairs, Ss complete example 8. Get feedback from the whole class.

Active grammar

8   We love it when tourists come to stay.

8 ▶ Ss match the sentence endings and beginnings. Ss check their answers with a partner.

Answers							
1	h	4	b	7	f
2	a	5	g	8	e
3	c	6	d		

9a ▶ Ss work alone to complete six of the sentences with their own ideas.

b ▶ Put Ss in pairs. They compare their sentences with their partner. Get feedback from various Ss.

2 Vocabulary | Phrasal verbs

In this lesson, Ss look at phrasal verbs through the context of communities.

> **OPTIONAL WARMER**
>
> Write the following on the board: *hippy commune, rural village, surfing community, online book community*. In pairs Ss discuss what they know about these communities or think they might be like and the type of people who might belong to them.

1 ▶ Ss read the texts 1–4. Tell Ss to underline words or expressions they don't understand in the text and that you will deal with them later. In pairs Ss discuss whether they would like to join any of the communities or not and why/why not. Ss also discuss if they would be interested in joining any of the communities temporarily or permanently. Monitor conversations for errors. Ss compare ideas with another pair.

▶ Get feedback from various Ss. Ask Ss if they underlined any unknown words or phrases in the texts. Encourage Ss to work out the meanings from context or from an English–English dictionary before asking you. Finally, read out errors you have heard and discuss them with the class.

2 ▶ Ss read the texts again and match the phrasal verbs to the correct meanings.

Answers					
a	turn up	g	hold up	m	get away from
b	fit in	h	carry out	n	come down to
c	get by	i	get through	o	come up with
d	catch on	j	come across	p	keep up with
e	fill in	k	see to		
f	do up	l	take to		

3 ▶ Ss read through the rules and match the types of verbs (a–d) to the examples.

Answers			
a	2	c	1
b	3	d	4

4a ▶ Ss ask and answer questions 1–7 with a partner. Encourage Ss to ask each other follow-up questions. Monitor the conversations for correct use of phrasal verbs.

b ▶ Get feedback by asking Ss to tell the class one thing they learned about their partners. Write any important errors you have heard on the board and get different Ss to correct them for you. Finally, congratulate Ss on their correct use of the phrasal verbs.

5 ▶ Give Ss time to read through the Lifelong learning box. Get Ss to write five sentences about themselves or their friends/family with the phrasal verbs they have used in this lesson. Ss read out their sentences to the whole class.

Answers
catch up with – three-part phrasal verb
put me up – transitive (2)
looked after – transitive (2)
stayed on – intransitive

2 Communication

3 ► In groups of three or four, Ss discuss questions 1–10 to help them form the club. Monitor conversations and help the groups as necessary.

4 ► Ss present their ideas to the rest of the class. When all the groups have presented their ideas, Ss decide which of the clubs they would be interested in joining. Read out errors you have heard and get different Ss to correct them. Finally, congratulate Ss on interesting ideas or language they have used in the lesson.

> **OPTIONAL WARMER**
>
> Ss make a list of all the clubs or organisations they have been a member of in their lives. Ss then share their lists with a partner, explaining the type of clubs/organisations they belonged to and how important they were to them. Get feedback from different pairs.

1a ► Ss read about the club. Ss decide if the club is silly, funny or a good idea and talk about this with a partner. Ask Ss if there are any words or phrases they don't understand in the text.

b ► Ss think about a presentation they could give if they were joining The Not Terribly Good Club. Ss share their presentation idea with a partner. Get feedback.

> **OPTIONAL EXTENSION**
>
> Ss could prepare their presentations and present them to the rest of the class. When all the Ss have made their presentations, the class can decide whose presentation was the best.

2a ► 🔘 1.11 Ss look at the headings and predict what type of thing each club does and the type of people who might be members. Get feedback and discuss Ss' ideas as a class. Play the recording. Ss complete the notes.

b ► Ss compare notes with a partner.

Suggested answers

Old boys' club
the main idea of the club: keep in touch with old school friends, have reunions
other things that it does: gets involved in charity events
type of meeting: party
who can be a member: anyone who went to the same school
problems: difficult to keep in touch without meeting regularly, you rely on other people to run the club, and sometimes you don't hear anything for a year or two

Ballroom-dancing club
number and type of people in the club: 30, mostly older, retired people
how long she has been a member: six months
when and where it meets: once a week, sometimes in a school hall
problems: they meet in the evenings after work and it can be quite hard to get yourself out of the house again
things they have learned: waltz, foxtrot, Latin dances like the jive and the tango

---

Review and practice

1 ▶

Answers			
1	to consult	6	to paying
2	spending	7	to make
3	to hearing	8	living
4	to buy	9	to wear
5	applying	10	taking

2 ▶

Answers			
1	better	6	more
2	near	7	isn't
3	would	8	bit
4	like	9	the
5	same	10	than

3 ▶

Answers			
1	was carried out	7	came up with
2	vast	8	held up
3	get away from	9	keep up with
4	side-by-side	10	turn up
5	run-down	11	come across
6	bustling	12	stunning

2 Writing bank

1 ▶ Focus Ss' attention on the emails. Ss answer the questions. Get feedback from the whole class.

Answers	
1	to inform Ms Foong that her company has been shortlisted for an award; Demetri Leopoulos is the head of the judging panel
2	information as to how many of Ms Foong's team will be attending; a 150-word history of her company
3	in the email, she provides information as to how many of her team will be attending; in the attachment, she provides the 150-word history of her company
4	CEO

2 ▶ In pairs, Ss match the expressions. Get feedback from the whole class.

Answers	
1	I am pleased to inform you
2	We would like to invite you
3	We would be grateful if you could let us know
4	for inclusion in
5	We are happy to accept your kind invitation
6	you requested

3 ▶ Focus Ss' attention on the How to... box. In pairs Ss complete the phrases.

Answers	
1	pleased
2	accept
3	grateful
4	find
5	take

4a ▶ Individually, Ss plan and then write an email, inviting their partner to a formal occasion. Encourage Ss to use language from the How to... box. Go round and monitor Ss who need any help with the planning or writing stages.

b ▶ Ss read each other's emails.

c ▶ Ss write a response to the email they received.

d ▶ Ss read each other's responses. Get feedback from various Ss.

3 Tales

Overview

CEFR Can do objectives
3.1 Tell an anecdote
3.2 Describe a person in detail
3.3 Tell a humorous story
Communication Tell an extended story
Writing bank Write a detailed narrative

CEFR Portfolio ideas
a) Write a humorous article called 'The worst mistake I ever made' describing a real (or fictional) language mistake which you made when using English. Describe what happened as a result of your mistake. Share your article with your friends.
b) Choose an animal which represents your club, company, or school now. Choose an animal which represents what you would like your club, company or school to become. Use these metaphorical ideas in an amusing short presentation.
c) Write a story which includes a giraffe, a kettle, a pair of high-heeled shoes and a text message. Read your friends' stories. Are they better than yours?
d) Choose a photograph of a person from any page in the Students' Book. Describe the person and the photograph. Tell your friends. How long does it take for them to find the photograph?

Lead-in

OPTIONAL WARMER

Put Ss in pairs, A and B. Ss A open the book and describe two of the pictures on page 35 to Ss B. Ss B draw the pictures as Ss A describe them. Tell Ss B that they don't have to draw a perfect picture and that a representation will be adequate. When all of the pictures have been described, Ss B open their books and compare their drawings with the pictures on page 35. Ss B can also check any details that Ss A did not describe to them, and compare what they had imagined the picture to be like with the real picture.

---

1 ▶ Focus Ss' attention on the pictures. In pairs, Ss discuss how they think the pictures are connected and what type of story each of the pictures illustrates. Ss also discuss if they ever tell stories and if they are good at storytelling. Ss discuss what makes a good storyteller.

2a ▶ In pairs, Ss look at the phrases and discuss the differences between them. Tell Ss that they can use their dictionaries to help if necessary. Get feedback from the whole class.

b ▶ In pairs, Ss think of examples of the words and expressions. Ss then compare their examples with other pairs. Get feedback from the whole class and ask Ss to explain their examples to you.

▶ In a monolingual class, ask Ss to think of examples in their own language. In a multilingual class, Ss can do the same, but pair them so that Ss of different nationalities are working together. Ss share their examples with a partner. Get feedback by asking Ss to explain their partner's examples to the whole class.

3a ▶ In pairs, Ss read through questions 1–7 and check that they know the meaning of the underlined phrases. Encourage Ss to help each other with the vocabulary, or use an English–English dictionary. Help and answer their questions as necessary. Get feedback from the whole class, asking Ss to explain the meanings of the phrases.

b ▶ Put Ss in new pairs, so that they are working with a different partner. Ss discuss the sentences with their new partners. Monitor the conversations and take note of errors. Get feedback from the whole class. Write the errors on the board and ask Ss to correct them before writing the correct forms on the board.

EXTEND THE LEAD-IN

Put Ss in pairs. Ss look at the pictures again and decide what happens next in each of the stories. Encourage Ss to be imaginative and use humour if they can. Put Ss in new pairs so that they are working with a different partner. Ss share their ideas with their new partners. Get feedback from the whole class and decide who had the best ideas for what happened next in the stories.

3.1 Famous hoaxes

In this lesson, Ss read about some famous hoaxes. Through this context they look at the grammar of narrative tenses. Ss then tell a story about something that has happened to them. They look at synonyms, and how they can make what they say and write more memorable and interesting.

OPTIONAL WARMER

Write *April Fools' Day* on the board and ask Ss if they know what it is. If some Ss know, get them to explain to the rest of the class. If none of the Ss know, explain what it is. Ask Ss to discuss if such a day exists in their culture. In a monolingual class, Ss can tell you about their country. In a multilingual class, Ss of different nationalities can tell a partner about the days in their country. Encourage Ss to ask follow-up questions to find out more information before you get feedback from the class.

Reading

April Fools' Day (1 April) is the day in the UK, and in many other countries, when people play tricks on each other. Radio and TV stations often include hoax news stories to try to fool listeners and viewers. In France, people often try to attach a paper fish to other people's backs. In Spanish-speaking countries, tricks are played on 28 December, the day of the Holy Innocents. For examples of famous hoaxes and April Fools' Day tricks, see: www.museumofhoaxes.com.

1a ▶ Ask Ss to look at the photos and discuss questions 1–4. Get feedback from different groups and discuss Ss' ideas with the whole class.

b ▶ Ss read the article quickly to find the answers. You might want to give a time limit, for example five minutes. Tell Ss not to worry about any words they don't understand at this stage as you will deal with them later.

· Answers
1   In a remote part of the Philippines.
2   They are probably being filmed for a documentary.
3   Manuel Elizalde is the man who 'discovered' the tribe.
4   A hoax is an act of deception, a trick or practical joke.

---

2 ▶ Ss decide whether the statements are true or false. Ss read the text again to check if their answers are correct.

Answers
1   F   4   T
2   T   5   F
3   T

---

3 ▶ Put Ss in pairs to discuss questions 1–4. Monitor the conversations for important errors. Get feedback and discuss Ss' ideas with the whole class.

Grammar | narrative tenses review

OPTIONAL GRAMMAR LEAD-IN

Write the following gapped sentences on the board:
1 In 1971, while he _____ _____ (work) as a government minister, Manuel Elizalde _____ (announce) a great discovery.
2 They explained that they _____ _____ _____ (pretend) all along; Elizalde _____ _____ (pay) them to act like a Stone Age tribe.
Ss complete the sentences with the correct form of the verbs in brackets. When they have completed the sentences, get feedback from the whole class and write the correct forms on the board. Ss identify the tenses used to fill the spaces (Past Continuous, Past Simple, Past Perfect Continuous and Past Perfect Simple). Discuss why we use each of these tenses and write the names of the tenses beside the sentences on the board.

4a ▶ Focus Ss' attention on the first paragraph of the article. Ss underline examples of the tenses.

Answers
Past Simple: *announced, lived, used, could find, isolated, didn't speak, arrived, allowed*
Past Continuous: *was working*
Past Perfect Simple: *had found, had existed*
Past Perfect Continuous: *had been living*

---

b ▶ Focus Ss' attention on the Active grammar box. In pairs, Ss discuss the difference in meaning between the pairs of sentences.

Active grammar

1a) means Elizalde had left the country before the truth came out.
1b) means Elizalde was in the country at the time the truth came out, and then he left immediately. Here 1a) is more appropriate; the truth came out after Elizalde had left the country.
2a) uses the continuous to emphasise duration (the long period of time).
2b) is also possible but doesn't emphasise duration as strongly as 2a).
3a) and 3b) are similar in meaning.

---

c ▶ Focus Ss' attention on rules A–D in the Active grammar box.

> **Active grammar**
>
> A chronological   C before
> B progress   D length

▶ Refer Ss to the Reference on page 47 and give them time to read the notes.

5a ▶ Ss read about the hoaxes and put the verbs in brackets in the correct form. Check answers with the whole class.

> **Answers**
>
> 1 were picking   6 had been working
> 2 called   7 announced
> 3 had published   8 had
> 4 admitted   9 had been developing
> 5 had been joking   10 had invented

b ▶ ● 1.12 Play the recording and get Ss to check their answers.

> **OPTIONAL EXTENSION**
>
> If Ss have access to the Internet, ask them to find out more information about famous hoaxes for homework. In the following lesson, Ss share anything they have found out with the rest of the class. Ss also discuss if they think that these hoaxes are believable or not and which one is the most amusing.

Pronunciation | contractions (1)

6a ▶ Ask Ss if there are any contracted forms in the tenses they have just looked at. If they can't see that *had* is contracted, write it on the board and ask them how it could be contracted: *'d*. Ask Ss if they know any other word that can be contracted to *'d*. Answer: *would*. Tell Ss that sometimes when English is spoken quickly, it can be difficult to hear contracted words like *had* and *would*.

▶ ● 1.13 Play the recording and ask Ss to write down the sentences they hear. Ss compare the sentences they have written with a partner.

b ▶ Focus Ss' attention on audioscript 1.13 on page 169. Play the recording again and ask Ss to practise reading the sentences aloud in pairs, paying attention to the contracted forms.

Speaking

7a ▶ Ss think of an event in their lives that they can tell a story about. Tell Ss to think about topics 1–5 when preparing their stories and also think about how they can include narrative tenses. Encourage Ss to make notes. Monitor and help Ss where necessary.

b ▶ When Ss have finished preparing how to tell the real events of the story, tell Ss to invent two or three details to include in the story. Tell them it is important that they include these details in a natural way and give them time to think about how to include the false details.

c ▶ Ss tell their stories to a partner. Tell Ss listening to the stories to think of questions they can ask to try to guess which of the details are not true. Monitor conversations carefully for how Ss use narrative tenses. When Ss have finished telling the stories, their partners ask them the questions to try and discover the invented parts of the story.

▶ Get feedback from the whole class and check if the Ss have been able to discover the invented details. Write errors Ss have made with narrative tenses on the board and ask Ss to correct them. Focus Ss' attention on their correct use of the tenses and congratulate them on their use.

Vocabulary | synonyms

8 ▶ Focus Ss' attention on the article on page 36. Ask them to find synonyms for words/phrases 1–10.

> **Answers**
>
> 1 fooled   6 ancient
> 2 isolated   7 vital
> 3 destroy   8 liberated
> 4 pretending   9 extended
> 5 hoax   10 tragic

9a ▶ Ask Ss to work in pairs to read about the four hoaxes, and to think of synonyms for the underlined phrases. Encourage Ss to use the context to guess the meaning of any unknown words. Get feedback from various Ss.

b ▶ Ss match the words from the box to the underlined words and phrases which have similar meanings.

> **Answers**
>
> announcing – heralding   chased – pursued
> allegedly – supposedly   deceived – conned
> appearance – arrival   doing – performing
> attack – invasion   instructed – ordered
> authentic – genuine   led to – spawned
> carried out – perpetrated   rose – floated

10a ▶ Focus Ss' attention on the Lifelong learning box and give them time to read it. In pairs, they discuss possible ways to rewrite sentences 1–5. Get feedback from the whole class.

Suggested answers	
1	fool
2	genuine
3	ancient
4	ruin
5	carried out

b ▶ In pairs, Ss discuss the sentences from exercise 10a.

3.2 A good read

In this lesson, Ss look at vocabulary for describing books. They then listen to people describing characters from books before reading some book extracts. Ss then go on to look at the grammar of compound words.

> **OPTIONAL WARMER**
>
> Ask Ss to discuss in pairs when and where they like to read books, magazines or newspapers. Ask Ss if they sometimes read in situations like the ones shown in the photos. Get feedback from various Ss.

Vocabulary | books

1 ▶ Put Ss in pairs. Focus Ss on questions 1–3. In their pairs, Ss discuss the questions. Monitor conversations for any interesting language that Ss use. Get feedback and discuss Ss' ideas as a class.

> **OPTIONAL EXTENSION**
>
> For question 2, write the following prompts on the board: *books, music, luxuries, tools*. Organise Ss into pairs. Tell Ss that they are going to be on a desert island with a partner for a year and can only bring three of each of the things on the board to the island. Ss individually decide on three things for each category then try to, with their partner, agree on what to take to the island. Get feedback from the whole class and discuss Ss' choices.

2a ▶ Put Ss in pairs. Tell Ss to cover the words in a–h. With a partner, Ss think of a way of finishing sentences 1–8 if they are describing a book. Get feedback from various pairs and write possible sentences on the board.

▶ Ss uncover the phrases a–h. With a partner, Ss match these with the sentence halves 1–8.

Answers					
1	h	4	c	7	e
2	d	5	g	8	b
3	a	6	f		

▶ Ask Ss which of the expressions is negative. (*The characters are one-dimensional.*)

b ▶ Ss match the expressions with those from exercise 2a with a similar meaning. Ss compare their answers with a partner. Check answers with the whole class.

Answers
1 I'm an avid reader: 7 e
2 I was hooked: 1 h
3 It was gripping: 3 a
4 It depicts real events: 6 f
5 It has a nice, easy style: 2 d
6 It has sold a lot of copies: 8 b
7 I was emotionally involved in it: 4 c
8 They didn't really come alive for me: 5 g

3 ▶ Ss complete the book review. Then they compare answers with a partner.

Answers
1	c	4	b	7	a
2	a	5	b	8	b
3	a	6	c		

4a ▶ In groups of three or four, Ss think of different books, either in English or the Ss' language, which could be described by the words in the box.

b ▶ Ss discuss the books. If all the Ss in the group know the book, Ss decide if they agree with each others' descriptions. Get feedback from the class and discuss the books Ss have described.

Listening

5a ▶ Focus Ss on questions 1–6. Give Ss time to read through them and check understanding.

▶ ● 1.14 Tell Ss that they are going to listen to three people discussing these questions. Play the recording. Ss make notes on what the three speakers say. Ss compare what they have written with a partner.

b ▶ Play the recording again. Ss check their answers with a partner and complete any gaps they have. Check answers with the whole class.

Answers
1 *Who is your favourite fictional character?*
   Speaker 1: Philip Marlowe
   Speaker 2: Elizabeth Bennett
   Speaker 3: the old man from *The Old Man and the Sea*
2 *How do you visualise them (what do they look like)?*
   Speaker 1: like Humphrey Bogart: tall, good-looking, tough
   Speaker 2: quite tall with a very lively, mobile face and possibly dark hair
   Speaker 3: quite old, big strong hands that were cut and bruised, a little bit of grey hair
3 *What personal traits do they possess (type of character)?*
   Speaker 1: doesn't always say the right thing, always has a clever retort, has real problems, very clever, very tough, likes to get to the bottom of the problem
   Speaker 2: sparky, lively, feisty, lippy (talks back to men), takes control of her own life
   Speaker 3: wise, took pride in his job, did his best
4 *What memorable things do they do?*
   Speaker 1: unlike most modern characters, he doesn't always win/isn't always on top of the situation
   Speaker 2: takes control of her own life, goes for the guy that she really loves, wins her guy in the end
   Speaker 3: dragged himself out every night, cast his nets, hoped he would catch something
5 *What problems do they overcome?*
   Speaker 1: solves murder crimes
   Speaker 2: women had little control over what happened to them in the marriage market, people thought she was socially unacceptable
   Speaker 3: he was down on his luck in the story, hadn't caught anything for a long time, had little opportunity in life
6 *Do you know anyone like them in real life?*
   Speaker 1: doesn't say
   Speaker 2: doesn't say
   Speaker 3: the speaker's father

6a ▶ Ask Ss to think individually about their own favourite fictional character from a book. Give Ss a few minutes to think about how they would answer questions 1–6 from exercise 5a about their chosen character.

b ▶ In small groups, Ss take turns to describe their character. Monitor for any important errors. Get feedback from the whole class, then write the errors you have heard on the board and get various Ss to correct them.

▶ For homework, ask Ss to turn their notes into a full description of the character. In the following lesson, get the Ss to read out their character descriptions to the rest of the class.

> **OPTIONAL VARIATION**
>
> If Ss can't think of a favourite character from a book, they can describe a favourite character from a film or television programme.

Reading

7 ▶ Ss read through extracts 1–6 and match them with questions a–f. If there are any words or expressions in the extracts that Ss don't understand, tell them that you will deal with them later. Ss compare their answers with a partner. Check answers with the whole class.

> **Suggested answers**
> | | | | |
> |---|---|---|---|
> | a | 6 | d | 3 |
> | b | 4 | e | 1 |
> | c | 2 | f | 5 |

8 ▶ Put Ss in small groups. Ss discuss the questions. Point out that some of the vocabulary in the extracts might be challenging, so encourage Ss to work out the meaning from the context before using a dictionary or asking you. Get feedback from various pairs.

Vocabulary | compound words

> **OPTIONAL WARMER**
>
> Get Ss to re-read the six book extracts again and to look at the underlined words. Ask Ss to work in pairs to decide what these words have in common. (They are all compound words.) Ss discuss if they know of any characteristics of compound words. Get feedback from the whole class.

9 ▶ Focus Ss on the questions and the underlined words in the extracts. In pairs, Ss answer the questions. Ss compare their answers with another pair. Check answers with the whole class.

> **Answers**
> 1 extract 3 contains only a compound noun (*hell-raiser*)
> 2 *self-conscious* and *hot-headed* describe someone's character; *weather-beaten*, *far-seeing*, *hollow-cheeked*, *fast-moving*, *washed-out* describe something physical
> 3 works hard = *hard-working*; keeps an open mind = *open-minded*; looks good = *good-looking*; thinks freely = *free-thinking*; loves fun = *fun-loving*

▶ Refer Ss to the Reference on page 47 and give Ss time to read through the notes.

10a ▶ Ss read sentences 1–8 and discuss the meaning of the underlined compound adjectives with a partner. Get feedback from various Ss.

> **Suggested answers**
> 1 *single-minded* = determined/never gives up
> 2 *self-sufficient* = doesn't rely on other people/looks after herself
> 3 *thick-skinned* = doesn't get upset when criticised/doesn't take criticism personally
> 4 *kind-hearted* = good to other people/generous
> 5 *stand-offish* = not friendly/doesn't talk to other people
> 6 *career-orientated* = always thinks about his career/does a lot of things to enhance his career
> 7 *level-headed* = calm (in good and bad situations)/not too excitable
> 8 *absent-minded* = forgetful

b ▶ Ss divide the compound adjectives into three groups: positive, negative and neutral.

> **Answers**
> 1 positive
> 2 positive
> 3 positive (in this context, though it can also be negative in other contexts)
> 4 positive
> 5 negative
> 6 neutral
> 7 positive
> 8 slightly negative

Speaking

11a ▶ Ss look at the photos and write as many compound adjectives as they can think of to describe each person. You may want to give Ss a time limit for doing this. Help Ss where necessary.

b ▶ Ss compare their opinions with a partner. Get feedback from the whole class.

12 ▶ Tell Ss they are going to describe someone they know well. Focus their attention on the How to... box and get Ss to make notes about first impressions, physical details and character. Encourage Ss to use the expressions from the box and compound words where possible when making their notes. It may be a good idea to get Ss to describe someone who is unusual in some way, either physically or in character.

13 ▶ Each student describes their person to the whole class. Take note of any errors in using compound words. Ss decide if any of the descriptions had been about the same person and if any sound similar. Write any errors Ss have made with compound words on the board and get Ss to correct them.

3.3 Jokers

In this lesson, Ss read a text about Groucho Marx. Through this context they look at the grammar of participle clauses and gerunds. Ss go on to look at vocabulary connected with humour. They then listen to someone telling a joke before finishing the lesson by telling a joke themselves.

> Groucho Marx was an American comedian who appeared in many films both as a member of the Marx Brothers and on his own. He also appeared on American radio and TV shows. He was recognisable for his trademark greasepaint moustache, bushy eyebrows and cigar, as well as for his witty remarks both off and on-screen. In 1974 he was awarded a special Academy Award for his and his brothers' services to the film industry. Groucho Marx died in 1977. See www.marx-brothers.org for more information.

OPTIONAL WARMER

Show Ss the picture of Groucho Marx on page 42. In pairs, Ss discuss what they know about him. If Ss have never seen Groucho Marx before, they can guess who he is, what he is famous for, and in what period he was most famous. Get feedback from the whole class.

Reading

1 ▸ Ask Ss to discuss the questions in pairs. Get feedback on who the Ss' most popular comedians are.

2 ▸ Tell Ss they are going to find out information about Groucho Marx, the comedian in the picture. Tell Ss they are going to read the texts in sections. At the end of each section, Ss read through three possible answers to a question. Working with a partner, Ss discuss and then guess what might be the answer for each question. Ss then go the relevant next section, as instructed, to find out if they were correct. Monitor to check that Ss are reading the sections in the correct order.

Answers			
1	a	5	a
2	c	6	c
3	b	7	a
4	b		

3a ▸ Focus Ss on statements 1–6 about Groucho Marx. Ss decide whether each statement is true or not.

b ▸ Ss compare their answers with a partner. Monitor the conversations for errors. Get feedback from the whole class and check the answers the Ss have written. Write any important errors on the board and encourage Ss to correct them before you write the correct forms.

Suggested answers

1 Probably. His family was poor, and he suffered from insomnia.
2 Probably not. She stopped him from becoming a doctor and pushed him into show business.
3 Probably. They performed and made films together successfully.
4 Definitely. He started in 1904 and made a comeback in the 1970s.
5 Probably. He had a long, successful career.
6 It depends on your sense of humour.

4a ▸ ⬤ 1.15 Tell Ss that they are going to hear someone describing Groucho Marx's life but there will be some mistakes in the description. Play the recording. Ss take note of any mistakes the speaker makes.

b ▸ Ss compare their answers with a partner. Play the recording again for Ss to check their answers.

Answers
It wasn't during a radio show that they started making jokes. It was on stage.
The boys' mother died and the Great Depression began in 1929 not 1926.
Thalberg helped them get into the movie business, not television.
Their last film was *The Big Store*, not *A Day at the Races*.
He was in his 80s, not his 90s.
He died three days after Elvis Presley, not on the same day.

Grammar | participle clauses

OPTIONAL GRAMMAR LEAD-IN

Write the following sentences on the board:
1 Desperately attempted to win some money, Groucho met Irving Thalberg during a card game.
2 Thalberg, impressing with his new friend's act, helped the Marx Brothers to get established in the movie business.
Elicit the correct forms of the verbs from the Ss (*attempting* and *impressed*). Tell Ss that one of these forms is called the present participle and one the past participle and ask them to identify them (present participle: *attempting*, past participle: *impressed*). Explain that we often use participles to add extra information to the idea in the sentence. Refer Ss to the Active grammar box for more information about participle clauses.

5a ▶ Ss read rule A in the Active grammar box and then find examples in the article. Ss compare their answers with a partner. Check answers with the whole class.

> **Active grammar**
>
> past participle: *Thalberg, <u>impressed</u> with his ...*
> present participle: *Desperately <u>attempting</u> to win ...*

b ▶ Ss read rule B in the Active grammar box and then find an example in the article. Check answers with the whole class.

> **Active grammar**
>
> *<u>Having been</u> no more than a moderate success ...*

c ▶ Ss read rule C in the Active grammar box and then find an example in the article. Check answers with the whole class.

> **Active grammar**
>
> *<u>After hitting</u> the heights ...*

d ▶ Ss read rule D in the Active grammar box and then find an example in the article. Check answers with the whole class.

> **Active grammar**
>
> *<u>Growing up</u> with a comedian ...*

▶ Refer Ss to the Reference on page 47 and give Ss time to read through the notes. Monitor and answer any questions Ss might have.

6a ▶ In pairs, Ss correct the mistakes in sentences 1–7 so that they include participles. Check answers with the whole class and write the correct forms of the verbs on the board.

> **Answers**
> 1 When **telling** a joke, timing is very important.
> 2 **Working** as a comedian must be a great job because you make people laugh.
> 3 **Having** become famous, comedians usually get depressed.
> 4 **Made** to look out of date by modern comics, old comedians like Chaplin and Groucho Marx are not funny these days.
> 5 **Telling** jokes in a foreign language is extremely difficult.
> 6 On **being** told a joke, you should laugh even if you don't think it's funny.
> 7 After **watching** Mr Bean and Chaplin, etc., I think physical humour can be as funny as verbal.

b ▶ Ask Ss to read through the corrected statements in exercise 6a and mark whether they agree or disagree with them. Ss compare their answers with a partner and discuss why they agree or disagree with the statements. Monitor the conversations for errors.

Vocabulary | humour

7a ▶ Get Ss to cover definitions 1–8. Focus Ss on the words in the box. Working in pairs, Ss discuss if they have seen these words before and what they think they mean. Encourage Ss to use an English–English dictionary to look up any unknown words. Ss then match the types of humour in the box to definitions 1–8. Ss can check any words they are not sure of in dictionaries. Ss compare their answers with their partners. Check answers with the whole class.

> **Answers**
> 1 surreal   5 puns
> 2 farce   6 irony
> 3 cartoons   7 exaggeration
> 4 black humour   8 satire

b ▶ Ss discuss questions 1–4 with a partner. Monitor the conversations carefully for errors.

▶ In a monolingual class, Ss can discuss the questions in small groups before you get feedback from the class. In a multilingual class, put Ss in pairs so that they are working with someone of another nationality. Get feedback by asking Ss from different countries to talk about the humour of their country.

Pronunciation | speech units

8a ▶ ⏺ 1.16 Ss cover the text. Tell Ss that they are going to listen to someone telling a joke. Play the recording. Ss listen and if necessary take notes while doing so. Ss discuss the joke with a partner and tell each other if they find it funny or not.

b ▶ Ss discuss why they think the speaker pauses at certain moments. (To give dramatic effect and to keep the listeners interested.) Ss uncover the text. Play the recording again for Ss to read the joke as they listen. While they read, Ss mark the places on the text where the person telling the joke pauses.

> **OPTIONAL EXTENSION**
>
> Ss practise telling the joke to a partner, reading the text and pausing at the right moments. Get various Ss to tell the joke in front of the class, as long as they feel comfortable doing so.

Speaking

9a ▶ Put Ss in groups of three. Tell Ss that they are going to tell a joke to their partners. Refer Student A to page 149, Student B to page 151 and Student C to page 153. Give Ss time to read through their jokes two or three times. Tell Ss to try to memorise their jokes if possible. Monitor to check that Ss understand all the words and expressions in their jokes and help them where necessary. Encourage Ss to think about the best places to pause while telling the joke.

b ▶ Ss tell their jokes to the other Ss in their group. Monitor carefully to see if Ss pause at important moments while telling the joke and for any errors the Ss make. In their groups, Ss decide whose joke was the funniest and also who was the best at telling the joke. Finally, write important errors on the board and get different Ss to correct them. Congratulate Ss on telling the jokes, as it is not an easy skill in a foreign language.

OPTIONAL EXTENSION

Tell Ss that they are going to prepare to tell their own jokes, either in their own language or in English. Tell them to write the joke down and mark where they think the best place would be to pause while telling the joke. Collect the Ss' jokes and check there is nothing unsuitable, which might offend another member of the class. Also check the jokes for errors. Hand back the jokes in the following lesson and ask various Ss to tell their jokes to the rest of the class, reminding them to be aware of pausing for dramatic effect.

3 Vocabulary | Metaphors

In this lesson, Ss look at the language of metaphors. They then go on to create their own metaphors.

OPTIONAL WARMER

In a monolingual class, ask Ss if there are any famous chefs in their country. Ss can tell you who they are, why they are famous and if they appear on television or not. In a multilingual class, pair Ss so that they are working with a partner of a different nationality. Ss tell each other about celebrity chefs in their countries. Get feedback by asking Ss to tell the rest of the class about what they have learnt about celebrity chefs in their partner's country.

1a ▶ Focus Ss on the picture. With a partner, Ss discuss what they think the relationship is between the people in the picture and what they think happens in the story. Ss share their ideas with another pair. Get feedback from the whole class.

b ▶ Ss read the story to check their predictions and to find out who the narrator is describing and what made them the way they were.

2 ▶ Focus Ss on the underlined metaphors in the story. Ask Ss to discuss in pairs what they think the metaphors mean. Encourage Ss to work out the meaning of the metaphors from the context. Tell Ss to write the metaphors from the text next to meanings 1–12. Ss compare their answers with a partner. Check answers with the whole class.

Answers
1 follow in (his/her) footsteps
2 dead end
3 take off
4 reach a crossroads
5 warm personality
6 stormy (relationship)
7 frosty reception
8 feel under the weather
9 struggle
10 call the shots
11 in the firing line
12 have (my) sights set on

3 ▶ In pairs Ss complete sentences 1–8 using the metaphors from exercise 2. Ss compare their answers with another pair. Check answers with the whole class.

Answers
1 under (the) weather
2 a dead end
3 stormy relationship
4 call the (shots)
5 take off
6 in (the) firing (line)
7 set on
8 in (your mother's) footsteps

4 ▶ In pairs Ss think of and discuss examples of the different areas mentioned. Monitor the conversations for errors. Get feedback and write any errors on the board. Ask different Ss to correct the errors.

5a ▶ Tell Ss that they are going to create their own metaphors. Focus them on the topics in the box and the example. Monitor what the Ss are writing.

b ▶ Put Ss in pairs. Ss take turns to say their metaphors and guess what it is describing. Get feedback from the whole class.

3 Communication

In this lesson, Ss read the openings to some pieces of fiction. They then discuss in pairs or groups how the story could continue and tell their stories to other pairs/groups.

OPTIONAL WARMER

In pairs, ask Ss to discuss what they think makes a good opening to a book. Get feedback and discuss Ss' ideas with the whole class.

1 ▶ Put Ss in pairs or groups of three or four. Focus Ss on the openings to the pieces of fiction. Ss read extracts 1–8 and discuss questions 1–3 with a partner. Monitor the conversations for interesting language the Ss use. Get feedback from the whole class.

2a ▶ Working alone, Ss think of an opening sentence and think about how the story could continue. On a separate piece of paper, they write the opening sentence. Encourage Ss to use metaphors where possible.

b ▶ Ss pass their piece of paper to another Ss. On the piece of paper they received, they write the rest of the story.

c ▶ Ss check their stories and make any changes necessary.

d ▶ Ss tell their stories in small groups. Monitor the stories and take note of interesting language and metaphors that Ss use correctly. Get feedback and decide as a whole class which pair or group has told the most interesting and unusual story. Draw Ss' attention to any interesting language and metaphors they have used while telling the stories and congratulate them on its use.

OPTIONAL EXTENSION

For homework, ask Ss write up their stories. In the following lesson, collect the stories and photocopy them. Hold a competition for the best story which the Ss themselves can judge. If you prefer, you could ask another teacher to be the judge.

3 Review and practice

1 ▶

Answers

In April 2000 journalists at *Esquire* **decided** that life at the magazine was getting a bit boring. So they published an article about FreeWheelz, an Internet company that gave customers free cars which were covered in advertising. The article **claimed** that FreeWheelz 'will transform the auto industry more than Henry Ford did.' The company **hadn't yet become** famous but it would 'on 1 April, when FreeWheelz launches on the web for real.' Readers who **saw** the website, which had been created by the author of the article, were impressed. Within days, the site **had received** over a thousand hits and messages from other entrepreneurs who claimed they had been planning similar businesses. The website contained a questionnaire for potential clients which **included** a number of bizarre questions such as 'Does hair loss concern you?' In the following edition, the magazine owned up, explaining that the article had been an April Fools' hoax. The magazine **was preparing** to forget all about it when suddenly an offer for the domain name FreeWheelz came in. The author of the article sold the name for $25,000, splitting the profits with the owners of the magazine. The conclusion? Never trust a strange story which contains the date 1 April.

2 ▶

Answers

1 Doing things for other people is life's biggest pleasure.
2 Anyone wishing to take the exam must register in June.
3 Most of the dead animals found after the earthquake were domestic pets.
4 Feeling sleepy, Luisa went to bed.
5 When swimming, it is compulsory that you wear a bathing cap.
6 Having been famous for years, he finally wanted some peace and quiet.
7 Banned from exhibiting their paintings in the national exhibition, they decided to set up their own.
8 Waking up early as usual, David looked out of the window.

3 ▶

Answers

1 avid
2 page-turner
3 black humour
4 hooked
5 readable
6 one-dimensional
7 based
8 gripping
9 couldn't put it down
10 best-seller
11 puns
12 irony
13 moving
14 fictionalised
15 depict
16 surreal

4 ▶

Answers

1 the
2 relationship
3 off
4 footsteps
5 reached
6 firing

3 Writing bank

1 ▶ Focus Ss' attention on the photo and the title. Ss answer the questions. Get feedback from the whole class.

2 ▶ In pairs, Ss read the story and discuss the questions. Get feedback from the whole class.

3 ▶ Focus Ss' attention on the How to... box. In pairs, Ss add the phrases.

Answers
Use metaphors: *His hands were the size of Yorkshire hams*
Use personification: *spewing orange flames*
Use adjectives: *lush grass*
Use dialogue: *"Back to the sky," I said.*

4a ▶ Individually, Ss plan a story. Encourage Ss to use ideas from the How to... box. Go round and monitor Ss who need any help.

b ▶ Ss write their stories.

c ▶ Ss read each other's stories. Encourage Ss to give each other positive feedback.

4 Progress

Overview

CEFR Can do objectives
4.1 Describe the chances of something happening
4.2 Talk about plans and arrangements
4.3 Take detailed and accurate notes
Communication Present and argue a case for something
Writing bank Write a detailed article

CEFR Portfolio ideas
a) If there was a fire in the place where you live and you had to leave immediately, which three objects would you save from the fire? (We can assume that all the people are safe.) Discuss your answers with other people, explaining the reasons for your choices. Listen to the other peoples' choices. What do you think their choices reveal about their priorities and personalities?
b) Do you think there are intelligent life forms on other planets? If there are, do you think they would be friendly or hostile to humans on Earth? Write your ideas in an article for a popular magazine.
c) Choose a scene from a film in your own language. Write English subtitles for the scene.
d) Choose an animal with amazing abilities. Describe the abilities and explain why they are important for the animal's survival. Write a commentary for a TV documentary.

Lead-in

OPTIONAL WARMER
Organise Ss into three groups. Each group looks at one of the three smaller photos on page 49. Give Ss one minute to brainstorm as much vocabulary as possible connected to their photo. Ss then share their ideas with Ss from the other groups. Get whole class feedback and write any interesting vocabulary on the board.

1 ▶ Focus Ss on the photos. Get Ss to discuss the questions in pairs. Get feedback from the whole class.

2a ▶ Ss read through the news headlines 1–4 and match them with the photos. Check the answers with the class.

Answers
1 small photo, middle
2 small photo, top
3 small photo, bottom
4 large photo at top

b ▶ Focus Ss on the words and phrases in the box. With a partner, Ss match the words and phrases to the headlines in exercise 2a. Tell Ss that some of the words/phrases might go with more than one headline. Ss compare their answers with another pair and explain their choices. Check answers with the class.

Suggested answers
1 test tube, strain, superbug, analysis
2 network, crash a system, hacker, software, microchip, firewall
3 cell, organ, skin tissue, gene, genetic engineering
4 mission, orbit, scan, shuttle, launch

c ▶ ● 1.17 Tell Ss they are going to listen to the four news stories. Play the recording. Ss check their answers. Ss compare their answers with their partner.

3 ▶ Focus Ss on sentences 1–3. Get Ss to work in pairs to check the meaning of the underlined words in each sentence. If they do not know the meaning of the words, encourage Ss to help each other or check in their dictionaries before asking you. Ss discuss the questions with their partners. Get feedback from the whole class. Focus Ss' attention on any interesting language they have used, and praise them for its use.

EXTEND THE LEAD-IN
Put Ss in pairs to think of another type of progress that they would most like to see in the future and why. Ss justify their choices to the rest of the class. Get the Ss to try to reach an agreement as a class about which is the most important area of progress for the future.

4.1 Superpowers

In this lesson, Ss read an article about superheroes and about how scientists are trying to recreate superpowers artificially. Through this context, they look at the grammar of future probability. Ss finish by listening to an interview with Stan Lee, the creator of Spider-Man, and discussing future possibilities/probabilities.

> **OPTIONAL WARMER**
>
> Put Ss in pairs, A and B. Tell Ss A to turn their chairs round so that they can't see the board. On the board write the names of the following superheroes: *Spider-Man, Batman, The Incredible Hulk, Superman, The Invisible Woman*.
> Ss B describe the superheroes to their partners who try to guess their names from the descriptions. The winners are the pairs who describe and guess the superheroes first.

Speaking

1 ▶ Ss discuss the questions in pairs. Get feedback from the whole class.

Reading

2 ▶ Ss read the article and check their ideas for exercise 1. Get feedback from the whole class.

3 ▶ Focus Ss' attention on the article again, and the places with a * symbol. Point out that the * symbol means that information is missing. In pairs, Ss complete the article with sentences 1–6.

> **Answers**
> Regeneration paragraph: 5
> Super-strength paragraph: 6
> Force field paragraph: 2
> Web-shooter paragraph: 4
> X-ray vision: 1
> Flying paragraph: 3

4a ▶ Ss read the article and mark the research they think is important with a tick (✓), the research they think is less important with (✗), and any information that worries them with (!). Tell Ss not to worry about any words they don't know the meaning of at this stage as you will be dealing with them later. Ss compare their ideas with other Ss. Get feedback from the whole class.

b ▶ Ss compare their answers in small groups.

Grammar | future probability

> **OPTIONAL GRAMMAR LEAD-IN**
>
> Write the following sentence stem on the board:
> *One of the Ss in the class will …*
> Beside this, write:
> *… be president of his/her country.*
> *… be an international football player.*
> *… do his/her homework tonight.*
> *… take up studying another language in the next year.*
> *… buy a newspaper tomorrow.*
> In groups of three or four, Ss discuss these prompts and decide how likely it is that Ss in the class will do these things. Monitor carefully for Ss' use of expressions of probability. When Ss have finished talking, get feedback from the whole class and focus Ss' attention on the ways in which they expressed probability.

5 ▶ Ss add phrases from the article on page 50 to the Active grammar box. They compare their answers with a partner. Check answers with the whole class.

> **Active grammar**
>
> Sure to happen: *Are bound to …*
> Very likely to happen: *there is a distinct possibility that …*
> Likely to happen: *There is every likelihood that …; There is every chance that …*
> Unlikely to happen: *the odds are against …; It is doubtful that …; There is a slim chance that …; there is very little chance that …; it is unlikely that …*
> Impossible: *stands no chance of …; you don't stand a chance of …*

▶ Refer Ss to the Reference on page 61. Give Ss time to read through the notes and ask you any questions.

6a ▶ Get Ss to read the sentences and in pairs discuss and cross out the option which is *not* possible in each case. Ss compare their answers with another pair. Check answers with the class.

> **Answers**
> 1 option   5 hope
> 2 hopeless   6 doubt
> 3 doubt   7 any chance
> 4 chance   8 doubt

b ▶ Put Ss in different pairs so that they are working with a new partner. Ss discuss if there is any difference in meaning between the two correct options in each sentence. Get feedback from various Ss.

> **Answers**
> 1 *no chance* = no possibility; *no doubt* = certainty
> 2 *doubtful* = unlikely; *possible* = there is a chance
> 3 *haven't a hope/chance* = same meaning
> 4 *remote/slim* = same meaning
> 5 *bound/sure* = same meaning
> 6 *likelihood/chance* = same meaning
> 7 *every likelihood* = a slightly better chance than a distinct possibility
> 8 *chance/hope* both refer to possibility, *hope* implies a more personal involvement in the outcome

7 ▶ Ss close their books. Write *There is no chance that I'm lending her my laptop.* on the board. Write *stand* below this sentence. Ask Ss to rewrite the sentence using the word *stand*. Get feedback from the whole class and write the correct answer on the board.

▶ Ss open their books. Ss to rewrite sentences 1–8 in pairs. Ask Ss to compare their sentences with a partner and then check answers with the whole class.

> **Answers**
> 1 It is doubtful that they will make a breakthrough in the near future.
> 2 It is not inconceivable that we'll be able to travel to Mars by 2050.
> 3 They're bound to notice something is missing.
> 4 There is a chance that the family have already been informed. / There is a remote/slim chance that the family haven't already been informed.
> 5 We're being met at the airport so presumably we don't need train tickets. / Presumably we're being met at the airport so we don't need train tickets.
> 6 Unfortunately, he doesn't have a hope of getting the job. / Unfortunately, there's no hope of him getting the job.
> 7 There is a distinct chance/possibility that China will win the space race.
> 8 I doubt whether the relationship will improve.

Speaking

8 ▶ Ss discuss events 1–5 in pairs. Monitor conversations for errors and correct use of language to express probability. Get feedback from different pairs and discuss Ss' ideas as a whole class. Read out any important errors you have heard and get various Ss to correct them.

Listening

9a ▶ 🌐 1.18 Tell Ss they are going to hear an interview with Stan Lee, the creator of Spider-Man. Give Ss time to read questions a–d. Play the recording and ask Ss to write down the order in which Stan Lee answers the questions in the interview. Ss compare their answers with a partner.

> **Answers**
> 1 c   3 d
> 2 b   4 a

b ▶ Play the recording again and ask Ss to take notes about the different topics listed in the box. Check answers with the whole class.

10 ▶ In pairs, Ss discuss if they agree with what Stan Lee says about diseases, going to Mars and genetics. Monitor conversations for Ss' use of ways of expressing probability. Get feedback from the whole class and focus Ss' attention on any interesting language they have used.

4.2 Thinking ahead

In this lesson, Ss look at vocabulary connected with making arrangements. Ss then look at the grammar of future forms. Ss go on to listen to two telephone conversations and look at different ways of being vague and imprecise when we don't want to, or can't, give details. Ss finish by playing 'twenty questions'.

OPTIONAL WARMER

Write these questions on the board:
When was the last time you arranged to do something with a friend?
Who did you arrange to meet?
Where did you meet?
How did you arrange to meet?
Get Ss to discuss the questions in pairs. Get feedback from the whole class and tell Ss that they are going to be looking at vocabulary connected to making arrangements.

Vocabulary | arrangements

1 ▶ Ask Ss to discuss the questions in pairs. Monitor conversations for errors. Get feedback from the whole class. Write important errors on the board and encourage various Ss to correct them.

2 ▶ Ss read the emails to find out what Tom is trying to do and what happens in the end. Encourage Ss not to worry about words or expressions they don't understand at this stage. Ss compare ideas with a partner. Check answers with the whole class.

Answer
Tom is trying to organise a barbecue, but as no one can come, it is cancelled.

OPTIONAL VARIATION

Put Ss in groups of four. Ss take turns to read one of the emails and remember the information. Ss then tell the others in their group about the content of their email and what the purpose of it is. Ss then read all the emails and decide what Tom is trying to do and what happens in the end.

---

3 ▶ Before Ss look at definitions 1–12, ask them, in pairs, to try to work out from the context what the underlined words and phrases in the emails mean. Check with various pairs what they think the phrases mean.

▶ Focus Ss' attention on definitions 1–12. Ss match the underlined words and phrases to the definitions. Ss then compare answers with their partners. Check answers with the whole class.

Answers

1	(what) you're up to	7	call off
2	crop up	8	snowed under
3	tied up	9	fall through
4	(have something) lined up	10	go ahead
5	put my feet up	11	at a loose end
6	get out of (something)	12	wind down

▶ Ask Ss if they are any other words or phrases in the emails they don't understand. Encourage Ss to answer each other's questions or check in a dictionary before asking you.

4 ▶ Ss read sentences 1–12 and complete them by adding one word to each one. Check answers with the whole class.

Answers

1	off	5	up	9	went
2	Put	6	up	10	snowed
3	up	7	up	11	of
4	at	8	down	12	through

5a ▶ In pairs, Ss discuss questions 1–6. Monitor conversations and take note of interesting language Ss use.

b ▶ Ss think about two other Ss in the class and predict what their answers to the questions might be. Ss mingle and ask these Ss the questions to check their predictions. Read out errors you have heard and get Ss to correct them.

Grammar | future forms (review)

OPTIONAL GRAMMAR LEAD-IN

Write the following sentences on the board:
1 The class finishes at six o' clock.
2 I'll have a cigarette now.
3 Most of the Ss will do their homework this evening.
4 There's going to be a class party at the end of the week.
5 It's going to snow tomorrow.
6 I'm meeting the rest of the class for a coffee tomorrow morning.
7 I'll be flying over the Atlantic at this time tomorrow.
8 I'll have finished this book before the end of the month.
In pairs, Ss decide which of the sentences are true and which are false. Ss then decide what future forms are used and why they are used in each sentence. For example, in sentence 1 the Present Simple is used for a timetable in the future.

6a ▶ Focus Ss' attention on the emails on page 53. In pairs, they identify the different verb forms used to talk about the future. Get feedback from the whole class.

b ▶ Ss complete the tasks in the Active grammar box. Let them compare with a partner.

Active grammar

2	c	6	h
3	d	7	f
4	g	8	b
5	a		

▶ Refer Ss to the Reference on page 61 and give them time to read through the notes.

7a ▶ Individually, Ss complete sentences 1–12 using the correct future form of the verb in brackets.

b ▶ Ss compare with a partner and decide if any of the sentences can use more than one future form. Check answers with the whole class.

Answers
1 is going to faint
2 'll pick it up
3 are getting/are going to get (Present Continuous for intention or *going to* for arrangements)
4 are going to be
5 will have retired
6 am using/'ll be using/'m going to be using (Present Continuous for intention, Future Continuous for something that will be in progress during a period of time in the future, or *going to* for arrangements)
7 will be lying
8 will be doing
9 will have finished
10 starts
11 'll write
12 will have eaten

8 ▶ Ss complete questions 1–8 with the correct form of the verb in brackets. Check the questions as a class.

Answers
1	will still be studying	5	will have changed
2	will have	6	will have
3	will be living	7	will have
4	will have	8	will have seen

Pronunciation | auxiliary verb *have*

9a ▶ Focus Ss' attention on the sentences. Ss discuss the questions in pairs.

b ▶ 🔵 1.19 Now play the recording. Ss check with a partner.

c ▶ 🔵 1.20 Play the recording. Ss discuss the question.

d ▶ Play the recording again. Ss repeat the questions. Monitor for appropriate pronunciation of contractions.

10a ▶ Ss interview a partner with the questions from exercise 8, paying attention to contracted forms. Encourage Ss to ask follow-up questions. Monitor Ss for correct use of future forms and the use of contracted forms.

b ▶ Get feedback by asking Ss to share information about their partners with the whole class. Finally, write errors on the board and get different Ss to correct them. Focus Ss' attention on their use of contracted forms and praise them for correct usage.

Listening and speaking

OPTIONAL WARMER

Write these questions on the board:
How often do you talk on the phone?
Who do you talk to?
How long do you spend on the phone every day?
Which do you use more, a mobile or landline?
Ss discuss the questions in pairs. Get feedback from the whole class about who spends most time on the phone every day.

11 ▶ 🔵 1.21 Tell Ss they are going to hear two telephone conversations. Play the recording. Ss listen and decide what the relationship between the speakers is and what plans they are trying to make. Ss compare answers with a partner. If necessary play the recording again for Ss to check.

Answers
Conversation 1: they are friends. They are trying to meet on Saturday night.
Conversation 2: they are a couple. They are discussing arrangements for dinner at home.

12 ▶ Play the recording again. Ss complete the expressions in the How to... box. Ss compare answers with a partner. Check answers with the whole class.

> **Answers**
> 1 moon
> 2 time
> 3 less
> 4 loads
> 5 (number)
> 6 or so
> 7 pieces
> 8 thing
> 9 kind
> 10 way

13 ▶ Ss unjumble the sentences. Encourage Ss not to add punctuation to the sentences. Ss compare answers with a partner. Check answers with the whole class.

> **Answers**
> 1 We still go to that café from time to time.
> 2 We are going to do various bits and pieces before we leave.
> 3 I'm sort of pushed for time this weekend.
> 4 Her job involves solving problems whenever they crop up, that kind of thing.
> 5 They'll stay here for more or less a month.
>   (Note: 'They'll stay here for a month more or less' is wrong here because a comma is needed after month.)
> 6 Because I'm so busy, I only see my sister once in a blue moon.
> 7 By this time next year, I'll have met loads of new people.
> 8 We're hoping to meet at about four-ish.
> 9 I'll be arriving at ten or so.
> 10 In a way, I prefer staying at home on Saturday nights.

14a ▶ 🌐 1.22 Play the recording and ask Ss to write their own imprecise or vague answers to the questions they hear, using the phrases from the How to... box.

b ▶ Ss compare answers with a partner. Get feedback from the whole class, and comment on Ss' use of the phrases from the How to... box.

15 ▶ Ask Ss if they know how to play 'twenty questions'. If any Ss know how to play, they explain the rules to the class. If they don't, focus Ss on the instructions in the box. Ss then play the game in pairs. Encourage Ss to include imprecise or vague information in their answers. Take note of errors and Ss' use of expressions for being imprecise or vague.

▶ When Ss have finished, get feedback from the whole class and find out which Ss guessed their partner's famous person. If Ss finish quickly, they can repeat the activity with a different famous person. Draw Ss' attention to their use of expressions for being imprecise or vague. Read out errors you have heard and discuss them with the whole class.

4.3 Great expectations

In this lesson, Ss read an article about gifted children. They then look at ways of emphasising information in sentences through inversion. They listen to an expert on gifted children talking about a strange case.

> **OPTIONAL WARMER**
>
> Write these prompts on the board: *school, friends, food, TV, sports, games*. Tell Ss to think back to when they were ten years old and to remember the type of lives they had, using the prompts on the board to help them. Ss then tell a partner about their lives when they were ten years old. Get feedback from the whole class to see whose childhoods were the most similar/different.

Vocabulary | special abilities

1 ▶ In pairs, Ss discuss the question. Ss make three lists of things that they think are usual for children to be able to do by the time they are two, five and ten years old. Get feedback from various Ss.

2 ▶ In pairs, Ss discuss what they think words 1–7 mean. Ss then match the words to synonyms a–g. Check answers with the whole class.

> **Answers**
>
> | | | | | | |
> |---|---|---|---|---|---|
> | 1 | d | 4 | e | 7 | c |
> | 2 | a | 5 | g | | |
> | 3 | f | 6 | b | | |

> There are many characteristics of gifted children. They may learn to read early and tend to demonstrate high reasoning ability, creativity, curiosity, a large vocabulary and an excellent memory. However, they can sometimes have problems with teachers and other authority figures as they may frequently question authority. Gifted children often have problems in school as they are not challenged enough. Some famous gifted children: Ruth Lawrence – the youngest student to enter Oxford University at age 11; Steve Wozniak – started developing complex electronics while still at school, went on to develop the world's first screen and keyboard desktop computer; writer H.P. Lovecraft – recited poetry aged two and was writing poetry at the age of five; Mozart – wrote his first symphony at the age of eight.

Reading

3 ▶ In pairs. Ss look at the photos, and at the words and phrases from exercise 2. Ss make predictions about what the article is about using the photos and phrases. Ss compare predictions with another pair.

4 ▶ Ss read the article quickly to check their predictions. To ensure that Ss skim through the text you may want to give them a time limit for this first reading. Ss discuss with a partner if any of their predictions were correct.

5 ▶ Ss read the article more carefully and answer questions 1–5. Ss compare their answers with a partner. Check answers with the whole class.

> **Answers**
> 1 Because Son could play chess before he was three years old.
> 2 It's nothing special. It is natural for him.
> 3 They receive lots of attention, not all of it positive. They are labelled as overly demanding, treated as money-making machines, and scrutinised like lab rats.
> 4 The 'key question' is whether geniuses are born or made.
> 5 It is a combination of nature and nurture. ('Prodigies are half born, half made.')

6 ▶ In pairs, Ss discuss questions 1–5. Monitor conversations for errors and any interesting language that Ss use. Get feedback and ask different pairs to share their ideas with the rest of the class. Write errors on the board and get different Ss to correct them. Finally, read out interesting language that Ss have used and congratulate them on its use.

Grammar | inversion

> **OPTIONAL GRAMMAR LEAD-IN**
>
> Write two sentences on the board about things you are able to do. For example: *I speak English. I also speak French*. Underneath, write the prompt: *Not only … .* Ask Ss how you could make one sentence using the two original sentences and the prompt. Ss discuss this in pairs. If Ss can't give you the sentence, write it on the board: *Not only do I speak English, but I also speak French.* Tell Ss that this is an example of inversion and elicit why this structure is used (to add variety and to emphasise parts of the sentence). Focus Ss on the change in word order and how the order in this type of sentence is the same as in a question. Ask Ss to write two sentences about themselves and what they are able to do. Then get them to write a third sentence combining the information in the two sentences, but this time beginning with *Not only … .* Monitor the class and check Ss' sentences as necessary. Ss show their sentence to a partner, who helps them check if it is correct. Ss read their sentences to the rest of the class.

7a ▶ Ss work in pairs to find further examples of inversion in the article on page 56.

> **Active grammar**
>
> No sooner had he started playing than he was able to adopt complex strategies.
> Only if they are in a stimulating home environment will their natural talents flourish.

b ▶ Ss match the rules and examples in the Active grammar box. Ss compare answers with a partner. Check answers with the whole class.

> **Active grammar**
>
> C 6   E 5
> D 7   F 4

▶ Refer Ss to the Reference on page 61 and give Ss time to read through the notes.

8 ▶ Ss read the six pairs of sentences and tick the correct option in each case. Ss compare their answers with a partner. Get feedback from various Ss.

> **Answers**
> 1 b   4 a
> 2 a   5 b
> 3 a   6 a

Pronunciation | word stress (2)

9 ▶ 🔘 1.23 Tell Ss they are going to listen to the correct answers. Play the recording for Ss to check the sentences in exercise 8 they have chosen. Ask Ss to mark the stressed words in each correct sentence. Ss can then check the words they have marked against audioscript 1.23 on page 170. Play the recording again and get Ss to read along with the recording.

10a ▶ Ss complete the three sentences with their own ideas.

b ▶ Ss then practise saying the sentences they have written with a partner, paying attention to the word stress. Monitor while Ss are saying the sentences, and give praise for good pronunciation.

> **OPTIONAL EXTENSION**
>
> Put Ss into two groups, A and B. Tell Ss A they are journalists writing a report on child prodigies. The journalists are going to interview Nguyen Ngoc Truong Son. Tell Ss B they are Son. They are going to be interviewed by a journalist. Ss in group A prepare the questions they can ask in the interview, and Ss in group B prepare what they might say in an interview. Encourage Ss B to be imaginative and invent details about Son and his life. When Ss have finished preparing, pair them off so that Ss A are working with Ss B. Ss conduct the interview. Monitor for errors. If any pair feels confident enough, ask them to act out their interview for the rest of the class. When Ss have finished, write errors you have heard on the board and ask Ss to correct them.

Listening

11a ► Tell Ss they are going to listen to an expert on gifted children describing a strange case. Focus Ss on the notes and give them time to read through them. Ask Ss to decide what information they need to complete the notes.

b ► ● 1.24 Play the recording. Ss listen and complete the notes. Ss compare their answers with a partner. Play the recording again for Ss to check their answers. Check answers with the whole class.

> **Suggested answers**
> 1   John and Michael
> 2   tiny
> 3   laughed
> 4   the date and day of the week
> 5   numbers
> 6   the weather, what they did, and other events in the world
> 7   visual
> 8   We can see the **answers**

c ► Ss discuss the questions in pairs.

12a ► Ss discuss the questions in groups.

b ► Ss read the Lifelong learning box and match the techniques to the explanations.

> **Answers**
> 1   e   4   a
> 2   c   5   f
> 3   d   6   b

c ► Focus Ss' attention on the notes in exercise 11a.

> **Answers**
> 2, 3, 4

Speaking

> **OPTIONAL WARMER**
>
> Divide the class into two groups, A and B. Ss A look at the first picture, Ss B the second. Give Ss three minutes to brainstorm what they think the child in the photo is like. You may like to put the following prompts on the board: *age*, *nationality*, *family*, *special talent*. Put Ss in pairs so that Ss A are working with Ss B. Ss now share their ideas about the child in their photo. Tell Ss they are going find out about the children and what they are really like.

13a ► Divide the class into two groups, A and B. Refer Ss A to the text on page 150 and Ss B to the text on page 154. Ss complete the texts and then make notes following the advice in the Lifelong learning box.

b ► Put Ss in pairs, A and B. Ss tell their partner about the person in their text from the notes they have made.

4 Vocabulary | Two-part expressions

In this lesson, Ss look at different two-part expressions.

> **OPTIONAL WARMER**
>
> Write *bread and _____*, *black and _____*, *salt and _____* on the board. Ss discuss what words best fill the spaces. Get feedback and complete the expressions: *butter*, *white*, *pepper*. Explain that these are two-part expressions and that they go together in that order. Ss think of other two-part expressions. Write correct examples on the board.

1a ► In pairs, Ss discuss the questions.

b ► Focus Ss on the two-part expressions in the sentences.

> **Answers**
> 1   Now and again
> 2   By and large

c ► Ask Ss to cover definitions a–j. In pairs, Ss look at the two-part expressions in sentences 1–10 and discuss their meanings. Ss uncover definitions a–j and match the expressions with their definitions. Ss can then compare answers with another pair. Check answers with the whole class.

> **Answers**
> 1   c   5   b   9   h
> 2   j   6   d   10 g
> 3   a   7   i
> 4   e   8   f

2 ► Ss close their books. Divide the class into groups of three: A, B and C. Ss A start by saying the first word in one of the two-part expressions. Ss B and C race to say the rest of the expression. Whoever says the rest of the expression correctly first chooses another two-part expression and says the first part for other Ss to complete. Continue until the Ss have said all the two-part expressions.

3 ► Ss cover exercise 1. Ss complete sentences 1–10 with expressions from exercise 1 without looking. Ss compare answers. Check answers with the whole class.

> **Answers**
> 1   law and order
> 2   facts and figures
> 3   trial and error
> 4   rules and regulations
> 5   aches and pains
> 6   tried and tested
> 7   out and about
> 8   once and for all
> 9   ready and waiting
> 10 sick and tired

4 ▶ Ss discuss questions 1–7 in pairs. Encourage Ss to ask follow-up questions where possible. Get feedback from various Ss.

5a ▶ Ss write three questions using the two-part expressions from exercise 1. Monitor and check the questions that Ss write.

b ▶ In pairs, Ss ask and answer the questions. When Ss have finished, discuss errors you heard with the whole class.

4 Communication

In this lesson, Ss listen to different people talking about important discoveries and inventions. They then read some texts about discoveries and inventions before presenting a case for research funding to the rest of the class.

> **OPTIONAL WARMER**
>
> Ask Ss to think of the three most useful inventions that affect their daily lives. Ss explain to a partner why these inventions are important to them. Get Ss to ask follow-up questions where possible. Get class feedback.

1 ▶ 🔘 1.25 Play the recording. Ss write down the inventions and discoveries mentioned, and take notes about them. Ss compare what they have written with a partner.

> **Answers**
> Speaker 1: X-ray machine, penicillin and DNA
> Speaker 2: a rocket
> Speaker 3: computers and the Internet
> Speaker 4: domestic appliances (e.g. the washing machine, processes like freeze-drying food) and transport (e.g. the bicycle, car, aeroplane)

2 ▶ Play the recording again. Ss tick the expressions in the How to... box that they hear.

> **Answers**
> It changed ... completely
> It paved the way for ...
> It has had a huge impact on ...

3 ▶ In small groups, Ss discuss the questions.

4 ▶ Ss read the three texts and think about questions 1–3 while reading. Ss will probably need time to take notes to answer the questions. Monitor and help with vocabulary Ss don't know the meaning of. Encourage them to use an English–English dictionary or ask their partners if there are any unknown words. Ss compare ideas with a partner. Get feedback from the whole class.

5a ▶ Divide the class into groups: A, B and C. Tell group A they are going to present a case for research into space travel, group B they are going to present a case for research into how robots can help mankind, and group C they are going to present a case for research into genetic engineering. In their groups, Ss discuss questions 1–4. Monitor and take note of any errors.

b ▶ Ss decide how they are going to present a case for their research. Give Ss time to prepare what they are going to say and help where necessary.

c ▶ Groups take it in turns to present their cases. Give each group five minutes to present their case to the rest of the class. Encourage the Ss listening to take notes and write questions to ask the Ss about their case. When the groups have finished presenting the case, the other Ss can ask them questions.

▶ Decide as a class which group made the most convincing case. Read out errors Ss have made and encourage them to self-correct. Congratulate Ss on interesting ideas and language they have used while presenting their cases.

4 Review and practice

1 ▶

Suggested answers

1 There is a good chance the weather will improve in the coming months. / There is a distinct possibility that the weather will improve in the coming months. / The weather could well improve in the coming months.
2 There is a remote chance that they will succeed in contacting us. / They probably won't succeed in contacting us. / There is a slim possibility that they will succeed in contacting us.
3 There is every likelihood that we will move house in the spring. / There is a good chance that we will move house in the spring. / We're bound to move house in the spring.
4 He hasn't/doesn't have a hope of being offered the job. / He doesn't stand a chance of being offered the job./ There's a distinct possibility he won't be offered the job.
5 Presumably, attendance will be high this year. / There is bound to be a high attendance this year. / There is a strong possibility that attendance will be high this year.
6 It is almost inconceivable that Thompson will score a goal. / The odds are against Thompson scoring a goal. / Thompson could possibly score a goal.

2 ▶

Answers

1 retires; 'll be looking
2 'm just coming
3 'll be
4 be seeing
5 'm going to work
6 'll make; say

3 ▶

Answers

1 b
2 c
3 b
4 c
5 c

4 ▶

Answers

1 longer
2 Only
3 have
4 Not
5 did
6 On
7 account
8 Never
9 been

5 ▶

Answers
1   in a blue moon
2   bits and pieces
3   at a loose end
4   up to
5   more or less
6   cropped up
7   time to time
8   put my feet up
9   snowed under
10 fell through

6 ▶

Answers
1   genetic
2   pains
3   tissue
4   microchips
5   scan
6   once
7   antibiotics/drugs
8   viruses
9   regulations
10 cloning

4 Writing bank

1 ▶ Focus Ss' attention on the photo and the title. Ss answer the questions. Get feedback from the whole class.

2 ▶ In pairs, Ss read the article and discuss the questions. Get feedback from the whole class.

Answers
1   with a teacher standing at a blackboard, writing down information for the children to copy and memorise
2   smartboards, clickers
3   robot teachers, 'smart classrooms' which can track individual students' brain movements

3 ▶ Focus Ss' attention on the How to... box. In pairs, Ss add further phrases. Get feedback from the whole class.

4a ▶ Individually, Ss plan an article. Encourage Ss to use ideas from the How to... box. Go round and monitor Ss who need any help.

b ▶ Ss write their articles.

Overview

Lead-in	**Vocabulary:** Fortunes
5.1	**Can do:** Talk about professional relationships **Grammar:** Emphasis **Vocabulary:** Business **Speaking and pronunciation:** Emphasis (1) **Reading:** Starting up and starting over **Listening:** Choosing a business partner
5.2	**Can do:** Discuss financial decisions/ regrets **Grammar:** Conditional sentences **Vocabulary:** Finance and philanthropy **Speaking and pronunciation:** Contractions (2) **Reading:** Rags to riches
5.3	**Can do:** Express priorities **Grammar:** Sentence adverbials **Vocabulary:** Expressing quantity **Speaking and pronunciation:** How to... express priorities **Reading:** 100 best companies to work for **Listening:** Working conditions
Vocabulary	Idioms (1)
Communication	Negotiate
Writing bank	Write a persuasive piece How to... write persuasively
Extra resources	ActiveTeach and ActiveBook

CEFR Can do objectives
5.1 Talk about professional relationships
5.2 Discuss financial decisions/regrets
5.3 Express priorities
Communication Negotiate
Writing bank Write a persuasive piece

CEFR Portfolio ideas
a) You are organising a dinner party for eight people. Choose any historical figures to be your seven guests. You want your guests to be interesting, but you don't want them to fight with each other, so choose carefully! Since you cannot cook, choose a menu from take-away food available locally. Write an email to one of your guests inviting them to the party, saying who will be there and persuading them to attend.
b) Write an article about the best boss or manager you have ever had, explaining why this person was so good. End your article with 'Five tips for good managers'.
c) Prepare a magazine advertisement for an electrical appliance. List the benefits from using the appliance.
d) A friend wants you to look after his/her pet for two weeks. You do not want to accept this responsibility. Invent reasons why you cannot care for the pet. Write a dialogue in which finally, you either accept or reject this task.

Lead-in

OPTIONAL WARMER
Ss write the names of three famous wealthy people from their countries. In a monolingual class, get feedback as a class and Ss explain to you how these people became rich. In a multilingual class, pair Ss so that they are working with Ss of a different nationality. Ss share information about the names they have written with a partner, explaining how the people became so rich. Get feedback from the whole class.

1a ▶ Ss work in pairs to make a list of ways they can think of making a fortune. When Ss have written their lists, they compare what they have written with another pair. Ss then decide which of the ways of earning a fortune are the easiest, which are the most risky and which the quickest. Get feedback from the whole class.

b ▶ Focus Ss on sentences 1–8. Ask Ss to discuss in pairs the meaning of the underlined words and phrases. Check answers with the whole class.

Answers
1 inherited a lot of money
2 argued about the price
3 the business of buying and selling shares
4 an increase in wages
5 describes (people) who earn a lot
6 worth more than money can buy
7 paid according to how much you sell
8 couldn't pay its debts

---

c ▶ Ss decide if any of the words/phrases could be used to describe the photos. Get feedback from various Ss.

2 ▶ Ss discuss statements 1–6 in small groups. Get feedback from the groups.

EXTEND THE LEAD-IN
Write the following sentence on the board: *High-income families should pay higher taxes.* Divide the class into two groups: A and B. Tell group A that they are in favour of this idea, and group B that they are against the idea. Give the groups time to prepare what they are going to say. Invite one of the Ss in group A to start the debate by stating why they are in favour of high-income families paying higher taxes. Then get one of the Ss from group B to respond. Make sure that all the Ss in both groups contribute to the debate. You can decide at the end of the debate which group has been more convincing in their arguments.

5.1 A new leaf

In this lesson, Ss read about a television show in which ex-convicts are trained to become florists. Ss then look at how to add emphasis in sentences. Ss finish the lesson by listening to someone talking about business partnerships, and go on to discuss what makes such partnerships successful or not.

> **OPTIONAL WARMER**
>
> Ss write down occasions when they think it would be suitable to send or receive flowers in their countries. Ss compare what they have written with a partner, and discuss if they have ever given or received flowers on such occasions.

Vocabulary | business

1a ▶ Ask Ss to read the proposal. In pairs, they discus the question.

b ▶ In pairs, Ss try to work out the meaning of the underlined expressions from the context. Don't ask for feedback at this point.

c ▶ To test Ss' understanding of the expressions from exercise 1a, ask them to complete the sentences in pairs. Get feedback from the whole class.

> **Answers**
> 1   bail; out
> 2   start-up funds
> 3   make; living
> 4   fringe benefit
> 5   broken even
> 6   launch; company
> 7   profit-share
> 8   recruited

Reading

2 ▶ Ask Ss to discuss the questions in pairs or groups of three. Get feedback from the whole class.

3 ▶ Ss read the article again more carefully and answer questions 1–6. Ss compare their answers with a partner. Check answers with the whole class.

> **Answers**
> 1   T
> 2   T
> 3   F
> 4   F
> 5   T
> 6   F

Grammar | emphasis

> **OPTIONAL GRAMMAR LEAD-IN**
>
> Ask Ss who was the first person to arrive in class. Write the following sentence on the board, with the student's name: _____ *was the first to arrive in class today*. Underneath write: *The person … .* Ask Ss to complete the second sentence, using the information contained in the first sentence. Elicit the following and write it on the board: *The person who arrived first in class today was _____.* Ask Ss why the second sentence is written in this order and explain that this is one way to emphasise important information in a sentence.

4a ▶ Ss look at rule A in the Active grammar box and find further examples from the article. Ss compare answers with a partner. Check answers with the whole class.

> **Active grammar**
> 1   … really wanted their own shop
> 2   … it proved very difficult indeed
> 3   Paula was not in the least bit alarmed by working with criminals.
> 4   … even with the advantage of publicity …; … the project was by no means easy
> 5   … they did know an awful lot about credit card fraud

b ▶ Ss look at rules B and C in the Active grammar box and find further examples from the article. Ss compare answers with a partner. Check answers with the whole class.

> **Active grammar**
>
> Cleft sentences: The reason she could be so calm was that she'd deliberately avoided finding out what crimes they'd committed.; … The thing that amazed her was that they all wanted to be on TV …
>
> *What* clause: what they reminded her of was the children she used to teach in a British comprehensive school.

▶ Refer Ss to the Reference on page 75 and give them time to read through the notes. Monitor to answer any questions Ss have.

5a ▶ Ss rewrite sentences 1–10 to add emphasis using the words in brackets. Ss compare their answers with a partner.

> **Answers**
> 1 He can't complain. It's his own fault he lost the money.
> 2 We're by no means certain that it isn't the same man committing the crimes.
> 3 What I really miss is having enough time to spend with friends.
> 4 They didn't understand what we wanted at all.
> 5 He didn't even stop at the red light. He just drove straight through.
> 6 The costs were very high indeed.
> 7 It was always Sammy who got into trouble.
> 8 Keith wasn't in the least bit annoyed when we cancelled the meeting.
> 9 The reason we came home early was because it started raining.
> 10 The thing I find annoying is those pop-up ads.

b ▶ 🔘 1.26 Play the recording. Ss check their answers.

Pronunciation | emphasis (1)

6 ▶ 🔘 1.26 Play the recording again. Ss note the main words which indicate stress in each sentence. Ss practise saying the sentences with the same stress and intonation as the recording.

7 ▶ Ss discuss questions 1–3 in pairs. Encourage Ss to use different ways of adding emphasis when talking to their partners. Monitor for correct use of emphasis. Get feedback from the whole class, congratulating Ss on any correct use of emphasis.

Listening and speaking

> **OPTIONAL WARMER**
>
> Write the following first halves of famous business partnerships on the board: *Saatchi*, *Ben*, *Fortnum*, *Hewlett*, *Johnson*, *Marks*, *Rolls*. Ask Ss to work in pairs to see how many of these famous business partnerships they can complete. Get feedback and write the second halves on the board: *Saatchi and Saatchi* (advertising agency), *Ben and Jerry's* (ice-cream makers), *Fortnum and Mason* (quality English food shop), *Hewlett-Packard* (computer manufacturers), *Johnson and Johnson* (manufacturer of health care products), *Marks and Spencer* (English department store), *Rolls-Royce* (luxury car manufacturers). Ss then discuss what each company does and why they think it is successful.

8a ▶ Give Ss time to read through the notes and discuss what information might be missing.

b ▶ 🔘 1.27 Play the recording and ask Ss to complete the notes. Ss compare answers with a partner. Check answers with the whole class.

> **Answers**
> 1 friends or family members
> 2 buy them out of their share
> 3 a visionary
> 4 an operations person
> 5 skills
> 6 hire help
> 7 communication
> 8 long-term

9a ▶ Focus Ss' attention on the phrases in the five sections and give them time to read them. Tell Ss that they are going to listen to the recording again, but this time there will be pauses between sections. Play the recording, pausing after each section to give Ss time to take notes about how the phrases are used. Play the recording again if necessary. Ss compare their ideas with a partner.

b ▶ If there are any words or phrases that the Ss don't know the meaning of, encourage them to answer each others' questions or consult a dictionary before asking you. Working with a partner, ask Ss to reconstruct what each speaker said using the words and phrases in the boxes and their notes from exercise 9a. Get feedback from various Ss.

10 ▶ Ss discuss the questions in pairs. Monitor the conversations and take note of any errors. Get feedback from various Ss.

5.2 Rags and riches

In this lesson, Ss read two people's experiences with money. They share this information with a partner and then look at the grammar of conditional sentences. Ss go on to read about some of the world's greatest philanthropists.

OPTIONAL WARMER

Write *money, love, health, family* on the board. Ask Ss to put these four things in order of importance to them. Then tell them to compare ideas with a partner and give reasons for their order. Ss compare their ideas with another pair and justify their choices. Get feedback from the whole class and try to reach a consensus about the order.

Reading

1 ▶ Ss read the statements and decide whether they agree or disagree with them. Ss then share their ideas with a partner and justify their opinions.

2 ▶ Put Ss in pairs. Refer Ss A to the article on page 67. Refer Ss B to the article on page 154. Ss read their texts and make notes to answer the questions as they read. Tell Ss not to worry about any words or phrases they don't know the meaning of at this stage, as you will be dealing with them later.

3 ▶ Ss now tell their partners about the person from their text, using the notes they have taken.

4 ▶ In pairs, Ss discuss the questions. Monitor the conversations for errors. Get feedback from the whole class. Write up any errors you heard on the board. Ss correct the errors with a partner.

Grammar | conditional sentences

OPTIONAL GRAMMAR LEAD-IN

Write the following jumbled sentence on the board: *If the lawyer he hadn't given power wouldn't lost of attorney, he have all money his.* Ss unjumble the sentence with a partner. If they have trouble doing so, write the first three or four words. When Ss have unjumbled the sentence, write the answer on the board: *If he hadn't given the lawyer power of attorney, he wouldn't have lost all his money.* Ask Ss to identify the structures used in this type of conditional sentence: *If* + Past Perfect + *would have* + past participle. Elicit why we use this type of conditional sentence (to talk about a hypothetical past situation) and its name (Third Conditional). Tell Ss they are going to be looking at other conditional structures in this lesson.

5a ▶ Focus Ss' attention on the Active grammar box. Ss identify whether the sentences are about Leon Spinks or Zhou Xiaoguang.

Active grammar

1 Spinks
2 Xiaoguang
3 Xiaoguang
4 Spinks
5 Spinks
6 Spinks
7 Xiaoguang

b ▶ Ss match the examples in the Active grammar box to their descriptions.

Active grammar

1 b
2 c
3 d
4 a
5 g
6 e
7 f

c ▶ Focus Ss' attention on the articles on page 67 and page 154. They identify sentences with conditionals or *wish*.

Answers

Spinks wishes things had gone differently … (*wish* + Past Perfect to talk about the past)

If he had never been heavyweight champion … they would still love him. (Mixed Conditional)

… he might have been one of them if he hadn't taken up boxing. (Third Conditional)

… if they eat healthy … maybe one day they might become the champ, too. (Second Conditional)

It might have stayed that way if Zhou Xiaoguang had not seen the potential … (Third Conditional)

… she wishes she had not needed 'to become a vendor at such a young age'. (*wish* + Past Perfect to talk about the past)

… if she hadn't experienced those difficult times, she would not have become the extraordinary businessperson that she is today. (Third Conditional)

▶ Encourage Ss to look at the Reference on page 75. Give Ss time to read through the notes.

6 ▶ Ss rewrite the sentences using the prompts in brackets so that the meaning stays the same. Check answers with the whole class.

> **Answers**
> 1 Supposing we left immediately, would we get to the bank in time?
> 2 If the last question hadn't been so difficult, I might/would/could have passed the exam.
> 3 I would have bought some presents if I had had my credit card with me.
> 4 If only there wasn't so much competition, the business might be/would be doing better.
> 5 Should you have any problems, you can call me.
> 6 If it hadn't been for Dr Hyde, I might not have survived the operation.
> 7 If they hadn't fallen out over money, they might/would/could still be married now.
> 8 Should you arrive late, just ask for me at the desk.

Pronunciation | contractions (2)

7a ▶ 🔵 1.28 Play the recording and Ss identify the full form of the underlined words.

> **Answers**
> 1 had; would; have
> 2 would; had
> 3 would; have

b ▶ 🔵 1.28 Play the recording again. Ss listen and repeat.

Speaking

8 ▶ Ss discuss questions 1–5 with a partner. Encourage Ss to use conditional structures where possible. Monitor conversations for correct use of conditionals and any important errors. Get feedback from different pairs. Finally, write errors on the board and encourage Ss to correct them.

Vocabulary | finance and philanthropy

> **OPTIONAL WARMER**
>
> Focus Ss on the photo of Bill and Melinda Gates. Ask Ss to discuss in small groups what they know about the people and what the text might be about. Get feedback from the whole class.

9a ▶ Ss read the definition and identify any philanthropists they know. Get feedback from the whole class.

b ▶ Ss read the article and discuss the questions in pairs. Ask Ss if there are any words or phrases from the text that they don't understand. Encourage Ss to answer each others' questions or look in an English–English dictionary before explaining the vocabulary to the group.

10 ▶ Focus Ss' attention on questions 1–3. Put Ss in small groups to discuss the questions. Monitor the conversations closely for errors and any interesting language Ss use. Get feedback from the whole class. Write any errors you have heard on the board and encourage Ss to come up to the board and correct them. Finally, congratulate Ss on any interesting language they have used.

11 ▶ Put Ss in pairs to discuss the questions. Get feedback from the whole class.

12a ▶ Ss complete the sentences. They can look at the underlined phrases from the article to help them. Let them compare with a partner.

> **Answers**
> 1 a
> 2 to
> 3 giving
> 4 make
> 5 in
> 6 put

b ▶ In pairs, Ss discuss which statements from exercise 12a they agree with. Get feedback from the whole class.

13 ▶ Focus Ss' attention on the Lifelong learning box. In pairs, they complete the sentences. Explain that each pair of sentences should be completed with the same word.

> **Answers**
> 1 recruit
> 2 fund
> 3 benefit

▶ Ss write similar pairs of gapped sentences with the other five words. In pairs, they take turns to look at each others' sentences and complete the gaps.

5.3 In good company

In this lesson, Ss read an article about which companies are good to work for and look at vocabulary for describing jobs. Through this context, Ss look at the grammar of sentence adverbials. Ss listen to an interview with a company director. They finish the lesson by looking at vocabulary expressing quantity.

OPTIONAL WARMER

Write the following question on the board: *If you could work for any company in the world, what company would you work for?* Ask Ss to discuss this question in pairs. Get feedback from the whole class.

Vocabulary | describing a job

1 ▶ Ss list the five most important things for them in a job. Ss then compare their lists with a partner and reach agreement about the five most important things. Get Ss to share their lists with another pair and justify their choices. Monitor the conversations for errors. Get feedback from the whole class.

2 ▶ Focus Ss on the words and phrases from the box. Ss discuss with a partner how many they know the meaning of. Ss check the words and phrases they don't know in their dictionaries. Check answers with the whole class. Ss check if any of these words and phrases appeared in their original lists.

Speaking

3 ▶ Focus Ss on the words from the box. Ask Ss to discuss in groups of three or four if they know any expressions which use these words. Get feedback from different groups and write correct examples on the board.

▶ Ss complete the the How to... box with the words from the box. Check answers with the whole class.

Answers

Saying it's very important: My main priority is ...; This is absolutely vital; I couldn't do without ...

Saying it's not too important: I'm not really bothered/concerned about this; I could do without ...

---

4 ▶ In pairs, Ss discuss which of the factors in exercise 2 are, or are not, priorities for them. Encourage Ss to use the expressions from the How to... box. Monitor for correct use of the expressions. Get feedback from various Ss.

Reading

5 ▶ Focus Ss' attention on the article. Ss read the article and answer questions 1–4. Ask Ss to compare their answers with a partner. Check answers with the whole class.

Answers

1   It uses a survey, asking employees questions about their company, for example, about pay, benefits, etc. Then it compares the results for each company.

2   All of the top companies pay well, allow workers to make decisions, and offer a comfortable workplace, but the winners tend to offer things 'above and beyond the norm', which other companies don't.

3   'Employees first, customers second'. They also believe in giving responsibility to employees.

4   Because the staff, even if they are very young, can make decisions that keep the customers happy.

Grammar | sentence adverbials

OPTIONAL GRAMMAR LEAD-IN

Write the following sentence ending on the board: ... *the most important thing for employees is not money.* Tell Ss to scan the article quickly to find out how this sentence begins. When the Ss have found the sentence, write the adverbial phrase at the beginning: *Surprisingly enough.* Ask Ss what this adverbial phrase says about the writer's opinion of the workers' priorities (answer: the writer is surprised). Elicit that sentence adverbials are often used at the start of a sentence to show an opinion or attitude to a subject.

6a ▶ Focus Ss' attention on the article again. Ask Ss to say what purpose the underlined sentence adverbials serve.

Active grammar

Sentence adverbials can be used to make a comment (often an opinion) about the subject.

---

b ▶ Focus Ss' attention on the Active grammar box and to choose the correct options in rules A and B.

Active grammar

A   beginning
B   comma

---

c ▶ In pairs, Ss complete the table. Get feedback from the whole class.

> **Active grammar**
>
> Unexpected points: *surprisingly enough*; *believe it or not*
> Generalisations: *by and large*; *broadly speaking*
> How something appears: *seemingly*; *apparently*
> Contrast: *however*; *on the other hand*
> Reflection on the past: *looking back*; *with hindsight*
> Partial agreement: *to a certain extent*; *up to a point*

d ▶ Ask Ss if they know any other adverbial phrases to add to the table.

▶ Refer Ss to the Reference on page 75 and give them time to read through the notes.

7 ▶ Focus Ss on sentences 1–6. Ss decide which of the adverbials in each sentence does not fit the context. Let them compare with a partner. Get feedback from various Ss.

> **Answers**
> 1 Apparently
> 2 Seemingly
> 3 Broadly speaking
> 4 apparently
> 5 Believe it or not
> 6 surprisingly enough

Speaking

8 ▶ Put Ss in pairs or small groups. Ss discuss sentences 1–5 with a partner. Monitor the conversations for errors. Get feedback from the whole class. Read out any important errors you have heard and discuss them with the class.

Listening

9 ▶ Ask Ss to discuss the questions with a partner. Get feedback from the whole class.

10a ▶ 🔵 1.29 Tell Ss that they are going to listen to an interview with a company director. Play the recording. Ss listen and take notes if they wish. Ss discuss with a partner what they think of the conditions the company director describes.

b ▶ Play the recording again. Ss listen and make notes on the different topics.

c ▶ Ss compare what they have written with a partner. Check answers with the whole class.

> **Answers**
> **type of business:** recruitment agency that trains and places graduates in sales jobs; a small, London-based company
> **staff:** 60 employees, young, mostly highly qualified graduates, energetic, out-going, like-minded people
> **incentives:** parties, annual skiing holiday, present for most-appreciated employee of the month, negotiated incentives, e.g. company cars, free breakfasts and cappuccino, help with accommodation
> **salaries:** good, with monthly, performance-related cash bonuses
> **atmosphere:** staff laugh a lot with their team, there is a great deal of energy, a fun atmosphere, a company bar, with free breakfasts and coffee
> **personal involvement:** giving people a say in the company, with monthly meetings to discuss big issues and where food is offered free; help with accommodation means that working for the company becomes a lifestyle choice

11 ▶ Ask Ss to discuss the questions in small groups. Get feedback from the whole class.

Vocabulary | expressing quantity

12a ▶ Focus Ss on phrases 1–10. Ask Ss to complete the phrases using the words from the box.

> **Answers**
> 1 as **many** as
> 2 a **little** bit more
> 3 a **great** deal of energy
> 4 **plenty** of benefits
> 5 **not** much of an expert
> 6 for the **most** part
> 7 an **awful** lot of time
> 8 The **vast** majority
> 9 **quite** a few staff
> 10 only a **handful** of people

b ▶ 🔵 1.30 Play the recording for Ss to check.

c ▶ Tell Ss that they are going to listen to the phrases again. Play the recording again while Ss mark the stressed words and underline the weak forms. (See answers for exercise 12a. Stressed words are in bold. Weak forms are underlined.)

d ▶ Ask different Ss to read out the phrases again, paying attention to the stressed words and weak forms.

13 ▶ Focus Ss on sentences 1–8. Ss rewrite the sentences so that they have a similar meaning. Tell Ss they should use the words in brackets. Ss compare their answers with a partner. Check answers with the whole class.

Answers
1 The government spends a great deal of money on defence.
2 Surprisingly few people turned up to see the race.
3 For the most part, customers appreciate our top-quality service.
4 It isn't much of a fee if you consider the amount of work involved.
5 There are plenty of bottles on the rack.
6 Only a handful of people asked questions at the end.
7 The vast majority of workers joined the strike.
8 There were an awful lot of people (there).

14a ▶ Ss complete sentences 1–6.

b ▶ Ss compare their answers with a partner and explain what they have written. Get feedback from various Ss.

OPTIONAL EXTENSION

Ss choose one of the sentences from exercise 14a to write a paragraph about. Monitor and help Ss as necessary, and check what they are writing. When they have finished, invite different Ss to present what they have written to the rest of the class. Encourage the Ss listening to ask follow-up questions. When Ss have finished presenting their topics to the class, focus Ss on the example topic of getting the most from the course. Put Ss in pairs to make a list of other ways, apart from doing more homework, which would help them get the most from the course. Ss then share their lists with other pairs. Get feedback from the whole class and write Ss' ideas on the board. Discuss which of the ideas are the most practical and encourage Ss to put them into practice during the course.

5 Vocabulary | Idioms (1)

In this lesson, Ss look at different idioms connected to money.

OPTIONAL WARMER

Write the word *charity* on the board. Make sure that Ss know what a charity is by asking them to name some famous ones. Put Ss in groups of three or four. Tell each group that they have 100,000 dollars to give to charity and that they have to decide on three charities they would give money to. Get feedback from each group and ask different groups to explain to the whole class what charities they chose and why.

1 ▶ Ask two Ss to read out the short dialogue to the rest of the class. Ask Ss to discuss in pairs the two meanings of the word *fortune*. Ask a pair to explain the meanings to the rest of the class.

Answers
Fortune means (A) luck, (B) a large sum of money.

2 ▶ In pairs, Ss match the phrases. Let them compare their answers with another pair. Check answers with the whole class.

Answers

1	f	4	b	7	c
2	h	5	a	8	g
3	d	6	i	9	e

▶ You may want to write sentences on the board to show how *splash out on* and *treat myself to* can be used differently, e.g. *I splashed out on a new pair of jeans. I treated myself to a massage.* These sentences show how *splash out on* means buy something expensive, whereas *treat myself to* means give myself a treat.

OPTIONAL VARIATION

Divide the class into pairs, A and B. Ss A look at the phrases 1–9, Ss B look at the phrases a–i and decide what these phrases mean. Ss then tell their partners what they think their phrases mean and if any of the meanings are similar. Ss then match phrases 1–9 to phrases a–i.

3 ▶ With a partner, Ss discuss questions 1–3. In a monolingual class, ask Ss to discuss the questions before explaining any similar phrases in their own language to you. In a multilingual class, organise Ss so that they are working with a partner of a different nationality. Ss then explain to the rest of the class any similar expressions which their partners have in their language.

Answers
1 The phrases in a–i are more colloquial.
2 The phrases in 1–9 are neutral.

4 ▶ Focus Ss' attention on the photos. In pairs, Ss decide if any of the phrases they have looked at in exercise 2 could be used to describe the photos. Get feedback from the whole class.

5a ▶ Ss discuss questions 1–8 with a partner. Monitor conversations for errors.

b ▶ Ss compare their answers with another pair. Get feedback from the whole class. Write any important errors on the board and get different Ss to correct them.

5 Communication

In this lesson, Ss listen to people talking about what they would do if their company suddenly had a fortune to spend. Ss then do a role play, deciding how a company should spend a fortune.

1a ▶ ⬤ 1.31 Tell Ss they are going to hear two people discussing what they would do if their company suddenly had a fortune to spend. Play the recording for Ss to take notes about the ideas they hear.

b ▶ Ss compare their answers with a partner. Ss also discuss how they think the speakers' characters are different. Get feedback from various Ss. Play the recording again for Ss to check their answers.

> **Answers**
> He wants to: replace the chairs in the office; renovate the office; do something practical.
> She wants to: go on a company 'jaunt' (holiday) to the West Indies; get a house by the sea for all employees to use.

2 ▶ Divide the class into groups of four. In their groups, Ss discuss what their company/university/school would do if they had a fortune to spend. Get feedback from various groups and decide as a class which group had the best ideas.

3 ▶ Ss read through the profile of Fortune Foods and answer the questions. Check that Ss have the correct answers.

> **Answers**
> The company's strengths: It has an excellent reputation and is growing. Its clients are rich businesses.
> Main problems for employees: The workers often stay late at night preparing food and are stressed. It is difficult for employees to drive to work.

4a ▶ Put Ss in two groups, A and B. Tell Ss about the situation. Refer Ss A (workers) to page 150 and refer Ss B (management) to page 149. Give Ss time to prepare their arguments. Monitor and help Ss where necessary.

b ▶ When Ss are ready, they start the negotiation. Monitor the conversations for errors. When Ss have finished the negotiation, they discuss question 3 together. Note any important errors that Ss have made on the board ask them to correct them. Finally, congratulate Ss on their efforts during the negotiation.

5 Review and practice

1 ▶

Answers
1 They explained how the project would be too difficult to manage, and to a certain extent I agree.
2 They didn't know who I was talking about. Apparently, Georgia left the company years ago.
3 I decided to leave and change careers. With hindsight, I'm not sure that I made the right decision.
4 By and large, the new arrangements have worked out well. / The new arrangements have worked out well, by and large.
5 The new minister was faced with a seemingly impossible task. / The new minister was, however, faced with an impossible task.

2 ▶

Answers
1 a, c
2 b, c
3 a, c
4 a, b
5 b, c

3 ▶

Answers
1 We weren't in the least bit surprised to hear that she got the part.
2 What I couldn't believe was being told to leave!
3 It was very hot soup indeed.
4 Actually, it is surprisingly warm here. / It's actually very warm here.
5 She makes a lot of her own clothes.
6 It is by no means certain that the game will take place.
7 It was Rachel who had the courage to complain about the service.
8 They have done nothing at all to put the problem right.

4 ▶

Answers
1 pestering
2 challenging
3 execute
4 priority
5 promotion
6 splash
7 hard
8 treat
9 bankruptcy
10 rolling

5 ▶

Answers
1 founded
2 fortune
3 charity
4 remarkable
5 venture
6 vision
7 design
8 worth
9 mind
10 wealthy

5 Writing bank

1 ▶ In pairs, Ss read the essay and discuss the question. Get feedback from the whole class.

2 ▶ Ss read the possible structure and discuss the questions. Get feedback from the whole class.

> **Answer**
> Yes, it does.

3a ▶ Focus Ss' attention on the How to... box. In pairs, Ss tick the phrases used. Get feedback from the whole class.

> **Answers**
> The key question is ...
> The fact is ...
> One example of this is ...
> Some might say ...
> Perhaps
> might
> generally

b ▶ Ss' add further phrases to the How to... box. Get feedback from the whole class.

> **Answers**
> State your position: the main point is that; the fundamental issue is ...
> give examples or use lists to illustrate a point: for instance
> anticipate counter-arguments: a common misconception is that ...; it has been put forward that ... (but ...)
> use hedging devices: arguably; to a certain extent.

4a ▶ Individually, Ss plan a persuasive essay. Encourage Ss to use ideas from the How to... box. Go round and monitor Ss who need any help.

b ▶ Ss write their essays.

6 Power

Overview

CEFR Can do objectives

6.1 Describe an important building/structure
6.2 Take detailed notes from fluent connected speech
6.3 Write an autobiographical statement
Communication Argue your case
Writing bank Write about your personal history

CEFR Portfolio ideas

a) Listen to a good song in English. Try to write the words of the song. How many times do you need to listen to the song?
b) Describe a famous building. Use less than 30 words. Don't say the name of the building. Can your friends guess the building you are describing?
c) Imagine that you get a temporary job as a tour guide at a famous building. Prepare and record the commentary you will give on your tour.
d) You think young people should spend more time ****ing. (Choose your own verb.) Write a letter to a newspaper explaining why.

Lead-in

OPTIONAL WARMER

Ask Ss to list occasions when they exercise power or someone exerts power over them in their daily lives. To help, ask Ss to think about the following areas: *school/university, work, family, free time, sports.* Ss compare notes with a partner, and explain their ideas. Ask different Ss to tell the rest of the class what they have learned about their partners.

1 ▶ Put Ss in groups of three or four. Ss discuss the sort of power represented in the photos. Ss then think of other types of power. Get feedback from various Ss.

2a ▶ Focus Ss on the words in the box. Ss decide which of the words collocate with *power* and which collocate with *powerful.* Ss write the words in the relevant column in the table. Let them compare answers with a partner. Check answers with the whole class.

Answers
power: too; nuclear; spending; economic; solar; brain; world; political; people; consumer
powerful: tool; speech; medicine; argument; influence; people; army

---

b ▶ Ss think of other words which they can add to the two columns. Get feedback from the whole class and write correct collocations on the board.

3 ▶ Focus Ss' attention on the underlined phrases in questions 1–6. In pairs, Ss check that they know the meaning of the phrases. Get feedback from the whole class.

Answers
1 have power over – be in a position of control over someone/something
2 in positions of power – jobs with powerful responsibilities, e.g. politicians, heads of multinational companies, etc.
3 economic power – power which countries have because of their economic situation
4 special powers – powers that are not within their 'normal' powers
5 comes to power – start being in a position of power (usually after an election)
6 holds the power – be in a powerful position

▶ Ask Ss to discuss the questions in groups of three. Monitor conversations for errors. Get feedback from various Ss.

EXTEND THE LEAD-IN

In a monolingual class, ask Ss in pairs to list the five most powerful people in their country and explain why these people are so powerful. In a multilingual class, group Ss so that they are working with Ss from other countries. Ss list the five most powerful people in their countries. Ss share this information in pairs, explaining why these people are so powerful. Get feedback from various Ss.

6.1 Images of power

In this lesson, Ss look at vocabulary through the context of architecture. Ss then listen to information about some of the world's most important buildings. They go on to look at the grammar of articles.

> **OPTIONAL WARMER**
>
> Ss think of a famous building. Ss think what words and phrases they would need to describe this building. Ss can look in a dictionary or consult you for any words they don't know. Ss then describe this building to a partner who guesses what building is being described.

Reading

1 ▶ Draw Ss' attention to the text. Ss choose the best summary.

> **Answer**
> 2

2 ▶ Put Ss in pairs. In their groups, Ss discuss questions 1–4. Monitor conversations for errors. Get feedback from the whole class. Write important errors on the board and encourage Ss to correct them before writing the correct forms on the board.

Vocabulary | power

3 ▶ Ss use the words in the box to complete the definitions and related example sentences 1–8. Tell Ss to make sure that they use the correct verb tenses in the sentences. Check answers with the whole class.

> **Answers**
> a   gain
> 1   gained
> 2   gain
> b   win over
> 3   win over
> 4   won over
> c   be impressed by
> 5   were (very) impressed by
> 6   was impressed by
> d   play an important part in
> 7   plays (an) important part
> 8   played (an) important part

Listening

> **OPTIONAL WARMER**
>
> In pairs, Ss discuss the structures in the pictures, and write any information they know about them. Ss compare their ideas with a partner. Get feedback from the whole class.

4a ▶ Focus Ss on the photos and the information in questions 1–7. In pairs, Ss match the information with the structures. Get feedback from the whole class and ask Ss to justify their ideas.

b ▶ 🔵 2.01 Play the recording. Ss to listen and check their answers.

> **Answers**
> 1   The Millennium Dome   5   The Pentagon
> 2   Hassan II Mosque   6   The Forbidden City
> 3   The Great Pyramid   7   The Eiffel Tower
> 4   Sydney Harbour Bridge

> The Millennium Dome is often referred to colloquially as 'The Dome' or 'The O2 Arena'.

5a ▶ Play the recording again and ask Ss to make notes about each building/structure.

b ▶ Ss compare their notes with a partner.

> **Answers**
> The Great Pyramid of ancient Egypt: Built as tomb for the Pharaoh. Base 230m² (ten football fields). Took 400,000 men 20 years to build. Used 2.3 million blocks of stone, some weighed 50 tonnes.
> The Eiffel Tower: Built 1889 – 100th anniversary of French Revolution. Pure iron structure (influence of Industrial Revolution), very light, can withstand high winds. Was tallest tower in world when built; still tallest building in Paris.
> Sydney Harbour Bridge: World's largest, not longest, steel arch bridge. Stands 134m above Sydney harbour. Opened 1932. Groups of 12 people climb every ten minutes to see views.
> The Pentagon: Largest office building in world, covers 13.8 hectares. Takes 15–20 mins to walk around. Built in Washington, in five concentric rings, during WW2 to house war department.
> The Forbidden City: Built between 1406–1420, during Ming Dynasty, also called Purple Forbidden City. Located in centre of Beijing. 720,000 m². Home to 24 emperors of Ming and Qing dynasties. One of largest palaces in world, many valuable and rare objects in museum.
> The Millennium Dome: Opened Dec 31, 1999 to celebrate new millennium. 1km round and 50m high in centre. Covers 20 acres. Could fit Eiffel Tower inside. Expensive to build and controversial.
> Hassan II Mosque: Built Casablanca, Morocco, for 60th birthday of Moroccan king Hassan II. Second largest religious building in world (after Mecca). Space for 25,000 worshippers inside, 80,000 outside. 210m minaret (tower) tallest in world. Built to withstand earthquakes, has heated floors, electric doors, lasers which shine at night.

▶ Ss discuss which of the structures they think are most impressive or interesting, and whether they have visited or would like to visit any of them.

Grammar | articles

> **OPTIONAL GRAMMAR LEAD-IN**
>
> Write these sentences on the board: *Alan is accountant. He earns $400 the week. He lives on the Smith Street. He loves the dogs.* Tell Ss that there is one error in each sentence. Ss correct the errors and compare their new sentences with a partner. Write the correct sentences on the board: *Alan is an accountant. He earns $400 dollars a week. He lives on Smith Street. He loves dogs.* Ss discuss the use or non-use of articles in these sentences. Tell Ss they are going to look at the use and non-use of articles in more detail in this lesson.

6a ▶ In pairs, Ss list some rules for when we use articles.

b ▶ Refer Ss to the Reference on page 89 and give them time to read through the notes.

c ▶ Focus Ss' attention on audioscript 2.01 on page 172. In pairs, they find examples of each type of article use. Get feedback from the whole class.

d ▶ Draw Ss' attention to the Active grammar box. In pairs, they choose the correct options in rules A–C.

> **Active grammar**
>
> A   a/an
> B   the
> C   no article

7a ▶ Ask Ss to list in pairs what they know about the city of Barcelona. Get feedback from various Ss and tell Ss they are going to read about the designer of the Sagrada Familia church, Gaudí. Ss read the article and complete the gaps with *a*, *an*, *the* or leave the space blank if no article is needed. Check answers with the whole class.

b ▶ In pairs, Ss explain the use or non-use of articles in the text. Ask different pairs to report their explanations to the rest of the class.

> Answers
> 1   – (city)
> 2   – (name)
> 3   a (new information)
> 4   The (specific)
> 5   the (shared knowledge, we have already mentioned the building)
> 6   the (unique)
> 7   the (previously mentioned)
> 8   – (countable plural)
> 9   – (abstract noun)
> 10 the (expression – the completion of)
> 11 the (shared knowledge)
> 12 the (specific)
> 13 a (news, first mention), could also be 'the' if we already know of its existence.
> 14 a (news)
> 15 – (general)
> 16 the (groups)
> 17 the (specific)

8 ▶ Focus Ss on sentences 1–10. Ss find the mistakes in the sentences and correct them. Warn Ss that there may be more than one mistake in each sentence. Ss compare answers with a partner.

> Answers
> 1   She really enjoys ~~the~~ sport, and plays ~~the~~ tennis a lot.
> 2   If ~~the~~ Mr Hart phones, can you tell him I'm in **a/the** meeting?
> 3   There is ~~a~~ cold weather, especially in **the** north.
> 4   Go down ~~the~~ Forest Street, and turn right into New Road.
> 5   ~~The~~ Violent crime is definitely on **the** increase.
> 6   I went to ~~one~~ a restaurant there years ago.
> 7   ~~The~~ Life in London is getting more and more expensive.
> 8   Katia is **the** ideal candidate for the job. She has a great deal of ~~the~~ experience.
> 9   Maurice has ~~the~~ **a** cold and won't be coming back to work this week.
> 10 It's without doubt **the** best hotel in ~~an~~ **the** area.

Speaking and writing

9 ▶ In pairs, Ss make notes about two important buildings or structures they know. Monitor and help Ss where necessary.

10 ▶ Refer Ss to audioscript 2.1 on page 172. Ss complete the spaces in the How to... box. Check answers with the whole class.

> **Answers**
> 1 arguably
> 2 one of
> 3 thought
> 4 Occupying
> 5 covers
> 6 celebrate

11a ▶ Ss choose two important buildings or structures that they know about, then share what they know and make notes.

▶ Alternatively, set this as a homework task so that Ss have time to do research the buildings or structures on the Internet. In the following lesson, Ss share information they have found with their partners.

▶ Ss write a short text about the buildings or structures. Encourage Ss to use phrases from the How to... box where possible. Monitor and help Ss where necessary.

b ▶ In groups, Ss take turns to describe their buildings.

6.2 Kid power

> Big companies are well aware of the preferences of children and teenagers and they take these preferences into account when designing and marketing products. Corporations such as Microsoft, Sony and Nokia have led the way in researching what appeals to teenagers. Nokia in particular has a reputation for researching teenagers. Researchers from the communications company look at teenagers around the world, trying to spot fashions which may become the next big thing among teenagers. Sony was one of the first companies to research in detail what young people wanted. Some surveys have shown that it is thought to be one of the 'coolest' brands by teenagers.

In this lesson, Ss listen to an interview about the influence children and teenagers have over the fashion and technology industries. Ss then look at vocabulary connected with fashions and fads. Ss go on to listen to two parents and two teenagers discuss various issues. Through this context, Ss look at the grammar of *whatever*, *whoever*, *whenever*, etc.

> **OPTIONAL WARMER**
>
> Ss discuss with a partner how they think teenagers are different from adults. Ss share their ideas with another pair. Get feedback from various Ss.

Listening

1a ▶ Ss discuss the questions with a partner. Monitor conversations for errors and interesting language Ss use. Get feedback from various Ss. Read out any important errors you have heard and discuss them with the class. Finally, congratulate Ss on any interesting language they have used.

b ▶ ⬤ 2.02 Play the recording and ask Ss to listen to find out if their answers were correct.

2a ▶ Focus Ss on sentence beginnings 1–7. In pairs, Ss try to remember the listening script to complete the notes. Ss compare their notes with another pair.

b ▶ Play the recording again for Ss to check their answers.

> **Answers**
> 1 Microsoft began the trend for using teenagers to find out what is trendy in technology.
> 2 Kids drive technology because they have no fear of it and automatically home in on the new.
> 3 Kids want technology that can be carried around.
> 4 Text messaging caught on because kids wanted to pass notes to each other during class.
> 5 Teenagers influenced the ThinkPad because they took notes in the dark during lectures.
> 6 Collaborative computing will be useful because people will be able to work simultaneously on a project with someone on the other side of the world.
> 7 Converse trainers sent their market researchers to the basketball courts of New York, and other places where you find teenagers.

Vocabulary | fashions and fads

3a ▶ Ss look at extracts 1–8. In pairs, Ss discuss the meaning of the underlined phrasal verbs. Get feedback from the whole class.

▶ Ss match the underlined phrasal verbs to definitions a–h. Check answers with the whole class.

Answers					
1	e	4	g	7	d
2	a	5	f	8	b
3	c	6	h		

b ▶ Ss look at the phrasal verbs in exercise 3a again. Ss identify the phrasal verbs which are exact opposites and decide if these verbs are formal or informal. Ss also identify the phrasal verb which has a literal meaning connected with football. Check answers with various Ss.

Answers
1 *be in* and *be out* are opposites (both are informal)
2 *kick off* has a literal meaning connected with football

4 ▶ Ss read the article and find the mistakes. Tell Ss that the mistakes are all connected with phrasal verbs. Ss compare their answers with a partner. Check answers with the whole class.

Answers
A new trend is catching off **on**. ... Big business has always homed in at **on** talented youth – the phenomenon really kicked up **off** with Michael Jordan ... How did this situation go **come** about? ... Who knows what's coming off **up** next? ...

5 ▶ Put Ss in pairs. Ss discuss questions 1–5 with each other. Ss then share their ideas with another pair. Monitor conversations for errors and correct use of phrasal verbs. Get feedback from the whole class. Write any important errors on the board and invite different Ss to correct them. Finally, congratulate Ss' on their correct use of phrasal verbs.

Speaking and listening

6 ▶ Put Ss in pairs. Focus Ss on the three photos and questions 1–4. Ss discuss the questions with each other. Get feedback from the whole class.

OPTIONAL EXTENSION
Ask the class to choose one of the photos shown. Put Ss in two groups, teenagers and parents. The 'parents' think of typical things parents might say to the teenager(s) in the photo. The 'teenagers' think of typical things teenager(s) might say to the parents. When Ss have prepared what they are going to say, pair off the Ss so that teenagers are talking to parents. Parents start the role play. Monitor the conversations for errors. When Ss have finished, correct any important errors with the whole class.

7 ▶ Put Ss in groups of three or four. In their groups, Ss discuss whether teenagers should be allowed to do the things mentioned in 1–6. Monitor the conversations for errors. Get feedback from the whole class. Finally, write important errors you have heard on the board and encourage Ss to correct them.

8a ▶ 🔘 2.03 Tell Ss they are going to hear two parents and two teenagers discussing different issues. Play the recording. Ss note down which of the questions from exercise 7 are answered in each conversation. Ss compare what they have written with a partner. Check answers with the whole class.

Answers
Conversation 1: go wherever they want at night
Conversation 2: watch however much TV they want
Conversation 3: socialise with whoever they want
Conversation 4: stay up late whenever they want

b ▶ Play the recording again and Ss take notes about the opinions expressed in the conversations.

Answers
Conversation 1: It depends on the age. There are some places that are not suitable for young teenagers, like bars.
Conversation 2: It is not good for teenagers to watch whatever they want on TV as they can't evaluate what they are seeing. It is also bad for their eyes and a bit passive.
Conversation 3: They want to be able to choose who they socialise with.
Conversation 4: Leah thinks it's a good idea to have a time for teenagers to go to bed. Mark feels that teenagers can decide for themselves when to go to bed.

Grammar | *whatever, whoever, whenever, etc.*

OPTIONAL GRAMMAR LEAD-IN
Write the following sentences a parent might say to a teenager on the board:
Whatever you do, don't stay out too late.
Come home whenever you like, but don't walk home alone. In pairs, ask Ss to discuss whether their parents ever say/said things like this to them. Ss then discuss the use of *whatever* and *whenever* in these sentences with their partners. Tell Ss that we use these words when it doesn't make any difference.

9a ▶ Ss read through the examples in the Active grammar box and choose the correct option in rule A. Ss compare their answers with another pair. Check answers with the whole class.

Active grammar
are conjunctions that join two clauses together

b ▶ Ss read through the examples in the Active grammar box and choose the correct meaning. Ss compare their answers with another pair. Check answers with the whole class.

> **Active grammar**
>
> 3 = I know what you are doing and I want you to stop.
> 4 and 5 = I don't care what you are doing, but I want you to stop.

c ▶ Ss look at rule C and match the uses with the examples. Ss compare their answers with another pair.

> **Active grammar**
>
> a 6
> b 7

▶ Tell Ss to look at Reference page 89 and give Ss time to read through the notes.

10 ▶ Ss complete sentences 1–5 in pairs. Check answers with the whole class.

> **Answers**
> 1 Whatever
> 2 whenever
> 3 wherever
> 4 Whoever
> 5 However

11 ▶ Focus Ss on the pairs of sentences 1–8. Ss complete the second sentences so that they have the same meaning as the first sentences. Tell Ss they must include *whenever, however, whatever*, etc. in each space and that they must use three words in total in their answers.

> **Answers**
> 1 Whatever you do
> 2 However good you
> 3 Whenever you feel
> 4 Wherever we go
> 5 Whenever I can
> 6 Whoever we employ
> 7 However you fix
> 8 Whatever those children

Pronunciation | emphasis using *however, whatever*, etc.

12a ▶ 🔘 2.04 Play the recording. Ss decide which syllable is stressed in *whatever, however*, etc. Get feedback from the whole class.

> **Answer**
> The first syllable of *ever* is stressed.

b ▶ Play the recording again and ask alternate Ss to repeat the sentences.

13a ▶ Ss write down two pieces of advice, using *whatever, whoever*, etc.

b ▶ In pairs, Ss tell each other their advice, paying attention to stress and intonation.

Speaking

14a ▶ Ss read the quotes. In pairs, they discuss the question. Get feedback from the whole class.

b ▶ Ss write six sentences giving their opinions. Do not ask them to discuss the opinions at this point.

c ▶ Focus Ss' attention on the points in the Lifelong learning box. Ss prepare to talk about their opinions from exercise 14b. Put Ss in groups and ask them to discuss their opinions.

6.3 Charisma

Charisma refers to the 'magnetic' characteristic possessed by some people which can charm or influence others. Charismatic people usually project calmness and confidence and have excellent communication skills. There are many famous people who are said to have possessed charisma. Leaders such as Martin Luther King, John F. Kennedy and Winston Churchill are commonly thought of as having been charismatic. Bill Clinton, Mohammed Ali and Madonna are examples of living famous people who possess charisma.

In this lesson, Ss read a text about charisma and charismatic people. Through this context Ss look at the grammar of link words. Ss then look at vocabulary used for describing personal characteristics. They finish by writing an autobiographical statement for a scholarship award.

Reading

1a ▶ Write *charisma* on the board. Ask Ss to think of a definition for this word with a partner. They can use the photos for ideas. Get feedback from various Ss and decide who has the best definition.

▶ Ss read the definition. With their partners, Ss write a list of famous charismatic people. Ss compare names with another pair and explain why they think these people are charismatic. Ss then discuss if they think the people in the photos are charismatic and in what ways. Get feedback from the whole class.

b ▶ Ss discuss questions 1–3 in pairs. Monitor conversations for errors. Get feedback from the whole class and ask Ss to justify their answers. Write important errors you have heard on the board and ask different Ss to correct them.

2 ▶ Ss read the article quickly and choose the best title from the three given. Tell Ss not to worry about vocabulary they don't understand at this stage. Get feedback from the whole class.

> **Answer**
> The best title is probably 3, 'The Mystery of Charisma'.

3 ▶ Ss discuss questions 1–5 with a partner. Check answers with the whole class.

> **Answers**
> 1 No. The writer says 'the formula remains elusive'.
> 2 Education. It was a parents' evening in a school and education was common ground for everyone present.
> 3 No. He mentions that charisma is associated with politicians, businesspeople and celebrities, but other professions have charismatic people too.
> 4 Because of his love of his subject and his enthusiasm.
> 5 Because charisma can be learned.

4 ▶ Ss discuss the meaning of the words and expressions in pairs. Encourage Ss to work out the meaning from the context or to use a dictionary. Check answers with the whole class.

> **Answers**
> the formula remains elusive = there's no easy way/recipe. It is complex.
> a crowd-pleaser = something/someone that is very popular
> he infected everyone within earshot = everyone who heard him became enthusiastic
> a larger-than-life figure = someone who is very charismatic and noticeable, usually a popular or famous figure
> on the edge of their seats = extremely interested in and aroused by a performance
> star quality = with great potential to become famous

Grammar | link words of time and contrast

> **OPTIONAL GRAMMAR LEAD-IN**
>
> Write this jumbled sentence on the board: *to get a job although it is possible many it is vital without knowing English, for in securing a good position.* Ask Ss to unjumble the sentence: *Although it is possible to get a job without knowing English, for many it is vital in securing a good position.* Underline *Although* and ask Ss what function this word has in the sentence. Elicit that we use *although* as a way of contrasting parts of a sentence. In pairs, Ss make a list of any other contrast linking words or expressions they know. Get feedback from the whole class. Write correct expressions on the board.

5a ▶ Ss match the six underlined expressions to the descriptions in the Active grammar box. Check answers with the whole class.

> **Active grammar**
>
> while – 2
> During – 2
> at which point – 3
> On finding – 1
> You had no sooner begun – 1
> He'd hardly started – 3

b ▶ Ss match the words to the descriptions in the Active grammar box. Check answers with the whole class.

> **Active grammar**
>
> when – 2
> whilst – 2
> by which time – 3

c ▶ Ss match the five contast clauses in bold to the descriptions in the Active grammar box. Check answers with the whole class.

Active grammar

Hard as we try – 6
Even though – 4
Despite – 5
much as – 6
Although – 4

---

d ▶ Ss match the words to the descriptions in the Active grammar box. Check answers with the whole class.

Active grammar

in spite of – 5
while – 4
difficult as it was – 6

▶ Refer Ss to the Reference on page 89. Give Ss time to read through the notes and ask you any questions they have about the linking words.

6 ▶ Tell Ss they are going to read about two charismatic women. Ss read the texts and complete it with the phrases in the boxes. Tell Ss that some of the phrases are not needed. Ss compare their answers with a partner. Check answers with the whole class.

Answers

1	When	6	by which time
2	although	7	Despite
3	Hardly had she begun	8	when
4	Despite	9	even though
5	During	10	Much

OPTIONAL VARIATION

Put Ss in pairs, A and B. Ss A read the text about Queen Victoria, Ss B read the text about Oprah Winfrey, completing the texts with the words from the box as they read. Ss then tell their partners about the person they have read about and explain the link words they have chosen to complete the spaces. Check answers with various Ss.

Vocabulary | personal characteristics

7 ▶ Focus Ss on adjectives 1–8. Ask Ss to check the meaning of the adjectives with a partner. Ask Ss if they can think of an opposite word or expression for each of the adjectives. Get feedback from the whole class.

▶ Then ask Ss to match adjectives 1–8 to phrases a–h which have an opposite meaning. Ss compare their answers with a partner. Check answers with the whole class.

Answers

1	e	4	c	7	d
2	g	5	f	8	b
3	h	6	a		

Pronunciation | stress shift on long adjectives

8a ▶ ⬤ 2.05 Tell Ss to focus on the stress and to mark it on the words. Play the recording. Get feedback from the whole class.

b ▶ Play the recording again. Ss complete the rules.

Answers

1 -ic
2 -ional

---

9 ▶ Focus Ss on the photos of the famous people. In pairs, Ss discuss what they know about the people and why they are famous. Ss also decide which adjectives from exercise 7 they could use to describe the people. Get feedback from different pairs and write the adjectives on the board.

▶ Ss make a list of other famous people who could be described using the adjectives from exercise 7. Ss compare their lists with a partner.

▶ Draw four columns on the board and at the head of the columns write *a politician*, *a teacher*, *an actor*, *a businessperson*. Ask Ss to brainstorm in pairs a list of qualities which they think are important for each job. Get feedback from different pairs and write the qualities in the columns on the board. Ss can then discuss which of these jobs they think is the most difficult to do and why.

6 Vocabulary | Idioms (2)

In this lesson, Ss look at different idioms which contain parts of the body.

OPTIONAL WARMER

Give Ss one minute to write a list of all the parts of the body they can think of. When the minute is up, tell Ss to stop writing. Ask who has written the most parts of the body. Get the student who has written the most words to come to the board and write the words they have in their list. Ask the rest of the class if there are any other body parts they have written and add them to the list on the board. Ask Ss if they know of any idioms which use these parts of the body and write them on the board.

1a ▶ Focus Ss on the pictures. Ask Ss to work in pairs to make a story from the pictures. Ss compare their stories with another pair.

b ▶ Tell Ss to read the text and compare it with their stories from exercise 1a. Tell Ss to underline any words or expressions they don't know the meaning of and that you will look at them later.

2 ▶ Focus Ss' attention on the underlined idioms in the text. Ask Ss to discuss the meaning of the idioms with a partner, trying to work out the meaning from the context. Get feedback from various Ss.

▶ Ss match the idioms to the phrases with a similar meaning. Check answers with the whole class.

Answers
a have your hands full
b (be) an old hand
c rushed off your feet
d land on your feet
e have a good head for business
f it all comes to a head
g have (someone's) interests at heart
h (my) heart sank
i save face
j face the music

▶ Ask Ss if there are any words or phrases in the text they don't know the meaning of. Encourage Ss to answer each other's questions before explaining the vocabulary yourself.

3 ▶ Get Ss to discuss the questions in pairs. Monitor the conversations for errors and correct use of the idioms. Get feedback by asking different Ss to tell the rest of the class what they have learned about the other Ss. While doing so, Ss should be able to re-use the idioms. Write any errors you have heard on the board and get different Ss to correct them for you. Finally, praise Ss on their correct use of the idioms.

OPTIONAL EXTENSION

Ask Ss to look back through the book and, with a partner, use the idioms to describe some of the people that have appeared in previous units.

---

6 Communication

In this lesson, Ss role play a situation where they argue their case to be the leader of a new community.

1 ▶ Focus Ss on the picture. Ask Ss to work with a partner to guess the identities of the different people and label the picture. Get feedback from various Ss and ask them to justify their choices.

2 ▶ Tell Ss to choose one of the people in the picture. Ss write a short profile of that person using the phrases given. Monitor and help Ss as necessary.

▶ Alternatively, you could secretly assign a role to each student by handing out slips of paper with their role.

3 ▶ Tell Ss to imagine that the plane they were travelling in has crashed on a desert island. Tell Ss that everyone has survived the crash and that they have decided to start a new community. Tell Ss that their new characters all want to be the leader of the community. Give Ss time to think about how they are going to present their manifestos to the rest of the class. Refer Ss to the questions 1–4 to help. Monitor and help as necessary.

4 ▶ Put Ss in groups. Ss take turns to present their manifestos to the rest of the group, arguing their case to become the leader of the new community.

5 ▶ In their groups, Ss elect a leader. (They cannot vote for themselves.) Ss explain to other groups who they have elected leader and why. Write on the board any important errors you have heard. Discuss the errors with the class and get different Ss to come up to the board and correct the errors. Congratulate Ss on any interesting ideas they have had and language they have used.

Review and practice

1 ▶

Answers
This 492m high building consists of two elements that correspond to **the** Chinese concept of **the** Earth as **a** square and **the** sky as **a** circle. **The** hole in **the** top also has **a** practical use – to relieve **the** pressure of **the** wind on **the** building. **The** glassy tower is being built just blocks away from **the** 420m Jinmao Tower in **a/the** district of Shanghai that has been designated **the** Asian centre for international banking. **The** tower's lower levels will be used for offices, and its upper levels for **a** hotel, **an** art museum and restaurants.

2 ▶

Answers
1   wherever
2   whatever
3   Whichever/Whatever
4   whenever
5   whoever
6   However

3 ▶

Answers
1   keep up with
2   kicked off
3   catch on
4   is in
5   came about
6   homing in on

4 ▶

Answers
1   came to a head
2   have my hands full
3   land on your feet
4   an old hand
5   rushed off her feet
6   interests at heart
7   save face
8   a good head for business
9   his heart sank
10 face the music

5 ▶

Answers
An hour with the Body Earth Power Group was
enough for me. No sooner ~~but~~ had Carin Brook
entered than everyone became silent. Much as I
tried to keep my mind open – and despite ~~of~~ the
fact that I have been known to do a bit of tree-
hugging myself – I couldn't help thinking that
this was going to be a waste of time. Brook, even
~~and~~ though she is tiny, had a charismatic presence.
We started stretching in order to 'feel the Earth's
rhythm', but it didn't last long. I'd hardly ~~but~~ lifted
my hands up when she told us all to sit down, close
our eyes and 're-visualise ourselves from above'.
Hard ~~as~~ though I tried, I just couldn't imagine what
the top of my head looked like, and in ~~the~~ spite of
her promptings to 'relax', the hard floor was getting
very uncomfortable. Thankfully, four o'clock came,
by which ~~the~~ time I was desperate for a nice soft
chair and a cup of tea.

6 Writing bank

1 ▶ In pairs, Ss read the autobiographical statement and
discuss the question. Get feedback from the whole class.

Answer
c

2 ▶ Focus Ss' attention on the How to... box. In pairs, Ss
tick the phrases used. Get feedback from the whole class.

Answers
as a child ...
at the age of ...
during this time ...
I spent a month ...
it was at this time that ...
... for the foreseeable future
do an apprenticeship
enrol on a course
realise my true vocation was
work in this field
my application was successful
had an aptitude for
develop my skills

3a ▶ Ss read the advert and, in preparation for writing
their own personal statement, think of an area they would
choose to study.

b ▶ Individually, Ss make notes in preparation for their
application. Encourage Ss to use ideas from the How to...
box. Go round and monitor Ss who need any help.

c ▶ Ss write their statements.

Overview

Lead-in	**Vocabulary:** Nature
7.1	**Can do:** Explain procedures
	Grammar: Relative clauses
	Speaking and pronunciation: *to*
	How to... explain procedures
	Reading: Animals to the rescue
	Listening: Explaining how to do something
7.2	**Can do:** Make inferences based on extended prose
	Grammar: Verb patterns (2)
	Vocabulary: Descriptive language
	Listening: The Danakil Depression
7.3	**Can do:** Write an advert for an object
	Grammar: *as ... as* and describing quantity
	Vocabulary: Buying and selling
	Speaking and pronunciation: *as*
	Reading: Animals online
Vocabulary	Suffixes
Communication	Develop and justify your ideas
Writing bank	Write an advertisement
	How to... write a web advertisement
Extra resources	ActiveTeach and ActiveBook

CEFR Can do objectives

7.1 Explain procedures
7.2 Make inferences based on extended prose
7.3 Write an advert for an object
Communication Develop and justify your ideas
Writing bank Write an advertisement

CEFR Portfolio ideas

a) 'How can I remember all the words I learn in English class?' a young relative asks you in an email. Write a reply in simple English. Explain the procedures you use and tell your relative why the procedures help you. Compare your email with the emails written by your friends. Who has the best procedure?

b) You want to sell an object from your house. You can choose any object but it must be green in colour. Write an advertisement on a postcard. Describe the object, the reason for the sale and the asking price.

c) Tell the story of your life to your friend. Your friend will interrupt with questions beginning with the word 'Why?' Give helpful answers to your friend.

d) Write the story of your life but include three untrue pieces of information. Read your friends' stories. Can you identify the false statements?

Lead-in

OPTIONAL WARMER

Tell Ss that they have to think of an animal for each letter of the alphabet. In pairs, Ss race to write as many names of animals as they can within a time limit of three minutes. Get feedback from the class, giving one point for each correct animal name that another pair has, and two points for each correct animal that no other pair has. The winning pair is the one with the most points.

---

1 ▶ Focus Ss' attention on the animals in the photos. Ask Ss to discuss the questions in pairs. Get feedback from various Ss.

2 ▶ Ss look at the words in the box and discuss with a partner if they know the meaning of any/all of the words. Get feedback from the whole class.

▶ Ss put the words into the correct column in the table. Ss compare their ideas with a partner. Draw Ss' attention to the fact that *tame* can be used as an adjective as well as a verb and explain the difference in meaning. Get feedback from the whole class.

Answers

1	Types of animal (noun)	mammal, carnivore, breed (n), reptile, predator
2	Describes animals (adjective)	tame, rare, exotic, endangered
3	Where animals live	natural habitat, sanctuary, nature reserve, cage, nest
4	Things animals do	breed (v), hibernate, stalk, lay eggs
5	Animal issues	fur trade, animal rights, animal testing, over-hunting, over-fishing

---

3 ▶ Put Ss in small groups to discuss questions 1–4. Monitor the conversations. Get feedback from various Ss. Write any important errors you have heard on the board and get different Ss to come to the board and correct them.

EXTEND THE LEAD-IN

Put Ss in two groups, A and B. For homework, Ss A do research about the work of sniffer dogs using the Internet or any other resources they like. Ss B do research into working elephants. In the following lesson, Ss work in pairs: A and B. Ss share with a partner what they have found out about these animals and the work they do.

7.1 Animal instinct

In this lesson, Ss read about how animals can help warn us of natural disasters and how rats can be trained to help people in the event of a disaster. Through this context, Ss look at the grammar of relative clauses. They then listen to people giving explanations about how to do something before looking at language used to explain procedures.

OPTIONAL WARMER

Write *animal instinct* and *natural disaster* on the board. Put Ss in two groups, A and B. Ss A list words they associate with *animal instinct*, and Ss B list words they associate with *natural disaster*. Ss then share the words they thought of with a student from the other group. Get feedback from the whole class, and write words Ss have thought of on the board in two lists.

Reading

There have been many incidences of animals changing their behaviour before a natural disaster strikes. Perhaps the most famous recent incident was before the 2004 tsunami in the Indian Ocean, when many animals reportedly escaped without injury by running to higher ground before the wave arrived. Some scientists believe that animals have an early-warning sensory system which can detect disasters, such as earthquakes, before they happen. This may be due to the fact that animals have more sensitive hearing and smell than humans, and that they also have sensory organs that detect small tremors and changes that occur before a natural disaster.

1a ▶ Ss match words 1–6 to words a–f. Check answers with the whole class.

Answers
1 d
2 c
3 e
4 f
5 b
6 a

b ▶ Tell Ss that these expressions are taken from the text on page 92. In pairs, Ss discuss pairs what they think the article will be about. Get feedback from the whole class.

c ▶ Ss read the article quickly to check their predictions.

2 ▶ Ss read the article again more carefully and answer questions 1–8. Ss compare answers with a partner. Check answers with the whole class.

Answers
1 The elephants suddenly became nervous and left their habitat. The flamingos suddenly flew to higher ground even though it was the breeding season.
2 They move away from the danger area.
3 The sharks were electronically 'tagged', so they could be observed.
4 Their senses are sharper and they can feel changes in the environment.
5 The technology isn't always available and doesn't always work. We have lost our 'animal instincts' with the advance of technology.
6 Similarities: they both smell people when they are sent to disaster areas. Differences: the rats are smaller and can get into small spaces and crawl in damaged buildings more easily.
7 The rat's brain gives off a signal which is transmitted via a radio on the rat's back.
8 In destroyed buildings, places where there is no electricity source, places where there are a number of different smells.

3 ▶ Ss discuss questions 1–4 in pairs. Get feedback from the whole class.

Grammar | relative clauses

OPTIONAL GRAMMAR LEAD-IN

Write the following sentences on the board:
1 The cat <u>that had a white ear</u> was run over by the car. The cat <u>that had a stripy tail</u> was unhurt.
2 The cat, <u>which was sitting in the sun at the time of the accident,</u> was run over by the car.
Ask Ss how we know which cat was run over in 1. (Because of the underlined information.) Tell Ss that this information is vital to the meaning of the sentences and that this clause is a defining relative clause. Elicit, that in 2, the underlined information is not vital to the meaning of the sentence and is a non-defining relative clause.

---

4 ▶ Ss read the Active grammar box and do the tasks. Check answers with the whole class.

Active grammar

1 a) ... that were giving tourists rides ...
   b) ..., which should have been breeding at that time of year, ...
   c) ..., which were being observed by US biologists, ...
   d) ... that inhabit an Indian nature reserve, ...
   e) ... which can do this job.
   f) ..., whose noses don't work well ...
   g) ... which we rely on ...
2 defining relative clauses: a), d), e), g)
   non-defining: b), c), f)
3 defining
4 before and after the non-defining relative clause
5 g) The preposition goes at the end: ... *something which robots are not as good at*. In more formal English, the preposition can go at the beginning (*at which robots are not as good*).
6 *Of course there are already robots which can do this job, one of which looks and moves like a snake* ... The words *all, some, few, one, none, either, neither of which* can all come before *of which*.

▶ Refer Ss to the Reference on page 103 and give them time to read through the notes.

5 ▶ Ask Ss to discuss the pairs of sentences and decide if they have the same meaning, or if they are different and how. Let them compare with a partner.

Answers

1 different: a means only those monkeys whose DNA is similar to humans are used in research (other monkeys are not used because their DNA is not similar to humans'); b means that all monkeys may be used because all monkeys have similar DNA to humans.
2 b is wrong because it needs to be a defining relative clause, therefore without the comma.
3 b is wrong because there should be a comma after *seals*. It must be a non-defining relative clause (because all seals' blubber is used for fuel and food).
4 Both are correct.
5 b is wrong. You can't use *that* to begin a non-defining relative clause.

---

6 ▶ Ss put the phrases into the right sentences. Check answers with the whole class.

Answers

1 Should hunting which is done only for sport and not for food be allowed?
2 Should zoos, which take animals from their natural habitat, be banned?
3 Should the Amazon rainforest, which is being destroyed, be protected against industry? If so, how?
4 Should the use of fur for clothing, about which there has been much debate in the fashion industry, be banned?

Speaking

7 ▶ Ss discuss the questions, thinking of arguments for and against each issue. Get feedback from various Ss.

OPTIONAL EXTENSION

After the discussion Ss, choose one of the questions as the topic for a discursive essay. Ask Ss to write 150–200 words on the chosen topic for homework. In the following lesson, either take the essays in or ask Ss to swap their essays with a partner and comment on the content and language.

Listening

OPTIONAL WARMER

Put Ss in two groups, one in favour of rabbits as pets, the other in favour of dogs as pets. Each group thinks of reasons why their animal makes the better pet. Put Ss with a partner from the other group. Ss then try and convince their partners that their animals are better to have as pets than their partners'.

8a ▶ ⊙ 2.06 Tell Ss they are going to listen to two people giving explanations about how to do something. Play the recording and ask Ss to mark sentences 1–8 with a T if they are true, F if they are false, and DS if the sentence is not mentioned.

b ▶ Play the recording again for Ss to check their answers. Get feedback from the whole class.

Answers

1 F
2 F (they're picky eaters)
3 F (you need to get rabbits vaccinated)
4 DS
5 T
6 DS
7 T
8 DS

Pronunciation | *to*

9a ▶ Ask Ss to read clauses 1–4 aloud. Tell Ss to pay attention to how *to* is pronounced.

b ▶ ⊙ 2.07 Play the recording for Ss to check their answers.

Answers
/ tə/

10a ▶ Focus Ss on extracts 1–4. Tell Ss to underline the prepositions in each.

b ▶ 🔵 2.08 Play the recording for Ss to check their answers. Give Ss time to practise saying the clauses with a partner. Monitor and note any difficulties Ss are having with producing the weak forms. Highlight these on the board for Ss to correct in pairs. Give praise to the Ss for their efforts.

Speaking

11 ▶ Focus Ss on the words in the box. Ss use these words to complete the spaces in the How to… box. Ss compare answers with a partner. Check answers with the whole class.

```
Answers
 1  be
 2  first
 3  easy
 4  piece
 5  The
 6  step
 7  Without
 8  doesn't
 9  it
10  Any
```

12a ▶ Ss complete paragraphs 1–3 in their own words to explain three different procedures they are familiar with. Monitor and help Ss as necessary.

b ▶ In pairs, Ss take turns to explain their procedures. Encourage Ss listening to ask follow-up questions to find out what the instructions are for.

OPTIONAL EXTENSION

Tell Ss that a friend is going to stay in their house while they are on holiday. Ss write three notes to leave around the house explaining how to use the washing machine, feed the pet, etc. If Ss don't know anything about washing machines or pets, they can write instructions for something else. Ask different Ss to read their notes to the whole class.

7.2 Going to extremes

Here are some of the hottest places in the world: El Azizia in Libya, where the highest ever temperature was recorded as 58° C. Marble Bar in Australia once recorded a period of 160 days from 31 October 1923 to 7 April 1924, where the maximum temperature reached or exceeded 100°F (37.8°C) every day. In terms of annual average temperature, the warmest place in the UK is Scilly, Cornwall, with a mean temperature of 11.5°C. Death Valley, California, is the hottest place in the US. The record temperature there was 56.7°C in 1913. The hottest town in the world is Dallol, Ethiopia, with an average temperature of 34.4°C.

In this lesson, Ss speak about places they have been to. They then go on to listen to the story of a trip to the hottest place on Earth. From this context Ss look at descriptive language. Ss also at different verb patterns.

OPTIONAL WARMER

In a monolingual class, Ss discuss with their partners what the hottest and coldest places in their countries are. In a multilingual class, Ss tell a partner of a different nationality about the hottest and coldest places in their countries. Get feed back from various Ss.

Vocabulary | descriptive language

1a ▶ In pairs, Ss match the words to make common collocations.

```
Answers
 1  d
 2  c
 3  g
 4  a
 5  f
 6  b
 7  e
```

b ▶ Focus Ss' attention on the photos. Ask Ss to discuss the places in the photos in pairs and decide where they might be. Ss then decide which of the collocations from exercise 1a could be used to describe the photos. Ss compare their ideas with another pair. Get feedback from the whole class.

OPTIONAL EXTENSION

Ss choose one of the photos and write a description of it using collocations from exercise 1a. Encourage Ss to be imaginative and invent details of the place if necessary. Monitor as Ss are writing, helping as necessary. Ss read out their descriptions to the rest of the class. Ss listen to compare their descriptions of the same photo.

2 ▶ Focus Ss on sentences 1–7. Ss complete the sentences with the collocations from exercise 1a. Ss compare their answers with a partner. Check answers with the whole class.

> **Answers**
> 1 tourist site
> 2 active volcano
> 3 permanent settlement
> 4 below sea level
> 5 ghost town
> 6 spectacular landscapes
> 7 inhospitable land

Speaking

3 ▶ Ask Ss to discuss the questions in pairs. Monitor conversations for errors. Get feedback and discuss Ss' ideas with the whole class.

4 ▶ Tell Ss to imagine they are going to take a trip to the desert and spend a month there. In pairs, Ss choose five of the things from the box that they would take with them. Ss compare their list with other Ss and justify their choices. Get feedback from the whole class and get the Ss to try to reach agreement about the best five things to take.

Listening

5a ▶ ⬤ 2.09 Tell Ss that they are going to listen to the first part of a story about a trip to the hottest place in the world. Ss read questions 1–3. Play the recording and ask Ss to answer the questions. Give Ss time to compare their answers with a partner. Check answers with the whole class.

> **Answers**
> 1 a visa
> 2 He thinks that David's trip is a very strange one. He says that the Danakil Depression is not a tourist site.
> 3 He shows his sense of humour when he says, 'Typical British. Obsessed by the weather.'

b ▶ Ss discuss the questions with a partner. Ss compare their answers with another pair. Get feedback from various Ss.

c ▶ ⬤ 2.10 Play the recording for Ss to check their predictions. Ss discuss if their predictions were correct. Check answers with the whole class.

6 ▶ In pairs, Ss discuss questions 1–5. Monitor and make note of any important errors you hear, as well as examples of interesting language Ss use. Get feedback and open the discussion to the whole class. Write the errors on the board and invite different Ss to come to the board and correct them for you. Finally, draw Ss' attention to any interesting language used, and congratulate them on its use.

7a ▶ Focus Ss' attention on audioscripts 2.09 and 2.10 on page 173. Ss decide what things/people the words in the box describe. Ss compare their answers with other Ss. Check answers with the whole class.

> **Answers**
> *zig-zag* describes how the flies in the office fly
> *crumble* describes ruined buildings made of salt blocks
> *warped*: the air
> *vibrant*: colours of the salt statues
> *hunched*: volcano

b ▶ Write the words from the box on the board. Ss work in pairs to try to define the words. Encourage Ss to check the words in a dictionary before asking you.

> **Suggested answers**
> *zig-zag*: with abrupt alternate right and left turns
> *crumble*: break and fall into small pieces
> *warped*: bent or twisted and changed from its usual shape
> *vibrant*: full of life
> *hunched*: bent and arched

c ▶ In pairs, Ss make a list of things that they can describe using the adjectives. Ask different Ss to read out their lists to the whole class.

> **OPTIONAL VARIATION**
> Ss think of other things you can talk about using the adjectives but only write down the thing and not the adjective. Ss A read out the things they have written to their partners who guess what adjectives Ss A is thinking of: A: *Barcelona*. B: *Do you think Barcelona is a vibrant city?* Continue until Ss A have read out all of their things, then Ss B read out their things for Ss A to guess.

8 ▶ Ss read through the Lifelong learning box and discuss the questions in pairs. Discuss the usefulness of reading descriptive writing for helping to extend Ss' understanding of English. Encourage Ss to read books in English throughout the course.

> **OPTIONAL EXTENSION**
> If Ss have been reading books in English during the course, in future lessons you could get different Ss to present a talk to the rest of the class about the books they are reading. Encourage Ss listening to ask follow-up questions about the books being presented. Alternatively, if a class set of one book is available, reading and discussion could be incorporated into the lesson cycle. This could also serve as a basis for the filming of a scene from the book or writing a book review.

Grammar | verb patterns (2)

> **OPTIONAL GRAMMAR LEAD-IN**
>
> Organise the Ss into two groups, A and B. Tell Ss A to write a list of things that they have to remember to do every day in their daily lives. Tell Ss B to write a list of things they remember doing as children. Get feedback from the two groups and write them on the board under two headings: *I must remember to …* and *I remember + -ing*. Ask Ss what the difference in meaning is between the two columns. Elicit that *remember + infinitive* is something that you need to do and that *remember + ing* is something you remember doing in the past.

9 ▶ Focus Ss' attention on the Active grammar box. Ss read through the notes and answer the questions. Ss compare their answers with a partner. Check answers with the whole class.

> **Active grammar**
>
> 1   intended = *meant to write*; involved = *means walking*
> 2   responsibility or something you need to do = *remember to drink*; memory of the past = *remembers experiencing*
> 3   feeling of sadness about something in the past = *regret going*; formal apology = *regret to inform*
> 4   paused in order to do something = *stopped to visit*; completely finished something = *stopped looking*
> 5   experiment to see what will happen = *tried drinking*; an effort to do something difficult = *tried to build*
> 6   continued an action = *went on riding*; did something after finishing something else = *went on to write*

▶ Refer Ss to the Reference on page 103 and give them time to read through the notes. Monitor and help Ss with any questions they have.

10 ▶ Ss add two words to sentences 1–12 to complete them. Tell Ss to follow the patterns from the Active grammar box. Ss compare their answers with a partner. Check answers by asking various pairs to read out their sentences.

> **Answers**
> 1   taking the
> 2   stopped to
> 3   tried to
> 4   on speaking/talking
> 5   getting/waking up
> 6   giving up
> 7   to break
> 8   to bring/buy/get
> 9   stopped writing
> 10   went on
> 11   to inform
> 12   try drinking

11a ▶ In pairs, Ss choose the correct option in sentences 1–6. Check answers with the whole class.

> **Answers**
> 1   lying
> 2   going
> 3   to spend
> 4   travelling
> 5   exploring
> 6   going

b ▶ Ss read through the sentences again and mark them T if they are true for them and F if they are false. Ss compare their answers with a partner and explain their views. Get feedback from the whole class.

7.3 Perfect pets?

In this lesson, Ss read a text about buying live animals online. Through this context, Ss look at the grammar of *as … as* and describing quantity. Ss then look at vocabulary connected with buying and selling.

OPTIONAL WARMER

Write the following jumbled names of animals on the board: *rilolga, gtier, cmpzanhiee, kteitn, rafgife, okenmy*. Get Ss to unjumble the words and tell you the names of the animals, then write them on the board: *gorilla, tiger, chimpanzee, kitten, giraffe, monkey*. Ask Ss to work in pairs to rank these animals in order of how dangerous they are, 1 being the most dangerous, 6 the least dangerous. Ss justify their order to another pair.

Reading

Nowadays, it is possible to buy endangered or potentially dangerous animals online. The International Fund for Animal Welfare, an organisation dedicated to the protection of animals and the environment, is trying to stop online trade in wildlife. Their website is: www.ifaw.org. For specific information on the online wildlife trade, see: www.caughtintheweb.co.uk.

1a ▶ In pairs, Ss discuss which statements might be true. Don't ask for feedback at this point.

b ▶ Ss read the article quickly to check their predictions.

Answers
1 true
2 true
3 false
4 false
5 true
6 true

2a ▶ Focus Ss on sentences 1–6. Ss read the article again more carefully and select the best option in each sentence. Don't ask for feedback at this point.

b ▶ Ss read the article again to check. Check answers with the whole class.

Answers
1 toys
2 rare animals
3 at the size of the illegal market for wild animals
4 can't look after it
5 sell the animals on the Internet
6 illegal hunting

---

3 ▶ Ss discuss the questions in pairs. Monitor and take note of interesting ideas or language used. Get feedback from various pairs. Congratulate Ss on any interesting ideas or language heard during their discussions.

Grammar | *as … as* and describing quantity

OPTIONAL GRAMMAR LEAD-IN

Write the following sentence beginning on the board: *Virtually all of the students in the class …* Ask Ss to complete the sentence with their own idea (as long as it is true). Get feedback from various Ss, and discuss the use of *virtually all* as a way of describing quantity. Ask Ss to write down other ways of describing quantity they know of. Get feedback from the whole class and write correct expressions on the board.

4a ▶ Focus Ss on rule A in the Active grammar box. Ss read through the article again quickly and find further examples. Check answers with the whole class.

Active grammar

bought and sold for as little as a few hundred dollars
there are as few as 150,000 left
buying wildlife online is as damaging as killing it yourself
(The first two examples show surprise about a statement. The last example means the two things are equal.)

---

b ▶ Focus Ss on phrases a–h in the Active grammar box. Ss discuss the questions in pairs. Check answers with the whole class.

Active grammar

1 a) as much as – as little as
    b) well under – well over
    c) not very much – a great deal
    d) a tiny minority – a large majority
    e) virtually all – virtually none
    f) precisely – approximately
    g) as many as – as few as
    h) a minimum – a maximum
2 not very much, a great deal, a tiny minority, a large majority, virtually all, virtually none, a minimum, a maximum
3 as much as, as little as, well under, well over, precisely, approximately, as many as, as few as, a minimum, a maximum
4 as much as, as little as, not very much, a great deal

▶ Refer Ss to the Reference on page 103 and give Ss time to read through the notes.

5a ▶ Ss identify the mistakes and correct them. Check answers with the whole class.

> **Answers**
> 1 Pet rabbits usually live for approximately eight years, but **a** small minority live longer.
> 2 Hamsters can give birth to as many **as** 20 offspring at a time.
> 3 A **large** majority of domestic parrots are able to repeat human speech.
> 4 correct
> 5 Koala bears spend virtually **all of** their lives asleep: 18 hours a day.
> 6 Horses usually die at around 20 or 25, but can live a **great** deal longer.
> 7 Tortoises can live to **well over** 100 years, a great deal longer than humans.
> 8 correct

b ▶ Ss discuss whether they think the sentences are true or false. Get feedback from the whole class and refer Ss to page 149 to check their answers. Get feedback about any information that Ss find surprising.

Pronunciation | as

6a ▶ 🔘 2.11 Play the recording. Ss listen to how *as* is pronounced in the three sentences.

b ▶ 🔘 2.12 Tell Ss they are going to hear some questions. Play the recording for Ss to answer using *I'm as …* and the prompts.

> **Suggested answers**
> 1 I'm as free as a bird.
> 2 I'm as strong as an ox.
> 3 I'm as quiet as a mouse.

Speaking

7 ▶ Put Ss in groups of three or four. Focus Ss on questions 1–3. Ss discuss the quotes in their groups. Monitor conversations for important errors.

▶ Get Ss from each group to report back to the class. Encourage Ss to use some of the phrases from the Active grammar box while doing so. Write any important errors you have heard on the board. Ask Ss to discuss the errors in pairs. Ask different Ss to come to the board and write the correct forms.

Vocabulary | buying and selling

8a ▶ Ss discuss the questions. Get feedback from the whole class.

b ▶ Focus Ss on phrases 1–10 and ask Ss, in pairs, to discuss their meanings. Ss match expressions 1–10 to an expression with a similar meaning in a–j. Ss compare answers with their partners. Check answers with the whole class.

> **Answers**
>
> | | | | | | |
> |---|---|---|---|---|---|
> | 1 | h | 5 | f | 9 | a |
> | 2 | j | 6 | g | 10 | e |
> | 3 | b | 7 | i | | |
> | 4 | c | 8 | d | | |

c ▶ In pairs, Ss look at the phrases again. Ss A close their books. Ss B say one of the phrases and Ss A respond with a phrase with a similar meaning. After Ss B have said a few phrases, Ss change roles.

Speaking

9 ▶ Focus Ss on the photos. Ask Ss to discuss in pairs what phrases from exercise 8b they could use to describe these things and what animals were used to make them.

10 ▶ Put Ss in pairs, A and B. Ss A take a possession from their bag and think of a way to make it sound wonderful to 'sell' it to their partners. Encourage Ss to use expressions from exercise 9a while doing so. When Ss A have finished 'selling' their objects to Ss B, change roles. Get feedback from various Ss about how they tried to make their objects sound attractive.

7 Vocabulary | Suffixes

In this lesson, Ss look at different suffixes and how they affect root words. Ss then do a crossword where the answers are all words with suffixes.

OPTIONAL WARMER

On the left-hand side of the board write the following words in a column: *elephants*, *gorillas*, *jaguars*, *dinosaurs*, *giant pandas*, *environment*. On the right-hand side write these words in another column: *ivory tusks*, *fur*, *climate change*, *natural resources*, *forest habitat*, *greenery*. Ss decide which words in the left-hand column are connected with the words in the right-hand column and why. Get feedback from the whole class and ask various Ss to justify their choices.

1a ▶ Tell Ss to find the words in sentences 1–7 that need to have a suffix added, remembering that they may need to omit some letters from the original word when adding the suffix. Ss compare their answers with a partner. Check answers with the whole class.

Answers
1. profitable
2. destruction
3. illegally
4. disappearance
5. dependent
6. emphasise
7. afterwards

b ▶ Ask Ss what type of words they created by using the suffixes. Ss find two nouns, two adjectives, two adverbs and two verbs. Check answers with the class.

Answers
Nouns: *destruction* and *disappearance*
Adjectives: *profitable* and *dependent*
Adverbs: *illegally* and *afterwards*
Verbs: *signifies* (the example) and *emphasise*

2 ▶ Ss read through the Lifelong learning box and do the tasks in pairs. Discuss how useful it can be to break up words when trying to work out the meaning. (Words ending in *-able* are usually adjectives. A *refund* is the money given to a customer who returns goods in a shop. The word *non-refundable* would often be seen on items in shops.)

3 ▶ Put Ss in groups of three or four. Ss work together to add one example for each suffix in tables 1–4 using the words in the boxes.

▶ Ask Ss to compare the words they have written with another group.

Answers
1. globalisation, retirement, sadness, tendency
2. motivator, entrant, psychologist, doorman
3. tolerate, satirise, testify, broaden
4. phenomenal, permanent, hopeful, Polish

▶ Draw Ss' attention to word stress rules with suffixes: with words ending in *-ation* the stress is on the *a* of *-ation*, with words ending in *-ment* the stress is on the syllable before *-ment*.

OPTIONAL EXTENSION

Put Ss in pairs. Each pair writes a short news item using as many of the words with suffixes from page 101 as possible. Tell Ss to write a story which has been in the news recently. Monitor what Ss are writing, then ask various Ss to read out their news stories to the whole class.

---

4 ▶ Focus Ss' on the crossword on page 151. In pairs, Ss decide which words are being described. Tell Ss to write only the suffixes in the spaces in the crossword. Check answers with the whole class.

Answers
1. argu<u>ment</u>
2. happi<u>ness</u>
3. opt<u>ion</u>
4. auth<u>or</u>
5. fisher<u>man</u>
6. special<u>ise</u>
7. radi<u>ate</u>
8. fluen<u>cy</u>
9. immig<u>rant</u>
10. sign<u>ify</u>
11. person<u>al</u>
12. differ<u>ent</u>
13. grate<u>ful</u>
14. guitar<u>ist</u>
15. wid<u>en</u>
16. Dan<u>ish</u>

7 Communication

In this lesson, Ss read a fact file about an island and discuss with a partner/in groups what they could do with the land. Ss then listen to two people discussing what they could do with the land, and finish with a role play.

> **OPTIONAL WARMER**
>
> Write the following prompts on the board: *situation, weather, people, vegetation, buildings*. Ask Ss to look at the picture of the island and discuss in pairs what they think life on the island is like, using the prompts to help. Get feedback from different pairs.

1 ▶ Focus Ss on the photo of the island and the notes. Ss read the fact file.

2 ▶ In pairs or small groups, Ss make a list of all the things they could do with the land. Ss compare their ideas with other pairs/groups. Get feedback from various Ss.

3 ▶ ⬤ 2.13 Tell Ss they are going to listen to two people discussing what they could do with the island. Play the recording while Ss listen and make notes about what the people say. Ss compare their notes with a partner and decide if their ideas were similar to those on the recording.

4a ▶ Put Ss in groups of three, Ss A, B and C. Refer Ss A to page 148, Ss B to page 150 and Ss C to page 152. Give them time to read and memorise their roles.

b ▶ Ss discuss what to do with the island, trying to convince the others of their point of view. Tell Ss that they must agree on something and this might mean a combination of their ideas. Monitor conversations for errors and interesting language that Ss use.

c ▶ Get the different groups to report their decisions back to the rest of the class. Decide as a whole class whose solution is the best one for the island.

7 Review and practice

1 ▶

Answers
One great problem for prison inmates, **who spend** most of their time locked up, is how to develop self-esteem and find a purpose to their days. One idea, **which has** been piloted at a prison in Washington, US, is to get the inmates to train dogs **that will** eventually help disabled people. The project has been a great success. The relationship between the inmates and the warders **who work** at the prison has improved considerably. Many of the inmates, **when they** leave the prison, go on to work with animals.
In another scheme, Pilot Dogs, a company **which trains** dogs for the blind in Ohio, US, put five dogs into the hands of prison inmates, **who trained** the dogs successfully.

2 ▶

Answers
1 I tried on ten pairs of shoes, of which one pair fitted me perfectly.
2 She called her classmates, none of whom had done the homework.
3 We found two good candidates, either of whom could have done the job.
4 We test-drove six cars, all of which cost over $20,000.
5 Sixteen people came camping with us in 2006, some of whom returned the following year.
6 I worked with the two children, neither of whom spoke any English.

3 ▶

Answers
1 to say
2 to think
3 speaking
4 to lock
5 to tell
6 to talk
7 drinking
8 to become

4 ▶

Answers
1 as
2 large
3 deal
4 approximately
5 virtually
6 precisely
7 maximum
8 well
9 much
10 none

5 ▶

Suggested answers

Eco-car for sale, in excellent **condition**. This state **of** the art vehicle runs on water-power, and is **the** latest model. There is some wear **and** tear on the seat. Ring Jerry for further details.

Cat boxes for sale. Perfect for large or small cats. Plenty of space and beautiful decoration. You can choose from a selection **of** styles and a wide **range** of colours. These wooden boxes were made **by** hand, and painted individually. They are **one** of a kind. £20 per box.

Animal Magic books on **the** market, as good **as** new. Just $2.50 per book. Buy the books in a set of four and receive a generous discount. The books are **in** perfect condition (some of them are still **in** their packaging).

7 Writing bank

1 ▶ In pairs, Ss read the advertisements and discuss the question. Get feedback from the whole class.

2 ▶ In pairs, Ss discuss the features. Get feedback from the whole class.

Suggested answers

1 T
2 T
3 T
4 F
5 F
6 T

3 ▶ Focus Ss' attention on the How to... box. In pairs, Ss add examples from advert 3. Get feedback from the whole class.

Answers

Give concise details about size, age, etc.: *7-inch portable; (Ramashay Model DVR30); Battery life is 3 hours; 2-inch scratch*

Describe condition (positive): *in good working order*

Describe condition (negative): *some wear and tear; scratch on the cover; rather tatty*

4a ▶ Individually, Ss make notes in preparation for their advert. Then Ss write their statements. Encourage Ss to use ideas from the How to... box. Go round and monitor Ss who need any help.

b ▶ Put Ss in small groups. Ss take turns to show their adverts and ask questions to find out more information.

Overview

Lead-in	**Vocabulary:** Issues
8.1	**Can do:** Stall for time when asked a difficult question **Grammar:** Reported speech **Vocabulary:** Contrasting opinions **Speaking and pronunciation:** **How to...** stall for time (when you're asked a difficult question) **Reading:** Future inventions **Listening:** Inventions
8.2	**Can do:** Discuss lifestyle in detail **Grammar:** The continuous form **Vocabulary:** Lifestyles **Listening:** Work/life habits
8.3	**Can do:** Explain everyday problems **Grammar:** Fronting **Vocabulary:** Cause and effect **Speaking and pronunciation:** Fronting **How to...** describe problems **Reading:** Advice.com **Listening:** Describing problems
Vocabulary	Academic English
Communication	Present different points of view
Writing bank	Write an essay that describes cause and effect **How to...** organise information in an essay
Extra resources	ActiveTeach and ActiveBook

CEFR Can do objectives
8.1 Stall for time when asked a difficult question
8.2 Discuss lifestyle in detail
8.3 Explain everyday problems
Communication Present different points of view
Writing bank Write an essay that describes cause and effect

CEFR Portfolio ideas
a) Choose a scene from a film or play in English or in your own language. Report what the characters say in the scene.
b) Which activities connected with using English make you feel stressed? Make a list of your problems. Ask your friends if they can suggest solutions.
c) Imagine you get sick during a vacation abroad. You go to the doctor and describe how your illness affects you. Write the dialogue.
d) How does the weather influence the economy of your country? What might be the effects of global warming? Prepare a formal lecture answering the two questions, using academic English.

Lead-in

OPTIONAL WARMER

Ask Ss to research an important issue which has been in the news in the previous week. This can be a news issue from their own country or an international news issue. Ss can research on the Internet or through newspapers. Encourage Ss to bring in newspaper cuttings or print-outs from the Internet if possible. Ss present the news issue to the the class. Encourage those Ss listening to ask follow-up questions.

1 ▶ Ask Ss to discuss in pairs what is happening in the photos, what issues the photos represent and if these issues are important or not. Get feedback from the whole class.

2a ▶ Ss make nouns from the words and phrases 1–10. Check answers with the whole class and write the nouns on the board.

Answers			
1	biotechnology	6	global warming
2	censorship	7	immigration
3	poverty	8	identity theft
4	democracy	9	space exploration
5	globalisation	10	pollution

3 ▶ Focus Ss on the words and phrases in the box. Tell Ss to check the meaning of the words in a dictionary. Ss decide which of the nouns in exercise 2 are associated with the words and phrases here. Tell Ss there may be more than one answer. Ss compare their answers with other Ss.

Answers
unemployment: poverty/immigration
depletion of the ozone layer: global warming/pollution
ID cards: identity theft/immigration
cloning: biotechnology
the right to vote: democracy
freedom of speech: censorship/democracy
giant corporations: globalisation
cost and safety issues: space exploration
multiculturalism: immigration

4 ▶ Ask Ss to discuss questions 1–3 in pairs. Monitor conversations for errors or any interesting language Ss use. Get feedback from the whole class and discuss the Ss' ideas.

EXTEND THE LEAD-IN

Ask Ss to work in pairs to write a short news report about one of the news issues they talked about in exercise 4. When they have finished, Ss swap their reports with another pair. Ss read each others' reports and write comments on the content of the news report. Ss return the reports to the Ss who wrote them so they can read the comments. Collect the reports for correction and display them on the wall.

8.1 A better future

> There has always been speculation about what the inventions of the future will be and how they will help the world. Necessity has always been the mother of invention, and this will be true of inventions of the future which will have to tackle problems such as the depletion of the world's oil, processing of the world's waste and identifying future illnesses. In the US, there is an organisation called the Da Vinci Institute which is dedicated to finding important future inventions and which has designed a museum dedicated to them. (See: www.davinciinstitute.com)

In this lesson, Ss discuss different issues of global importance. They then read a text about future inventions and through this context look at the grammar of reporting verbs. Ss go on to listen to people talking about inventions they would like to see and discuss these inventions.

> **OPTIONAL WARMER**
>
> Put Ss in groups of three or four. Ss make a list of the top three inventions the world has ever seen. Ss share their lists with another group, justifying their choices and explaining why these inventions have been so important for the world. Get feedback from each group and then try to reach agreement as a class about the most important inventions in history.

Vocabulary | contrasting opinions

1a ▶ Ask Ss to describe with a partner what they can see in the photos. Ask Ss to read sentences 1–6 and match each sentence to a photo. Ss compare their answers with another student. Check answers with the whole class.

Answers											
1 F	2 C	3 B	4 E	5 A	6 D

b ▶ In pairs, Ss read sentences a–f and match these sentences to the issues in exercise 1a. Ss compare their answers with another pair. Check answers with the whole class.

Answers											
1 d	2 c	3 a	4 e	5 f	6 b

2a ▶ Put Ss into pairs, A and B. Ss A give an opinion on one of the issues from exercise 1 and Ss B respond with an alternative opinion. Monitor the conversations for use of expressions for giving opinions and expressing contrasting opinions. Continue until Ss have discussed all the issues. Write good examples of these expressions being used by the Ss on the board. Congratulate Ss on accurate usage of the expressions.

b ▶ Put Ss in groups of three or four. Ss tell the other Ss in their groups about inventions that they wish had never been invented and why they would prefer for them not to have been invented. Ss also discuss if they would replace these inventions with anything else. Monitor the conversations for errors. Get feedback from various Ss.

Reading

3a ▶ Ss discuss statements 1–5 with a partner. Ss mark the statements T if they think they are true, F if they think they are false. Ss compare their answers with another pair. Don't ask for feedback at this point.

b ▶ Tell the Ss they are going to check their answers by reading an article about future inventions. Give the Ss a time limit of three minutes to read through the article quickly. Tell Ss not to worry about any words or phrases they don't understand at this stage as you will deal with them later. Check answers with the whole class.

> **Answers**
> 1 False ('He was wrong by a few million years. Once our oil is gone, it's gone forever')
> 2 True ('We have about 50 years' worth left, less if rates of industrialisation accelerate.')
> 3 True ('Once the jungles disappeared, we started burying our waste underground or chucking it into the sea.')
> 4 False ('ID theft is the fastest-growing type of crime.')
> 5 True ('Now we are examining people's genes for signs of future illness.')

4 ▶ Focus Ss on sentences 1–6. Ss read the article more slowly and choose the correct option in each sentence. Check answers with the whole class.

> **Answers**
> 1 are interested in things that haven't been invented yet
> 2 solar power might provide a source of energy to replace oil
> 3 there is too much rubbish for the space available
> 4 use our rubbish productively
> 5 microchips in every object we own
> 6 a way to predict the illnesses a person is vulnerable to

▶ Ask Ss if there are any words or phrases in the text they don't understand. Encourage Ss to answer each others' questions or to look unknown words up in the dictionary before explaining the vocabulary yourself.

5a ▶ Ask Ss to discuss in pairs what they think of the article and if it contains any good ideas.

b ▶ Ss look through the text for further examples of irony and humour. Get feedback from the whole class.

Grammar | reported speech

> **OPTIONAL GRAMMAR LEAD-IN**
>
> While Ss are discussing the article, take note of an exact sentence that one of the Ss says. Write this sentence on the board with inverted commas round it to show that it is direct speech. Ask the class if they remember who said this sentence and write the student's name beside it. Now ask Ss to report what the student said. Write the reported sentence on the board and discuss the differences between the original sentence and the reported version.

6 ▶ Ss read through the Active grammar box and answer the questions. Ss compare their answers with a partner. Check the answers with the whole class.

Active grammar

1 *He warned that whatever hadn't happened would happen and no one would be safe from it.* (He actually said 'Whatever hasn't happened will happen and no one will be safe from it')

Hilary Craft said we had already found the answer: solar power. She said we could expect enormous mirrors in the sky ... ('We have already found the answer: solar power. We can expect enormous mirrors in the sky.')

Clara Petrovic, said she was working on a prototype ... ('I am working on a prototype.')

Alexis Smithson said that in the past thieves had always taken objects. ('In the past, thieves always took objects.')

The verb tenses shift back one tense when we report speech.

2 *Glen Hiemstra of Futurist.com recently claimed that somewhere on planet Earth there is a young child who will be the first person to live forever.* ('Somewhere on planet Earth there is a young child who will be the first person to live forever.')

The example doesn't shift the tenses back and it uses a reporting verb.

4 1 admit – confess

2 remember – recollect

3 tell – inform

4 answer – respond (We *answer* a question, but we can *respond* to other things, e.g. a piece of music.)

5 suggest – imply (*suggest* has different meanings: it can mean *make a suggestion*, which is different from *imply*.)

6 threaten – warn (*threaten* suggests a punishment, *warn* might be to help someone.)

7 insist – maintain

8 assume – presume

Expressions a–h are more formal than expressions 1–8.

▶ Refer Ss to the Reference on page 117. Give Ss time to read through the notes.

7 ▶ Focus Ss on sentences 1–6. Ss delete the options which are not possible. Ss compare their answers with a partner. Check answers with the whole class.

Answers

1 threatened

2 implied discussing

3 informed

4 told

5 remember to visit

6 suggest

---

8 ▶ Put Ss in pairs. Ss report the dialogues using the correct words from the boxes. Tell Ss to leave the non-reporting verbs in the same tense if possible. Tell Ss that in one sentence they need to change a positive adjective to a negative one. Check answers with the whole class.

Answers

Sarah warned that if they/we don't start recycling, the consequences will be serious for the planet.

David suggested that they should start (OR suggested starting) a recycling group in the community.

Sarah remembered that there's one already.

Mike confessed that there had been one. He started it, but then it became really hard work, so they stopped.

David assumed that no one drives if they can walk these days.

Mike responded by saying that he drives everywhere.

Sarah implied that this is bad for the environment.

Mike threatened to kick them out of his flat if they didn't shut up about the environment.

Speaking and listening

9 ▶ Focus Ss on the pictures. Ask Ss to discuss each of the inventions shown with a partner and what they think the inventions do/are. Don't get feedback at this point.

10a ▶  2.14 Tell Ss they are going to listen to seven people talking about the invention they would most like to see. Play the recording and ask Ss to match the inventions with the pictures. Check answers with the whole class.

Answers

Speaker 1 – A   Speaker 4 – F   Speaker 7 – E

Speaker 2 – G   Speaker 5 – C

Speaker 3 – B   Speaker 6 – D

---

b ▶ Focus Ss on the statements about the different speakers 1–7. With a partner, Ss write T beside the statements they think are true and F beside the statements they think are false. Don't ask for feedback at this point.

c ▶ Play the recording again for Ss to check their answers.

Answers

1 T   2 F   3 F   4 T   5 T   6 F   7 T

---

11 ▶ Focus Ss on the How to... box. Ss complete the phrases. Tell Ss to check their answers with a partner and then with audioscript 2.14 on page 173.

Answers

1 question   2 see   3 tricky   4 about   5 a

12a ▶ Ss discuss questions 1–5 with a partner. Encourage Ss to use the expressions in the How to... box while doing so. Monitor the conversations for Ss' use of the expressions and make a note of any important errors. Discuss correct usage of the expressions that you heard and note any errors on the board for the Ss to correct.

b ▶ Put Ss in new pairs so that they are working with a different partner. Ss report to their new partner what their original partner said. Monitor for Ss' use of reported speech features. Write any important errors on the board and elicit corrections from the Ss.

8.2 Idlers and strivers

> Modern life is increasingly stressful and there are many people who become disenchanted with the way they live and the jobs they do. This can result in health problems. Some people have found an answer to the problems of their stressful lives in 'downshifting', a term which refers to when people give up their jobs and lead a different life, often in the country. This change normally results in a reduction in earnings but can bring about an improvement in the quality of life.
> See: www.thedownshifter.co.uk for information about downshifting.

In this lesson, Ss listen to two people talking about their work/life habits. Ss then look at vocabulary connected with lifestyles before looking at the grammar of the continuous aspect. Ss finish the lesson by interviewing their partners to find out if they are 'idlers' or 'strivers'.

OPTIONAL WARMER

Give Ss time to think about any areas of their life they would like to change. Ss can take notes about how they would like to change these areas. Ss then share this information with a partner, and discuss what they would have to do to make these changes and if it would be easy to make these changes to their lives or not. Get feedback from various Ss.

Listening

1 ▶ Ss work in pairs to discuss the people in the photos by answering questions 1–5. Monitor conversations and take note of important errors. Get feedback from different pairs. Write any important errors you have heard on the board and get different Ss to correct them.

2 ▶ 🔘 2.15 Tell Ss that they are going to hear the people in the photos talking about their work/life habits. Play the recording and ask Ss to take note of how the two lifestyles differ. Ss compare their notes with a partner. Check answers with the whole class.

Answers
Thomas leads a relaxed lifestyle, living by the sea. He believes that money isn't everything and that there is no point in hurrying.
Elise has a hectic city lifestyle. She believes that she wouldn't like living in the country, and that she would miss the noise of the city.

3a ▶ Focus Ss on questions 1–5. Ask Ss to read the questions and possible answers in pairs and choose the best answer for each question. Don't ask for feedback at this point.

b ▶ 🔘 2.15 Play the recording again for Ss to check.

Answers			
1	b	4	c
2	c	5	b
3	a		

Vocabulary | lifestyles

4a ▶ 🔘 2.15 Refer Ss to audioscript 2.15 on page 173. Play the recording again and ask Ss to read along with the audioscript.

▶ Focus Ss on the idiomatic expressions 1–10. In pairs, Ss try to work out the meaning of the expressions from the context of the audioscript. Get feedback from various Ss.

b ▶ Ss match expressions 1–10 to definitions a–j. Check answers with the whole class.

Answers			
1	f	6	i
2	c	7	b
3	g	8	d
4	e	9	h
5	j	10	a

5 ▶ Ask Ss to discuss questions 1–4 in small groups. Get feedback from various Ss. In a monolingual class, Ss can tell you whether they think people in their country work hard compared to other countries. In a multilingual class, Ss can tell a partner of a different nationality about whether people work hard in their country. Ss can then tell the rest of the class what they have learned about their partner's country.

OPTIONAL EXTENSION

Ss work in pairs or small groups. Ss prepare and write a survey addressing work/life habits to ask the other Ss in the class. Ss then ask their questions and make notes on the answers. The results can be presented in the form of charts or tables and displayed around the classroom.

Grammar | the continuous form

OPTIONAL GRAMMAR LEAD-IN

Prepare a short paragraph about yourself which includes an example of the following structures: Present Continuous, Past Continuous, Present Perfect Continuous, Past Perfect Continuous, Future Continuous and present participle clause. Tell Ss you are going to read the paragraph once at normal speed and that they should try to write down as much as they can. If they can't write everything, they should leave a space and continue. Read the paragraph. Ss then compare what they have written with a partner. Get feedback and write up on the board any parts of sentences Ss can give you. As a class, Ss try to fill in the spaces to reconstruct the text. Help the Ss until the full text is on the board. Ask Ss to look at the verb forms and decide what they have in common. (They are all continuous forms.) Ss discuss the use of the continuous form with a partner.

6a ▶ Focus Ss on the Active grammar box. Ask Ss to match the headings with the examples. Let them compare answers with a partner. Check answers with the whole class.

Active grammar

1 f
2 b
3 e
4 a
5 d
6 c

---

b ▶ Focus Ss on rule A in the Active grammar box. They complete parts 1–4. Check answers with the whole class.

Active grammar

1 c
2 e
3 d
4 f

---

c ▶ Focus Ss on rule B in the Active grammar box. In pairs, Ss think of examples. Get feedback from the whole class.

d ▶ Focus Ss on rule C in the Active grammar box. They complete parts 1–4. Check answers with the whole class.

Active grammar

Verbs of personal feeling: like, love, hate, want, prefer, dislike, wish
Verbs of thought: know, believe, imagine, mean, realise, understand, doubt, feel (have an opinion)
Verbs of the senses: hear, sound, appear, taste, see, smell, resemble, seem

---

▶ Refer Ss to the Reference on page 117. Give Ss time to read through the notes and answer any questions the Ss have.

7a ▶ Focus Ss on sentences 1–8. Ss change the verb forms into the continuous. Ss then discuss with a partner if this changes the meaning of the sentences and, if so, how. Ss compare their ideas with another pair. Check answers with the whole class and discuss how the meaning of the sentences can change with the use of the continuous forms.

Answers

1 I've read that book. – I've been reading that book. (Simple = she's finished the book. Continuous = she hasn't finished it.)
2 He gets bored. – He's getting bored. (Simple = this usually happens. Continuous = at this particular moment it's happening.)
3 I'll work till about 8 p.m. tonight. – I'll be working till about 8 p.m. tonight. (Simple and continuous = basically the same meaning here.)
4 She hit me. – She was hitting me. (Simple = she did it once. Continuous = she did it repeatedly.)
5 The first chapter is written. – The first chapter is being written. (Simple = it is finished. Continuous = it isn't finished.)
6 What music do you listen to? – What music are you listening to? (Simple = generally. Continuous = at this particular moment it's happening.)
7 He had lost his hair. – He had been losing his hair. (Simple = the hair was all gone. Continuous = the hair was in the process of going. He still had some left.)
8 The coach leaves at 11 p.m. – The coach is leaving at 11 p.m. (Simple and continuous = basically the same meaning here, BUT Simple = for a formally organised timetable. Continuous = may be a decision made by an individual.)

---

b ▶ Focus Ss' attention on the replies to the sentences in exercise 7a. Ss decide if these could be replies to the simple or the continuous forms in exercise 7a, or a reply to both of the forms. Ss compare their answers with a partner. Check answers with the whole class.

Answers

3 Both (as either form could be used in the sentence from 7a)
4 Continuous (the phrase 'go on' in the reply indicates a continued/repeated action)
5 Simple (the reply indicates the action is finished)
6 Continuous (the reply refers to the music playing now, not in general)
7 Simple (the reply indicates that there is no hair left – a finished action)
8 Both (as either form could be used in the sentence from 7a)

---

8 ▶ Focus Ss on the words in the box. Ask Ss to discuss the meanings of these words with a partner and look up any new words in a dictionary if necessary. Get feedback from different pairs by asking different Ss to give explanations of the words to the whole class.

▶ Ss read through the text and complete it with the words from the box. Tell Ss they may need to change the verb form to fit the context. If both the simple and continuous forms are possible, tell Ss to use the continuous form. Ss compare answers with a partner. Check answers with the whole class.

> **Answers**
> 1 were going back
> 2 were beginning
> 3 is pondering/has been pondering
> 4 Will we be working
> 5 seem
> 6 is growing/has been growing
> 7 are urging
> 8 have been advocating
> 9 quotes
> 10 was driving

9 ▶ Focus Ss on the Lifelong learning box. Ask them to work through the questions in pairs. Get feedback from the whole class.

Speaking

> **OPTIONAL LEAD-IN**
> Write the following words on the board: *shop assistant, anthropology student, work in a bar, jogging, studying for an exam, learning German, MA, play squash, go dancing*. Ask Ss to discuss in pairs if they have ever done or been any of these things. Get feedback by asking different Ss to share their experiences with the class. Then ask Ss to cover the profile of Dana Kolansky and look at her photo, and predict which of these things she does. (She does all of these things.) Tell Ss to read the text and check if their predictions were correct.

10 ▶ Ss read the profile and decide if Dana is an 'idler' or a 'striver'. Get opinions from different Ss and ask them to explain why they think this.

> **Answer**
> She is a 'striver'.

11a ▶ Focus Ss on the profile outline. In pairs, Ss discuss and decide what questions they would need to ask to complete the profile. Get feedback from different pairs and write the correct questions Ss give you on the board.

b ▶ Put Ss in pairs, A and B. Ss interview their partners using the questions they have written. Monitor the interviews for errors.

c ▶ Get feedback from various pairs and ask Ss to tell the rest of the class if their partners are 'idlers' or 'strivers' and why. Write any important errors you have heard on the board. Invite different Ss to come to the board and write the correct forms. Congratulate Ss on any interesting language they have used while doing the interviews.

> **OPTIONAL EXTENSION**
> Divide the class into two groups, 'idlers' and 'strivers'. In their groups, Ss decide why this is the best lifestyle to lead and write down a list of reasons. Put Ss in pairs so that they are working with Ss from the other group. Ss try to convince their partners that their lifestyle is better than their partner's. Get feedback and discuss with the whole class whether it is better to be an 'idler' or a 'striver'.

8.3 Everyday issues

In this lesson, Ss read problems and advice on a web page called advice.com. Ss then study the grammar of fronting. They then listen to people complaining about problems they have had with machines. Ss then look at the vocabulary connected to cause and effect. Ss finish the lesson by writing an essay about a problem or issue.

OPTIONAL WARMER

Ss make a list of machines they come into contact with in their daily life. Ss then share their lists with their partners. Get feedback from the class and write the list of machines on the board. Discuss with the whole class which of these machines they would most miss if they stopped working.

Reading

Problem pages have always been a traditional part of magazines. People can write to the magazine with a problem and an expert (or other readers) writes back in an open letter, giving advice about what to do in this situation. The advent of the Internet has meant that it is possible to ask for advice on the Internet in the same way.

1 ▶ In pairs, Ss discuss what is happening in the photos. Ss then tell their partners if they have ever been in situations like the ones shown. Ss describe to their partner what happened and how they resolved the problem. Write any errors you hear on the board. Get feedback by asking Ss to tell you what they have learned about their partners.

2a ▶ Focus Ss' attention on problems A and B from advice.com. Tell Ss not to worry about difficult vocabulary at this stage as you will be dealing with it later. Ss discuss the problems with a partner and decide which of the problems is more serious and why. Ss then think of advice which they would give to Silvana and Jake. Get feedback from the whole class.

b ▶ Ss read the advice in posts 1–4. Ss compare this advice with the advice they came up with earlier, and decide if they agree with the suggestions given. Get feedback from the whole class. Ask Ss if there are any words or phrases in the posts they don't understand. Encourage Ss to answer each other's questions before explaining the vocabulary to the class.

OPTIONAL EXTENSION

Assign Ss an area of life (love, family, friends, money) to write a 'problem letter' about. Give Ss time to prepare and write their letters. Then Ss swap letters with a partner, read the letter, and write some advice in reply. Ss return the letters of advice to their partners.

Grammar | fronting

OPTIONAL GRAMMAR LEAD-IN

Write the following sentence beginning on the board: *I get really irritated …* . Ss finish the sentence with their own ideas, so long as it is true for them. Get feedback and discuss Ss' 'pet hates' as a class. Now write: *What … * on the board. Ask Ss to complete this sentence so that it has the same meaning as the first sentence they completed. Elicit the following beginning of the sentence: *What I get really irritated by is …* . Discuss what effect this structure has on the sentence. Explain that we use this type of order to emphasise the subject of the sentence or to provide a clear link with a previous sentence.

3a ▶ Focus Ss on rule A in the Active grammar box. Ask Ss to rewrite example 2. Check answers with the whole class.

Active grammar

Why you insist on fooling yourself, I really don't know.

b ▶ Focus Ss on the website article. Ask Ss to find further examples of fronting. Check answers with the whole class.

Active grammar

What you need to do is to put yourself in your friend's shoes.
What might also work is having some games available for the children.
There's not much you can do.
What they really care about isn't the morals or ethics of you embellishing your CV …

c ▶ Focus Ss on rule B in the Active grammar box. Ask Ss to find further examples of fronting in the website article. Check answers with the whole class.

Active grammar

The fact remains that you …
The truth is …
The point is …
The fact of the matter is …

▶ Refer Ss to the Reference on page 117 and give them time to read through the notes.

4 ▶ Focus Ss on sentences 1–6. Ss change the sentences so that the meaning stays the same. Tell Ss to start the sentences with the word in brackets. Ss compare their sentences with a partner. Check answers with the whole class and write the sentences on the board.

> **Answers**
> 1   She didn't discipline them – that was the problem. – The problem was that she didn't discipline them.
> 2   I'm not sure how long he hoped to get away with this lie. – How long he hoped to get away with this lie I'm not sure.
> 3   I don't know how she manages with those kids. – How she manages with those kids I don't know.
> 4   Their behaviour was completely unacceptable. – Completely unacceptable was their behaviour.
> 5   My colleague lost his job because his work was so bad. – So bad was my colleague's work, he lost his job.
> 6   I really didn't know why they wanted to check up on me. → Why they wanted to check up on me, I really didn't know.

5a ▶ Put Ss in groups of three, A, B and C. Refer Ss A to page 148, Ss B to page 150 and Ss C to page 152. Give Ss time to read through their problems. Monitor to make sure that Ss understand their problems. If Ss prefer, they can make up their own problem. If so, monitor to check what problems the Ss come up with.

b ▶ Ss tell the other two Ss in their group about their problem. Tell the Ss listening to offer advice and to use fronting expressions where possible. Monitor the conversations, taking note of errors and correct use of fronting expressions. Get feedback from various groups and decide as a class if the advice given by Ss was good advice or not. Write any errors you have heard on the board and ask different Ss to come to the board and write the correct forms. Finally, congratulate Ss on their use of fronting expressions.

Pronunciation | fronting

6a ▶ ⬤ 2.16 Play the recording. Ss notice which words are stressed. Get feedback from the whole class.

b ▶ Play the recording again. Ss listen and repeat.

7a ▶ Ss write three more sentences based on the situations in exercise 5.

b ▶ In small groups, Ss take turns to read out their sentences.

Listening and speaking

8a ▶ Ask Ss to discuss with a partner what can go wrong with everyday machines and if they have any experiences of these or any other machines going wrong. Get feedback from various Ss.

b ▶ ⬤ 2.17 Tell Ss they are going to hear three people complaining about problems they have had with machines. Play the recording and ask Ss to take notes about which machines the people are talking about and what the problem is in each case. Check answers with the whole class.

> **Answers**
> 1   photocopier – keeps getting jammed
> 2   computer – won't shut down
> 3   fan – can't switch it on

9a ▶ Focus Ss on the How to... box. Ask Ss to discuss with a partner if the expressions are followed by a verb + -ing, an infinitive with to, or an infinitive without to.

b ▶ ⬤ 2.17 Play the recording again for Ss to check their answers and complete the expressions.

> **Answers**
> 1   getting jammed.
> 2   make any copies.
> 3   coming up with the same message.
> 4   shut down.
> 5   switching it on.
> 6   to be stuck.
> 7   go round.

10a ▶ Put Ss in pairs. Tell Ss to imagine that there is a problem with an item of technology in their home. Ss make notes about the problem. Ss describe the problem to their partners without mentioning the name of the item. Encourage Ss to use phrases from the How to... box.

b ▶ The Ss listening have to guess what the item is and come up with a solution if possible. Monitor conversations for errors and discuss the solutions to the problems Ss have offered. Write any errors you have heard on the board and ask different Ss to correct them.

> **OPTIONAL EXTENSION**
>
> On the board, write the following prompts: *where?*, *when?*, *how much?*, *problems*, *expected action*. Ss write a letter of complaint to the shop where they bought the machine they have described. Ss should include the prompts on the board in their letters.

Vocabulary | cause and effect

11a ▶ Focus Ss' attention on the eight statements. In pairs, Ss discuss the question.

b ▶ Focus Ss' attention on the underlined phrases. Ss complete the table.

> **Answers**
> Nouns: major source; cause of; far-reaching implications; influence on
> Verbs: brought about; results in; give rise to; stems from

12 ▶ Ss delete the words which cannot be used. Get feedback from the whole class.

> **Answers**
> 1 root   4 results in
> 2 implications   5 rise
> 3 influence on   6 results

13a ▶ Ss finish sentences 1–6 so they are true for them.

b ▶ Ss compare their answers with other Ss. Encourage Ss to ask each other follow-up questions where possible. Monitor the conversations for errors. Get feedback from the class. Read out any important errors you have heard and get different Ss to correct them for you.

Speaking

14a ▶ Focus Ss on the problems and issues suggested. Ss choose one of the problems/issues and make notes about its causes, the effect it has had on them or others, and possible solutions to this problem. Monitor and help Ss as necessary. Ss compare ideas with a partner.

b ▶ Put Ss in small groups. They discuss their ideas.

c ▶ Get feedback from the whole class.

8 Vocabulary | Academic English

In this lesson, Ss look at different examples of Academic English.

> **OPTIONAL WARMER**
> Put Ss in pairs. In a monolingual class, Ss discuss the differences in their own language between everyday speech and formal academic writing. Draw two columns on the board with the headings *Everyday speech* and *Formal academic writing*. Get feedback from the whole class and write characteristics of each type of language in the two columns. In a multilingual class, Ss of different nationalities tell each other about the differences between everyday speech and academic writing in their languages. Get feedback by asking Ss to tell you what they have learned about their partner's language.

1 ▶ In pairs, Ss choose the correct words/phrases in italics in the boxes. Tell Ss that of the three options, two are correct. Ss compare answers with another pair. Ss put the words in italics into the correct columns in the tables. Check answers with the whole class.

> **Answers**
> 1 with regard to; regarding
> 2 notably; namely
>   Introducing a topic: in terms of; with regard to
>   Being specifc: notably; namely; in particular; to be precise
> 3 Nevertheless; However
> 4 What's more; Furthermore
>   Contrast: nevertheless; however; and yet; on the other hand
>   Saying more: furthermore; what's more; in addition
> 5 highlight; underline
> 6 suggest; hint at
>   Verbs of direct focus: highlight; point out; emphasise; stress; underline; focus on
>   Verbs that focus indirectly: hint; imply; infer; suggest
> 7 evaluate; appraise
> 8 formulate; construct
>   Verbs for judging: assess; evaluate; appraise
>   Verbs which mean 'create': generate; construct; formulate
> 9 To sum up; In conclusion
>   Arranging data: for X days/hours running; in order of + (age, importance, etc.); in alphabetical/chronological order
>   Finishing: to sum up; in conclusion

2 ▶ Ss read the text and choose the correct words in italics. Ss compare answers with a partner. Check answers with the whole class.

> **Answers**
> 1 Furthermore
> 2 In terms of
> 3 On the other hand
> 4 infer
> 5 implied
> 6 pointed out
> 7 in particular
> 8 however
> 9 construct

3 ▶ Ss discuss questions 1–3 with a partner. Encourage Ss to use words and expressions from the lesson in their discussions.

▶ Put Ss with new partners. Ss tell their new partners what they have talked about. Get feedback from various Ss.

8 Communication

In this lesson, Ss give and exchange opinions about five different topics they have chosen.

> **OPTIONAL WARMER**
> Write the following expressions on the board: *I agree, I'm not sure about that, I don't think so, I agree with you up to a point, but ..., That's rubbish!, I disagree, I suppose you're right, You could have a point there*. With a partner, Ss divide the expressions into two groups: agreeing and disagreeing. Ss can also decide if any of these expressions are particularly formal or informal. (*That's rubbish!* and *I suppose you're right* sound more informal than the others.)

1a ▶ Ss discuss with a partner whether they have ever been in situations or places like the ones shown in the photos, and in which situation or place they would most like to be now. Get feedback from various Ss.

▶ Ss read statements a–j and decide if any can be used to describe the photos. Get feedback from the whole class.

b ▶ Ss give the statements a number from 1 to 5; 1 being something they completely disagree with, 5 something they completely agree with.

c ▶ Individually, Ss choose five of these topics they would be interested in discussing.

2a ▶ In groups, Ss compare the topics they have chosen. Tell Ss not to express their opinions about the topics at this stage, but to decide which five of the topics their group is going to discuss.

b ▶ When each group has decided on the topics to discuss, Ss compare the numbers they have written beside each statement and explain why they agree or disagree.

c ▶ Get feedback by asking each group to report to the class about what they talked about and what the group's views and opinions were. Ss could refer to the academic vocabulary on the previous page for useful phrases to make their points. Monitor Ss and note any important errors.

▶ Write errors you have heard on the board and ask Ss to correct them. Finally, congratulate Ss on their use of interesting language during the lesson.

8 Review and practice

1 ▶

Answers
We propose ... explained **to** us ... people **to** think ...
for **destroying** the local ... deliberately **harming** the ...
We **suggest adopting** this ... to **consider** spiritual ...
guaranteed to **open** our ...

2 ▶

Answers
1 Were you thinking
2 Why are you wearing
3 Where were you going
4 How long have you been playing
5 Had he been living
6 Why didn't you understand
7 Where have you been staying
8 Do you see

3 ▶

Answers
1 The **problem** is ... but the fact of the **matter** is that ...
   Quite **what** we're going ...
2 What **surprises** me ... thing **is,** she has ...
3 **Why** you're complaining ... idea **would** be to ...

4 ▶

Answers
1 influence
2 resulted; harm
3 consequences/results
4 gives; for
5 bring; force
6 from; cannot
7 sources/causes
8 roots

5 ▶

Answers
line 1: a
line 2: ✓
line 3: to
line 4: really
line 5: their
line 6: the
line 7: up
line 8: ✓
line 9: them
line 10: an

8 Writing bank

1 ▶ In pairs, Ss read the essay and discuss the question. Get feedback from the whole class.

Answer
a

2 ▶ In pairs, Ss discuss the questions. Get feedback from the whole class.

Answers
1 It is stated in the first sentence.
2 three
3 two
4 They are usually short.
5 It refers back to the effects of insomnia.

3 ▶ Focus Ss' attention on the How to... box. In pairs, Ss tick the expressions used in the essay. Get feedback from the whole class.

Answers
it has been estimated that ...
recent research points to the fact that ...
many people report that they ...
This paper will first examine ...
We will then ...
The primary cause of insomnia is ...
The second ...
Another aspect to take into consideration is ...
A further effect is ...
Regarding ...

4a ▶ Individually, Ss make notes in preparation for their essay. Encourage Ss to use ideas from the How to... box.

b ▶ Ss write their essays. Go round and monitor Ss who need any help.

Overview

CEFR Can do objectives
9.1 Express a degree of certainty
9.2 Use colloquial expressions to explain your tastes
9.3 Respond to hypothetical questions
Communication Present a proposal
Writing bank Write a detailed proposal

CEFR Portfolio ideas
a) Play a game with your partner. Ask questions. Try to make your partner say 'Yes' 'No'. Your partner will try to avoid using these words by expressing uncertainty. Can your partner answer questions for four minutes without saying *Yes* or *No*? Change roles and play again.
b) Is there an art form from your culture which foreigners do not understand or appreciate? Prepare the script for a TV programme which explains why this art form is so popular in your culture.
c) Life is full of 'What if...' questions. Write five 'What if ...' questions and do a survey amongst your friends. Make notes of their answers. Summarise the responses in a report. Mention the answers which surprised you.
d) As you know, in Britain, people drive on the left side of the road. Prepare a proposal for the British government suggesting a change to driving on the right. Think about the advantages of this proposal, the difficulties and the cost for the British population.

Lead-in

OPTIONAL WARMER

Ss talk to a partner about famous painters from their country. Get feedback from the whole class and ask different Ss to tell you about the different painters from their countries.

1 ▶ Focus Ss on the photos. Ss discuss which art forms they can see represented in the photos. Ss then think of other forms of visual arts and discuss with a partner which they prefer and why. Get feedback from various pairs.

2a ▶ Ss discuss sentences 1–8 and decide if they refer to books, films, theatre, art or architecture (there may be more than one answer). Draw five columns on the board and write *books*, *film*, *theatre*, *art* and *architecture* at the top of the columns. Get feedback from various Ss, write the words and phrases in the correct columns, and discuss which might go in more than one column.

Answers
1 film/theatre
2 film/theatre
3 book/film/theatre/art
4 film/theatre
5 book
6 architecture
7 film
8 art

b ▶ Ask the class which of the words and phrases might refer to the photos and why.

3 ▶ Put Ss with a different partner. In their new pairs, Ss talk about how often they do the things mentioned. Monitor conversations for errors.

▶ Ss then talk about their favourite paintings, buildings, films, novels, etc. Encourage Ss to use the vocabulary from exercise 2 while doing so. Get feedback from various pairs. Write important errors you have heard on the board and encourage Ss to self-correct.

EXTEND THE LEAD-IN

In a monolingual class, Ss think of five cultural or artistic places that a tourist to their city/town should visit. Ss compare their places with a partner and justify their choices. Get feedback by asking Ss what they have learnt about their partner's city/town.

9.1 Ahead of their time

In this lesson, Ss read a text about three important visionaries. Ss look at the grammar of dependent prepositions. Ss then listen to an interview with someone who is talking about famous inventors and go on to look at ways of expressing certainty and uncertainty.

Reading

1 ▶ In pairs, Ss discuss what the three people in the pictures have in common. Ss also talk about what they know about the three people and their achievements. Get feedback from various pairs.

2 ▶ Ss read the texts quickly to compare their ideas from exercise 1 with the information in the text and to find out more information. You may like to set a time limit for this initial reading to encourage Ss to skim the texts. Tell Ss not to worry about any words or phrases they don't understand at this stage. Get feedback from the whole class.

> **OPTIONAL VARIATION**
>
> Put Ss in groups of three, A, B and C. Having discussed what they know about the people in the pictures, tell Ss A to read the text about Leonardo da Vinci, Ss B to read about The Yellow Emperor and Ss C to read about Rachel Carson. Ss then tell the other Ss in their group what they have learned about the person they have read about.

3 ▶ Ss read the texts again more carefully and answer questions 1–6. Ss compare their answers with a partner. Check answers with the whole class.

> **Answers**
> 1   The Yellow Emperor and Rachel Carson
> 2   Leonardo da Vinci
> 3   Leonardo da Vinci and the Yellow Emperor
> 4   Rachel Carson
> 5   The Yellow Emperor
> 6   Leonardo da Vinci and the Yellow Emperor

▶ Ask Ss if there are any words or phrases in the text they don't understand. Encourage Ss to work out the meanings from the context or use a dictionary before you explain the vocabulary to the class.

4 ▶ Put Ss pairs. Ss discuss which of the people they think achieved the most. Ss also decide which of the three people they would most like to have met and why. Monitor conversations and take note of errors. Ss share their ideas with another pair. Get feedback from the whole class. Read out any important errors and discuss them with the class.

Grammar | dependent prepositions

> **OPTIONAL GRAMMAR LEAD-IN**
>
> Write the following sentence on the board: *Leonardo da Vinci immersed himself on painting for a time.* Ask Ss to spot the mistake and elicit the correct sentence: *Leonardo da Vinci immersed himself in painting for a time.* Ask Ss why the preposition *in* is correct here. (This prepositions collocates with this adjective and is 'dependent' on it.) Tell Ss that there is no rule for which prepositions go with which adjectives, verbs and nouns. Tell Ss to note collocations with prepositions they see when they are reading, and that it would be a good idea to have a separate section in their notebooks for examples of collocations.

5a & b ▶ Focus Ss on the Active grammar box and give them time to read through the notes and do the tasks. Ss compare their answers with a partner. Check answers with the whole class.

> **Active grammar**
>
> **verb + preposition:** range from … (to …); work on…; attribute to …; hope for …; succeed in …; improve on …; specialise in …
> **verb + object + preposition:** draw inspiration from …; made contributions to …; devote your life to …; make observations about …
> **noun + preposition:** in the fields of …; ideas for/of …; the development of …; a solution to …; admiration for … ; the quality of …
> **adjective + preposition:** (be) famous for …; (be) immersed in …; (be) obsessed with …
> **prepositional phrases (beginning with a preposition):** in a time of …; on one occasion …; of all time …; in later life …; in recognition of

c ▶ Ss match the definitions to the phrases in the Active Grammar box. Ss compare their answers with a partner. Check answers with the whole class.

> **Answers**
> a   devote your life to   d   (be) immersed in
> b   attribute to   e   improve on
> c   (be) obsessed with   f   admiration for

▶ Refer Ss to the Reference on page 131 and get them to read through the notes.

6 ▶ Ss read the text and choose the correct options. Ss compare answers with a partner. Check answers with the whole class.

> **Answers**
> 1   of   5   with   9   about
> 2   to   6   in   10   on
> 3   to   7   to   11   for
> 4   of   8   on   12   In
>
> (The scientist described is Albert Einstein.)

7 ▶ Ss complete the sentences. Let them check with a partner.

Answers

1	in	4	of	7	with
2	for	5	in	8	to
3	in	6	for		

8a ▶ In pairs, Ss think of other famous 'visionaries' or inspirational people and make notes.

b ▶ Ss ask and answer questions about them using phrases from the Active grammar box.

OPTIONAL VARIATION

Tell Ss to check the rules for *Twenty Questions* on page 55, Unit 4.2 again. Put Ss in pairs. Ss A think of a famous visionary and Ss B ask questions to find out the identity of the visionary. When asking questions, Ss should try to use expressions from the Active grammar box. When Ss have guessed the identity of the visionary, Ss change so that Ss A are asking Ss B questions.

Listening

9 ▶ Focus Ss' attention on the cartoon of the man in the bath. Ss discuss what is happening in the cartoon and who the man is. Ss also discuss when they think geniuses make their greatest discoveries.

10a ▶ 🔘 2.18 Tell Ss they are going to listen to a radio interview with someone who is talking about people who have invented or discovered something. Play the recording. Ask Ss to make notes under the three headings.

b ▶ Ss compare answers with a partner.

c ▶ Play the recording again for Ss to complete their notes/check their answers.

Answers

Discoveries made outside the laboratory
Archimedes was having a bath when he shouted 'Eureka!'
Physicist Richard Feynman saw a plate flying through the air in the college café, and was inspired to calculate electron orbits.
Alexander Fleming was making a mould for his hobby, microbe painting, when he accidentally discovered penicillin.
The psychology of high achievers
A study of high achievers (Nobel Prize winners vs other scientists) found that more than 50% were also artistic, and nearly all had a long-lasting hobby.
25% Nobel Prize winners played a musical instrument, 18 % drew or painted.
Less than 1% of normal scientists had a hobby.
Can only creative people be geniuses?
Not exactly. But creative thinking can help to solve scientific problems.
Often the solution to a problem will come when you are not thinking about it – you are asleep, or doing something different (a hobby).

The brain has the ability to make connections from one part of your life to another.
People who are good at making these connections, who have creative hobbies and interests, often excel in their fields.

11 ▶ Ss discuss questions 1–4 with a partner. Monitor the conversations for errors to correct after exercise 14. Get feedback and ask Ss to share their ideas with the rest of the class.

Speaking

12 ▶ Ss decide if the words and phrases in the box express certainty or uncertainty and write them in the correct column in the How to... box. Copy the How to... box onto the board. Get feedback from the whole class and write the words and phrases in the correct column.

Answers

certainty: indisputable; without a doubt; undeniably; unquestionably; irrefutable
uncertainty: it's not 100 percent certain; questionable; debatable; it's not clear-cut

13 ▶ Ss choose the correct option in sentences 1–8. Ss compare their answers with a partner. Check answers with the whole class.

Answers

1	debatable	5	clear-cut
2	not 100 percent certain	6	irrefutably
3	indisputably	7	questionable
4	unquestionably	8	irrefutable

14 ▶ In groups, Ss discuss statements 1–4, saying whether they agree or disagree with them. Encourage Ss to use phrases from the How to... box while doing so. Monitor for errors and correct use of the expressions from the How to... box. Ss share ideas with another group.

9.2 I know what I like

In this lesson, Ss look at language to express likes and dislikes. They listen to people talking about different pictures. Ss then look at the grammar of discourse markers. Ss go on to discuss exhibitions and their favourite artists. They finish the lesson by reading a text about art thieves.

OPTIONAL WARMER

Put Ss in pairs, A and B. Ss think of a famous painting. Ss A describe their paintings to Ss B. Ss B try to guess what the famous painting is. Ss B can draw what their partners are describing if it will help them. When Ss A have finished describing the painting, Ss swap so that Ss B describe their paintings to Ss A.

Vocabulary | describing art

Every year, the National Portrait Gallery in London holds a competition for the best portrait. For more information about the National Portrait Gallery, see: www.npg.org.uk.

---

1 ▶ Ask Ss to discuss in pairs the type of art that they like and don't like. Monitor conversations and take note of errors for later correction.

▶ Ss share their ideas with another pair. Get feedback from various Ss.

2a ▶ Focus Ss on sentences 1–6 and a–f. In pairs, Ss check they understand the meanings of the underlined phrases. Ss compare ideas with another pair. Check answers with the whole class.

b ▶ In pairs, Ss match sentences 1–6 with their opposites in a–f. Ss then decide which of the words underlined are used to show personal opinions and which are used to describe facts. Ss compare their answers with another pair. Check answers with the whole class.

Answers
1   f
2   d
3   a
4   c
5   b
6   e
personal opinions: striking, tranquil, plain, disturbing, dull, stunning
facts: abstract, avante-garde, colourful, traditional, monochrome, figurative

---

Listening and speaking

3a ▶ Focus Ss on the three pictures and the text. Ss read the text and decide with a partner which picture they like the best/least and which picture they think should win the competition. Get feedback from various Ss.

b ▶ 🔘 2.19 Tell Ss they are going to hear people talking about the pictures. Play the recording and ask Ss to decide which of the pictures the people are talking about in each conversation. Check answers with the whole class. Ss discuss with their partners which words/phrases helped them to decide which picture is being talked about. In pairs, Ss also decide which picture the people thought should win.

Answers
Conversation 1: Giulietta Coates
Conversation 2: Daniel
Conversation 3: La Familia
They think La Familia should win.

---

4 ▶ 🔘 2.20 Play the recording. Ss listen for which picture actually won and what the speaker thinks of the winner. Ss compare answers with a partner. Check answers with the whole class.

Answers
Giulietta Coates
It's good, but it's not the speaker's favourite.

5a ▶ Put Ss in groups of three or four. Focus Ss on the phrases in the box. In their groups, Ss check the meaning of these phrases. Ss put the phrases in the How to... box. Ss compare their answers with another group.

Answers
saying what you like: I'm really into her work; I've always admired her work; I'm a big fan of his stuff; He's one of my all-time favourites.
saying what you don't like: It's not my kind of thing at all; It's really not my taste; It's not my cup of tea; I can't relate to this type of thing.

---

b ▶ 🔘 2.21 Play the recording for Ss to check their answers. Ss mark the stressed words in each sentence.

c ▶ Tell Ss to describe a painting or a photograph that they like or don't like to their partners. Encourage Ss to use words and expressions from the How to... box in their descriptions. Monitor conversations for errors and correct use of words and expressions. Get feedback by asking various Ss to tell the whole class about the painting or photo their partners have described to them. Write important errors on the board and ask different Ss to correct them.

Grammar | discourse markers

6a & b ▶ Ss complete the tasks in the Active grammar box. Ss compare answers with a partner. Check answers with the whole class.

> **Active grammar**
>
> | **focusing on the main topic or returning to a previous line of discussion** | **introducing an opinion or criticism** |
> |---|---|
> | as far as ... is concerned | to be honest |
> | as regards/regarding | to tell you the truth |
> | as for | frankly |
> | as I was saying | |
> | anyway, what I was going to say was | |
> | **softening an opinion or criticism** | **making additional (often contrasting) points** |
> | is kind of | mind you |
> | it sort of | as a matter of fact |
> | more or less | in fact |

▶ Refer Ss to the Reference on page 131.

7 ▶ Ss complete statements 1–8 with one word using the Active grammar box if necessary. Check answers.

> **Answers**
> | | | | | | |
> |---|---|---|---|---|---|
> | 1 | To | 4 | At | 7 | of |
> | 2 | what | 5 | a | 8 | As |
> | 3 | the | 6 | concerned | | |

8 ▶ Ask Ss to underline the best options in dialogues 1–5. Ss compare answers with a partner. Check answers by asking different pairs to read out the dialogues to the class.

> **Answers**
> 1 A: To be honest
>   B: At any rate
> 2 A: kind of
>   B: Mind you
> 3 A: As a matter of fact
>   B: Frankly
> 4 A: As for
>   B: more or less
> 5 A: Regarding
>   B: To tell you the truth

Speaking

9 ▶ Ss discuss the questions with a partner. Encourage Ss to use discourse markers to help organise their speech and show their attitude to the subject. Monitor conversations for errors and use of discourse markers. Read out errors you have heard and discuss them with the class. Ask Ss which of the discourse markers they have used in their conversations and congratulate them on their use.

Reading

10a ▶ Ss discuss what is happening and what the famous painting is (Munch's 'The Scream').

b ▶ Ss read the text and answer questions 1–5.

> **Answers**
> 1 'Officials thought the painting was so famous that it wouldn't be stolen.'
> 2 Thugs. They were 'usually stealing wheels from cars a few years earlier'.
> 3 Paintings by famous artists Vermeer and Gainsborough. The paintings were stolen, and treated badly by the thieves.
> 4 He posed as a buyer for the J Paul Getty Museum. He also had to learn everything about the paintings. He even 'memorised the patterns of wax droplets left on one version of the painting'.
> 5 An art thief. He stole paintings for the love of art, not money.

11 ▶ Get Ss to discuss questions 1–4 in pairs. Monitor conversations. Ask various pairs to share their ideas with the whole class. Write errors on the board for Ss to correct.

12a ▶ Ss read through the Lifelong learning box. Discuss how it is useful to use contextual clues when working out the meaning of words in texts. Tell Ss that looking at the form of a word and relating it to other words in its family or to words in their own language can also be helpful. Tell Ss that if they can't work out the meaning of a word from context or form, they should check in a dictionary.

▶ Ss answer questions 1–4 about the word *thug*.

> **Answers**
> 1 *thug*: a violent person who may attack people
> 2 *Art thieves are ...*
> 3 *Thuggish* is the adjective used to describe a person or person's behaviour; *thuggery* is the noun used to describe violent behaviour.
> 4 Look at the phonemic transcription for a guide as to how the word is pronounced.

b ▶ With their dictionaries, Ss answer the same questions about the words/phrases.

> **Answers**
> 1 aesthetes: a person who knows about/appreciates beautiful art objects, like paintings, sculpture, etc.
> 2 mastermind: to organise a complicated plan
> 3 hideout: a place where you can hide
> 4 track down: find, after searching for a long time
> 5 stuffed: push something roughly into a small space
> 6 crack a case: solve a case (informal)
> 7 haul: amount of things that have been stolen

9.3 The bigger picture

In this lesson, Ss write a short paragraph about a photograph. Ss then talk about cameras and photography. Ss go on to read different texts and share information about these texts with a partner. Through the context of what they have read, Ss look at the grammar of unreal past. Ss then look at expressions for responding to hypothetical questions.

OPTIONAL WARMER

Ask Ss to bring a photo that is important to them to the next class. In the next class, write these questions on the board: *Who took the photo? Where were you? Who were you with? What time of day was it? What were you doing? How old were you? Why is this photo important to you?* Ss tell a partner about the photo they have brought in using the questions on the board. Get feedback and ask different Ss to explain to the class why the photo is so important to their partners.

Speaking

1 ▶ Focus Ss on the three photos. Ss discuss the questions with a partner.

Vocabulary | vision

OPTIONAL WARMER

Working in pairs, ask Ss to list words and expressions they know which are related to either cameras or photography. Get feedback from various Ss and write correct words and expressions on the board.

2a ▶ In pairs Ss discuss whether they agree with the writer.

b ▶ Ss match the words. Let them check with a partner.

Answers			
1	clichéd	4	novel
2	evocative	5	intriguing
3	quirky	6	breathtaking

Reading

3 ▶ In pairs, Ss discuss the questions.

4a ▶ Divide the class into two groups, A and B. Refer Ss A to the text on page 148 and Ss B to page 152. Ss read the texts and take notes about the different topics. When they have finished reading, Ss check their answers with the other Ss in their groups.

b ▶ Put Ss in pairs so that Ss A are working with Ss B. Ss tell their partners about the main ideas in the text and their answers to the topics from exercise 4a. Check the answers with the whole class.

Answers

A The best time to do it: early morning or late afternoon
Stories: people's eyes tell stories
The local culture: ask before photographing, take time to get to know the local culture, learn a few words of the language
Learning from professionals: spend time looking through big coffee-table books and magazines; watch for different uses of light, angle, line and texture

B The best time to do it: it doesn't matter what time of day you write as long as you do it every day
Stories: look for stories, find something unusual that has happened, look for a beginning, a middle and an ending; or find an original angle
The local culture: interact with the local culture; talk to people, try the food, haggle in the markets
Learning from professionals: travel writers don't just see the normal things; they spot things most tourists don't see

5 ▶ Ss discuss questions 1–5 in pairs or small groups. Ss compare ideas with another pair/group. Get feedback from the whole class.

OPTIONAL EXTENSION

Organise Ss into two groups, photographers and travel writers. In their groups, Ss imagine a typical day in the life of this person and make notes about it. Ss then pair off with someone from the other group and describe their days to the other student. Get feedback from the whole class and decide as a class whose typical day is more interesting.

Grammar | unreal past

OPTIONAL GRAMMAR LEAD-IN

Tell Ss that you had a problem today and they are going to guess the problem. Read out the following sentences to the class one by one: *If only I had woken up earlier. I wish I'd set the alarm clock. If only I'd got to the bus stop sooner. I wish I'd left the house sooner.* By listening to the sentences, Ss try to guess the problem you had: *I missed the bus and was late for work.* Write the sentences on the board and focus Ss on the verb tense used (Past Perfect). Tell Ss that when we are talking about imaginary situations in the present we use the Past Simple and that when we are talking about imaginary situations in the past we use the Past Perfect.

6 ▶ Focus Ss on the Active grammar box. Ss read through the notes and complete the tasks with a partner. Ss compare their answers with another pair.

Active grammar

1 article A: If only I could take good pictures, I wish I had a decent camera.
article B: Ah, if only I was a travel writer, I wish I could live like that.

2 (a) the present = *wish/if only* + Past Simple
(b) the past = *wish/if only* + Past Perfect

3 article A: it's high time you learnt a few basics.
article B: it's about time you started – no excuses.

4 something should be happening now, but it isn't

5 Past Simple

6 article A: the people would sooner you asked before photographing them
article B: Travel writers would sooner go to the jungle

7 *would sooner/would rather* + (a) infinitive without *to*
(b) Past Simple

8 article A: Suppose you see a beautiful landscape
article B: what if you could interview someone who lived in it

9 *what if/suppose* + (a) Past Simple (b) Past Perfect
(c) Past Simple

▶ Refer Ss to the Reference on page 131 and give them time to read through the notes. Draw Ss' attention to the contracted form of would: *'d*

7 ▶ Ss read sentences 1–8 and identify the mistakes. Tell the Ss that some of the sentences are correct. Ss correct the mistakes then compare their answers with a partner. Check answers with the whole class.

Answers

1 correct
2 correct
3 This scenery is so beautiful. If only **had** brought my camera.
4 I'd sooner you **didn't** write that down, please.
5 It's about time you **went** to bed.
6 What if **you** get ill when you go abroad?
7 I wish I **could** speak the language better. I'd ask them about their l lives.
8 Suppose **you had woken** up earlier yesterday. Would you have seen the sun rise?

---

8 ▶ Ss complete the second sentences in 1–8 so that they convey a similar idea to the first sentences. Tell Ss to include the verbs in brackets, but that they will need to change the tense. Ss compare their answers with a partner. Check answers with the whole class.

Answers

1 It's high **time we began** writing our journals.
2 Suppose someone **offered you** a job as a travel journalist?
3 We'd rather **you didn't take** photos inside the building.
4 If only **I had entered** the competition, I might have won!
5 I wish **I was a** good photographer.
6 I'd sooner **we chose** the photos together.
7 It's about **time you completed** that article.
8 What if **my camera jams** at the vital moment?

9a ▶ Ss complete the sentences so that they are true for them. Monitor and check the sentences Ss are writing and help as necessary.

b ▶ Ss mingle and compare their sentences with other Ss and explain what they have written. Encourage Ss to ask each other follow-up questions.

Speaking

10a ▶ Ss discuss the question in pairs.

b ▶Focus Ss on the words in the box. Ask Ss to work with a partner and write any expressions they know that contain these words. Get feedback and write correct expressions on the board. Focus Ss on the How to... box and ask Ss to complete the phrases with the words in the box.

c ▶ 🔘 2.22 Play the recording for Ss to check their answers.

Answers

1 I'd
2 to
3 doing
4 suppose
5 wouldn't
6 unlikely
7 way

Pronunciation | emphasis (2)

11a ▶ 🔘 2.23 Play the recording. Ss notice where the intonation rises in each sentence.

Speaking and writing

12a ▶ Ss discuss situations 1–6 in pairs. Encourage Ss to extend the conversations for as long as possible by asking each other follow-up questions. Monitor the conversations for errors and correct use of language from the How to... box.

b ▶ Ss think of two more hypothetical questions. Ss ask a partner the questions, starting with *What if ...?* or *Suppose ...?* Read out important errors you have heard and elicit the corrections from the class. Congratulate Ss on their use of the phrases from the How to... box.

> **OPTIONAL VARIATION**
>
> Ss write their two or more hypothetical questions on slips of paper and the teacher collects them. Ss take it in turns to choose a question and tells their answer to the class. The rest of the class then guess the question that they answered. Continue so that all Ss have a taken a question and told their answer to the class.

13 ▶ In pairs, Ss choose one of the situations shown in the pictures. Ss write the story of what happened in about 150 words. Tell Ss to use at least four of the words/ phrases from the How to... box in their story. Monitor and check what the Ss are writing, correcting and helping where necessary. Ask various Ss to read out their stories to the class.

9 Vocabulary | Commonly confused words

In this lesson, Ss look at some commonly confused words.

> **OPTIONAL WARMER**
>
> Ss think about the last time they went for a job interview. If they have never been to a job interview, Ss can imagine what they think it might be like. In pairs, Ss discuss how they prepared/would prepare for the interview.

1a ▶ Ss read the text quickly and discuss the questions with a partner. Get feedback from various Ss.

> **Answer**
> A post for a visionary thinker was created because the university department's educational goals were far too sensible and boring, no one took risks any more. The imaginative freelancer who was employed to advertise the vacancy got the job.

b ▶ Tell Ss to read the text again more carefully and choose the correct alternatives in the text. Ss compare their answers with a partner. Check answers with the whole class.

> **Answers**
>
> | | | | |
> |---|---|---|---|
> | 1 | meeting | 7 | actually |
> | 2 | sympathetic | 8 | advertising |
> | 3 | sensible | 9 | vacancy |
> | 4 | fit into | 10 | classic |
> | 5 | opportunity | 11 | attend |
> | 6 | test | 12 | in the end |

2 ▶ Ss read the pairs of definitions in 1–12. Without looking at the text again, Ss think of words that might suit these definitions with a partner. Ss read the text again and find words to match definitions 1–12. Check answers with the whole class. You may want to point out that we say *in the end*, but not *in the end of* and that *at the end (of)* always refers to something concrete (a day, a film, etc.).

> **Answers**
> 1 a) meeting, b) reunion
> 2 a) sympathetic, b) friendly
> 3 a) sensible, b) sensitive
> 4 a) suit, b) fit into
> 5 a) possibility, b) opportunity
> 6 a) test, b) prove
> 7 a) actually, b) at the moment
> 8 a) propaganda, b) advertising
> 9 a) vacation, b) vacancy
> 10 a) classical, b) classic
> 11 a) assist, b) attend
> 12 a) in the end, b) at the end

3 ▶ Focus Ss' attention on sentences 1–8. Ss complete the sentences with an appropriate word or phrase from exercise 1a. Ss compare their answers with a partner. Check answers with the whole class.

Answers
1   vacancy; suit
2   assist; reunion
3   opportunity; classical
4   At the end; sensible
5   In the; proved
6   at the moment; possibility
7   fit into; friendly
8   propaganda; actually

---

4 ▶ Ss choose a few of the confusing words that they have had problems with. Ss write their own sentences with these words. Monitor and check the Ss' sentences and help where necessary. Ask various Ss to read out their sentences to the rest of the class.

5 ▶ Ss discuss questions 1–3 with a partner. Monitor, taking note of any important errors. Write errors you have heard on the board and encourage Ss to correct them.

9 Communication

In this lesson, Ss listen to how two popular products were developed. Ss then present a proposal about a new product to the rest of the class.

1a ▶ ⬤ 2.24 Ask Ss to discuss the photos and what they know or can guess about the products shown. Ss read statements 1–6. Play the recording and ask Ss to listen and mark the statements **T** if they are true, and **F** if they are false.

b ▶ Play the recording again for Ss to check their answers.

Answers
1   F (He saw native people in the Arctic using the method.)
2   T
3   F (He sold the patent for 22 million dollars.)
4   F (It involved making multiple copies of patent documents by hand.)
5   T
6   T

---

2 ▶ Ss discuss questions 1–3.

3a ▶ Put Ss in pairs. With their partners, Ss choose one of the business ventures or come up with an idea of their own. Ss plan how they would 'sell' the venture to the rest of the class.

b ▶ Ss write a short summary of the main ideas behind the business venture. Monitor and help Ss as necessary.

c ▶ Ss take it in turns to present their proposals to the rest of the class. Encourage Ss listening to ask follow-up questions.

d ▶ Decide as a class which of the proposals are most interesting and which they would invest in if they could. Write any errors you have heard on the board. With their partners Ss discuss the errors and correct them. Finally, praise the Ss for any interesting language they have used.

OPTIONAL EXTENSION

For homework, Ss write an advertisement for the product, service, course or film. Check the advertisements in the following lesson. Ss then perform the advertisement for the rest of the class. If possible, record the advertisements on audio, video or DVD so that Ss can see and judge their own performance.

---

9 Review and practice

1 ▶

Answers
1 b
2 h
3 c
4 d
5 f
6 g
7 a
8 e

2 ▶

Answers
1 be honest
2 kind
3 As far as my work is concerned
4 As regards
5 more or less
6 In fact

3 ▶

Answers
1 left
2 know
3 could
4 went
5 had got up
6 run
7 learned
8 hadn't brought

4 ▶

Answers
1 appalling
2 over the top
3 heavy
4 contemporary
5 finest piece
6 incredible

5 ▶

Answers
1 vacation
2 advertising
3 sensitive/sympathetic
4 actually
5 sympathetic/sensitive
6 opportunity
7 classic
8 fit into
9 attended
10 meeting
11 in the end
12 tested

9 Writing bank

1 ▶ In pairs, Ss read the proposal and discuss the question. Get feedback from the whole class.

Answers
1 a photo competition
2 to help people look at their environment with fresh eyes

2 ▶ In pairs, Ss discuss the questions. Get feedback from the whole class.

3 ▶ Focus Ss' attention on the How to... box. In pairs, Ss complete the expressions. Get feedback from the whole class.

Answers
1 Description
2 objectives
3 borne
4 opportunities
5 believe

4a ▶ Individually, Ss make notes in preparation for their proposals.

b ▶ Ss write their proposals. Encourage Ss to use ideas from the How to... box. Go round and monitor Ss who need any help.

Overview

Lead-in	**Vocabulary:** Feelings
10.1	**Can do:** Discuss how feelings affect you **Grammar:** Modals (and verbs with similar meanings) **Vocabulary:** Outlook/attitude **Speaking and pronunciation:** Connected speech **Listening:** Lucky and unlucky people
10.2	**Can do:** Make guesses about imaginary situations **Grammar:** Modal verbs of deduction (present and past) **Vocabulary:** Strong feelings **Reading:** So what does it feel like …? **Listening:** Speculating
10.3	**Can do:** Describe a childhood memory **Grammar:** Uses of *would* **Speaking and pronunciation:** How to... talk about memories/experiences **Reading:** Holloway Street **Listening:** Childhood memories
Vocabulary	Phrasal verbs and particles
Communication	Express strong feelings
Writing bank	Write a personal anecdote **How to...** write about a personal experience
Extra resources	ActiveTeach and ActiveBook

CEFR Can do objectives
10.1 Discuss how feelings affect you
10.2 Make guesses about imaginary situations
10.3 Describe a childhood memory
Communication Express strong feelings
Writing bank Write a personal anecdote

CEFR Portfolio ideas
a) Think of a doctor, an athlete and an artist from your country. Write three paragraphs speculating about what each had for breakfast this morning. Give reasons for your ideas.
b) Tell a story about an lucky event in your life. Record it as an audio blog for your personal website.
c) How does your mood affect the clothes you choose to wear each day? Do you choose clothes which echo your mood or clothes which will make you feel better? Tell your friends and ask them if they can guess your mood from your clothes.
d) Choose three pieces of music which you link with different emotions. Share and compare your ideas with your friends.

Lead-in

OPTIONAL WARMER

Ss work in pairs. Ask them to discuss the last time they felt extreme emotions, such as anxiety, excitement, sadness, anger, etc. Encourage Ss to ask follow-up questions to find out more information when appropriate. Get feedback by asking different Ss to explain to the rest of the class what they have learned about their partners.

---

1 ▶ Ss discuss how they think the people in the photos are feeling and why. Take note of any important errors the Ss make. Get feedback from the whole class. Write any errors you have heard on the board and get different Ss to correct them.

2a ▶ Focus Ss on sentences 1–8. Ss check they understand the meaning of the underlined idioms and decide which idioms apply to the people in the photos. Ss compare their ideas with a partner and use a dictionary to look up unfamiliar words if necessary. Get feedback from the whole class.

b ▶ Ask Ss to work in pairs to match the sentences. Check answers with the whole class.

Answers
1   f
2   d
3   e
4   b
5   h
6   g
7   c
8   a

---

3 ▶ Ss choose some of the idioms and think of a time when they felt this way. Ss tell their partners. Monitor conversations for Ss' use of the idioms. Get feedback from various Ss. Write any errors you have heard on the board and get different Ss to correct them. Finally, congratulate Ss on their correct use of the idioms.

EXTEND THE LEAD-IN

Ask Ss to work in pairs to think of famous people whose current feelings might be described by the idioms. You could collect pictures of famous people from magazines to help Ss think of examples. Ss write a list of the names of the famous people and show them to another pair who guess which idiom can be matched with the feelings of each famous person, for example, *You wrote 'David Beckham' because he's over the moon about a goal he scored …* .

10.1 Feeling lucky?

In this lesson, Ss listen to an interview about 'lucky' and 'unlucky' people. Ss then look at the grammar of modals and verbs with similar meanings. Ss go on to work on expressions connected with being lucky. Ss finish the lesson by talking about a dream or a goal they would like to realise.

OPTIONAL WARMER

In a monolingual class, Ss list objects or actions considered lucky and unlucky in their country. Ss compare lists with a partner. Get feedback from the whole class and list the 'lucky' or 'unlucky' things on the board. In a multilingual class, ask Ss to work with a partner of a different nationality. Ss tell their partners about what is considered lucky or unlucky in their countries. Get feedback by asking various Ss what they have learned about luck from their partner.

Listening

1 ▶ Ask Ss to discuss questions 1–3 in pairs. Get feedback from the whole class.

2a ▶ 🔵 2.25 Tell Ss they are going to listen to an interview with someone talking about lucky and unlucky people. Ss read sentences 1–6. Play the recording and get Ss to underline the correct options in the sentences. Ss compare answers with their partners. Check answers with the whole class.

Answers			
1	different	4	different
2	unrealistic	5	Extroverts
3	help improve	6	receive praise

b ▶ In pairs, Ss discuss what the speakers say about each statement.

Answers

1 Lucky people are more open to opportunity and tend to be more optimistic and expect good fortune. When things go wrong, they are robust and resilient and they won't give up.
2 Lucky people have what psychologists call 'a positive delusion' and have boundless optimism.
3 Training aimed at making business people learn how to be 'lucky' can help business improve.
4 Research has shown that there are genetic differences between lucky and unlucky people, and that some people are born lucky or unlucky.
5 Lucky people are likely to create opportunities for good fortune by being extrovert, sociable and using open body language that gets people to respond to them.
6 Children showered with extra praise and encouragement do better at school.

3 ▶ 🔵 2.25 Play the recording again. Ss listen and make notes about what the speakers say about the different topics. Ss compare their answers with a partner. Check answers with the whole class.

Answers

1 Rhode Island – Maureen Wilcox would have won the Rhode Island lottery with her Massachusetts numbers and vice versa.
2 1993 – Lawyer John Woods escaped the bombing of the Twin Towers in 1993 and 2001.
3 being robust and resilient – 'Lucky' people don't give up when things go wrong.
4 having boundless optimism – 'Lucky' people expect to win the lottery more often. They believe they will win, so they keep playing.
5 failed business ventures – Some people are good at making a business work (they 'have the knack'). Others go from one failed business venture to another.
6 developing drive and focus – The business training was not the usual business motivational training, but was designed to make people think and behave like 'lucky' people.
7 sales figures – The company's sales figures increased by 20% each month.
8 a particular colour – One man breaks his routine by thinking of a particular colour when on his way to a party, and then only speaking to people wearing that colour.
9 gifted children – There was an American high school experiment in which teachers were told that some children in their class were specially gifted. There was nothing remarkable about the children. However, the teachers gave these children extra praise and encouragement, and as a result, the children performed better at school.

4 ▶ Ss discuss questions 1–4 in pairs. Get feedback from various Ss.

OPTIONAL EXTENSION

Divide the class into two groups and tell one group they believe in the idea of 'luck.' Tell the other group that they do not believe in the idea of 'luck.' In their groups, Ss have to prepare arguments for their point of view, using both the issues from the recording and their own ideas. Ss then pair up with Ss from the other group and try to convince them of their point of view.

Grammar | modals (and verbs with similar meanings)

> **OPTIONAL GRAMMAR LEAD-IN**
>
> Write the following prompts on the board: *punctuality, language spoken, homework, contact with English outside class.* Tell Ss that you want to make a list of rules for the class. With a partner, Ss write a list of rules, using the prompts. Monitor for Ss' use of modals of obligation. Ss then compare their list of rules with another pair. Get feedback from each pair and write examples of modals of obligation used by the Ss on the board. Get feedback from the whole class about how modal verbs such as *must* and *can't* are used to express obligation.

5 ▶ With a partner, Ss talk about the use of the underlined words in sentences 1–12. Get feedback and discuss Ss' ideas. Ss then match the underlined words to their correct usage in the Active grammar box. Ss compare answers with their partners. Check answers with the whole class.

> **Active grammar**
>
> 1   c
> 2   f
> 3   a
> 4   b
> 5   l
> 6   h
> 7   j
> 8   g
> 9   d
> 10 k
> 11 i
> 12 e

▶ Refer Ss to the Reference on page 145 and give them time to read through the notes.

6 ▶ In pairs, Ss discuss the differences in meaning between the three options in italics in each sentence. Check answers with the whole class.

> **Answers**
> 1   *might try catching* is a suggestion,
>   *needn't catch* shows a lack of necessity
>   *won't catch* expresses impossibility (It is too late to catch the bus.)
> 2   *Can* explains possibility
>   *must be able to* is deduction
>   *not supposed to* explains the rule (No Smoking)
> 3   *ought* and *'s supposed* express an expectation
>   *'s likely to* is a possibility (less likely than the first two)
> 4   *can't* is deduction (She is younger.)
>   *must* is deduction (She is older.)
>   *'s bound to* is a deduction (The speaker thinks she is probably older than him.)
> 5   *didn't need to get* shows lack of necessity (It wasn't required, and we don't know if the marks were good or not.)
>   *needn't have got* shows lack of necessity (We got good marks, but it wasn't necessary.)
>   *were supposed to get* shows that according to the rules, we needed good marks
> 6   *is bound to* is a certain prediction
>   *is supposed to* is talking about what should happen
>   *must* is talking about deduction
> 7   *Do you need to* talks about necessity
>   *Are you likely to* talks about probability
>   *Will you* talks about willingness

7 ▶ Ss rewrite the sentences. Let them check with a partner.

> **Answers**
> 1   This can't be the right direction.
> 2   Is she likely to pass the exam?
> 3   There must be a mistake on this bill.
> 4   He's bound to cheer up soon.
> 5   Aren't we supposed to register at the front desk?
> 6   You ought to make up your mind.

Pronunciation | connected speech

8a ▶ 🔘 2.26 Play the recording. Ss listen to the sentences and discuss the questions. Get feedback from the whole class.

> **Answers**
> 1   'd' and 't'
> 2   They are not pronounced.

b ▶ 🔘 2.27 Play the recording. Ss listen to the phrases and repeat.

Speaking

9 ▶ In pairs, Ss tell their partners about the things in 1–4. Get feedback from various Ss.

Vocabulary | outlook/attitude

10a ▶ Check with Ss that they understand the meaning of the underlined phrases in the questionnaire.

> **Answers**
> have a tendency to worry = tend to worry
> open to new experiences = happy to try out new things
> gut feelings and hunches = a feeling that you are sure is
>   right although you cannot give a reason for it
> intuition = feelings rather than the facts
> to get what I want from life = decide what is important in
>   life and obtain it
> chances of success seem slim = a strong possibility that
>   this will not work
> look on the bright side = be optimistic
> work out well = a situation will turn out for the better
> in the long run = in the long term
> dwell on things = think for too long about something
>   unpleasant

▶ Ss complete the questionnaire by writing a number between 1 and 5 in each box, depending on how strongly they agree or disagree with the statements.

b ▶ Ss read the results of the questionnaire on page 151.

c ▶ Ss compare their results. Ss discuss whether they agree with the rating they received or not.

11a ▶ Ss complete the article. Let them compare with a partner.

> **Answers**
> 1   out
> 2   long
> 3   slim
> 4   had
> 5   feeling
> 6   on
> 7   side

b ▶ In pairs, Ss discuss the question. Get feedback from the class.

Speaking

12a ▶ Ss complete the sentences. Monitor and help Ss as necessary.

b ▶ Ss tell their group about their sentences. Get feedback from various Ss.

10.2 What does it feel like?

In this lesson, Ss listen to three people talking about the first people to see or experience something amazing and how they might have felt at the time. Ss then study the grammar of modals of deduction. Ss go on to read a book review before looking at vocabulary connected with strong feelings.

Listening

> **OPTIONAL WARMER**
>
> Ask Ss to work in groups to put the three photos in order of excitement. Ss share their ideas with another group and justify their order.

1 ▶ Ss discuss in pairs what is happening in the photos. Ss talk about what it would be like to be in each situation and what problems there might be. Get feedback from various Ss.

2 ▶ ⬤ 2.28 Tell Ss they are going to listen to three people discussing similar situations to the ones shown in the photos. Play the recording and ask Ss to note down what the three speakers think the people who experienced the 'firsts' must have felt at the time. Ss compare their ideas with a partner. Get feedback from the whole class.

> **Answers**
> Speaker 1 thinks it must have been amazing to be the first
>   modern person to see Machu Picchu. It must have had
>   more of 'a mysterious air' because it was hidden in
>   vegetation.
> Speaker 2 thinks it must have been 'incredibly
>   exhilarating', but that the pilot must have had a
>   lot of doubts as well about controlling and landing
>   the plane.
> Speaker 3 thinks that Yuri Gagarin must have had 'mixed
>   emotions'; the thrill and excitement of space travel
>   as well as 'absolute awe', but he must have also felt
>   alone and probably quite scared.

3 ▶ Play the recording again and ask Ss to answer questions 1–5. Ss compare their answers with a partner. If necessary, play the recording again for Ss to check their answers. Check answers with the whole class.

> **Answers**
> 1   There's a train.
> 2   It was covered in vegetation and hidden. Now you can
>   see it as soon as you arrive.
> 3   Aircraft were not sophisticated – difficult to fly,
>   physically and mentally – lots of calculations to do,
>   how to control the crash landing.
> 4   How would it work out? Would he be able to control
>   the plane when it landed?
> 5   Positive: thrill/excitement, awe of what he's
>   experiencing, seeing Earth from space and being the
>   first person to see that. Negative: didn't know if he
>   would get back home, alone and probably quite scared.

4 ▶ Put Ss in pairs so that they are working with a different partner to discuss the questions. Ss discuss ideas with another pair. Get feedback from the whole class.

Grammar | modals of deduction (present and past)

> **OPTIONAL GRAMMAR LEAD-IN**
>
> Take a photograph into the class. It can be any type of photo, the bigger, the better, so Ss can see it. Put a piece of paper in front of the photo and hold this up for the class. Ask Ss to speculate what is in the photo. Move the paper so that Ss can only see a small part of the photo. Ss discuss with a partner what they think they can see. Ask a pair what they think the photo shows. If Ss don't use a modal verb of deduction in their predictions, elicit *might* and encourage Ss to use it. Ask Ss if there are any similar verbs to *might* to elicit *may* and *could*. Continue slowly revealing the photo and Ss continue making deductions until the whole photo is uncovered.

5 ▶ Ss complete the tasks in the Active grammar box. Ss compare their answers with a partner. Check answers with the whole class.

> **Active grammar**
>
> 1 Speaker 1: It **must have been** amazing to be the first modern person ..., I think it **must have been** pretty hard to get there ..., ... so they **must have been** really driven people ...., ... But, although they **might have felt** the same atmosphere when they were arriving, it **couldn't have been** quite as spectacular ..., ... but it **must have had** more of a mysterious air ...
> Speaker 2: It **can't have been** easy because you have to realise ..., They **must have been** difficult to fly physically ..., ... and that too **couldn't have been** easy.
> Speaker 3: I think Yuri Gagarin **must have had**, I think ..., never even had any concept of what it **might look** like from space ..., just how amazing that **must be** ..., ... anything **could have happened** up there ..., He **must have felt** alone ...
> 2 *might, could, may*
> 3 *can't be, can't have had, couldn't, couldn't have taken*
> 4 *must be, must have been*
> 5 *must be* describes something in the present, *must have been* describes a situation in the past.

▶ Refer Ss to the Reference on page 145 and give Ss time to read through the notes.

6 ▶ Ask Ss to discuss in pairs the difference in meaning (if any) between the two options in sentences 1–8. Ss compare ideas with another pair. Check answers with the whole class.

> **Answers**
> 1 same meaning
> 2 different: *can't* is a deduction about how he feels, *shouldn't* is a statement about how he should feel, *normally does much* is a statement about how he usually performs, *could've done* means it was possible for him to have done better
> 3 same meaning
> 4 different: *might be* is about the present, *could have been* is about the past
> 5 same meaning
> 6 different: *must* is much surer than *might*
> 7 different: *couldn't* is much surer than *might not*
> 8 same meaning

Speaking

7a ▶ Put Ss in pairs. Ss discuss pairs what they think is happening in each of the photos on page 153 and why. Encourage Ss to use their imaginations when looking at the photos. Get feedback by asking different pairs to share their ideas with the rest of the class. Decide as a class which pair has come up with the best story.

b ▶ Refer Ss to the stories behind the photos on page 150. Ss read through the stories and check if any of their speculations about the photos were correct.

Reading

> **OPTIONAL WARMER**
>
> Write the following questions on the board:
> *Where would you normally see a book review?*
> *Do you often read book reviews? Why/Why not?*
> *How do you choose a book to read?*
> *Would you buy a book because you saw a good review?*
> Ss discuss these questions in groups of three or four. Monitor the Ss' discussions for any interesting language they use. Get feedback from different groups. Draw Ss' attention to interesting words or phrases you heard while monitoring and discuss their meaning.

8 ▶ Ss read the introduction to a book review and discuss with a partner what they think 'some of the biggest highs' and 'some of the biggest lows' might be. Get feedback by asking various Ss to share their ideas with the class.

9 ▶ Ss read the rest of the review and decide with a partner if statements 1–8 are true or false, and why. Ss compare answers with another pair. Check answers with the whole class.

> **Answers**
> 1 T
> 2 F (it also covers stories of normal, unexceptional people who find themselves in exceptional circumstances)
> 3 F (he says how responsible he felt 'If we made a mistake, we would regret it for quite a while.')
> 4 T
> 5 T
> 6 F (it has a humorous tone)
> 7 F (he was the editor)
> 8 F (he doesn't care because he's just happy to be alive)

10 ▶ Ss discuss the questions in small groups. Monitor the conversations. Get feedback from the whole class. Write any errors you have heard in the board and encourage Ss to self-correct.

> **OPTIONAL EXTENSION**
>
> Put Ss in pairs. Ss A are reporters from *Esquire* magazine. Ss B choose one of the people mentioned in the article (Buzz Aldrin, Max Dearing, Craig Strobeck or Geoffrey Petkovich). Give Ss five minutes to prepare the interview between the reporters and the interviewees. Monitor and help Ss where necessary. When Ss are ready, they conduct the interview.

Vocabulary | strong feelings

> **OPTIONAL WARMER**
>
> Before the lesson, look through some magazines and newspapers to find faces showing strong feelings. Bring these to class to show the Ss and elicit any adjectives to describe feelings that they already know.

11 ▶ Focus Ss on sentences 1–16. Ss put the underlined adjectives into the correct column in the table. If Ss are not sure of the meaning of any of the adjectives, tell them to check them in a dictionary. Ss compare their answers with a partner. Check answers with the whole class.

> **Answers**
>
> | **happy** | **unhappy** | **neither happy nor unhappy** |
> |---|---|---|
> | thrilled | miserable | indifferent |
> | ecstatic | upset | uninterested |
> | chuffed | | |
> | delighted | | |
>
> | **scared** | **surprised** | **angry** |
> |---|---|---|
> | terrified | taken aback | furious |
> | petrified | flabbergasted | outraged |
> | | dumbstruck | livid |

12 ▶ Ss answer the questions 1–4 with a partner.

> **Answers**
> 1 chuffed
> 2 upset
> 3 taken aback
> 4 outraged

13 ▶ Focus Ss on sentences 1–6. In pairs, Ss discuss how they would feel in these situations and why. Encourage Ss to use the adjectives they haven't used before in their discussions. Monitor conversations for use of the adjectives and for errors. Get feedback from the whole class.

> **OPTIONAL VARIATION**
>
> Ss look at the different situations and write an adjective to describe how they would feel in each one. Tell Ss to write the adjectives in a different order from the order of the questions. Ss then swap their list of adjectives with a partner. Ss guess which adjective their partner has written to go with each situation: *Would you feel dumbstruck if you were offered a job as a model for a clothing company in Milan?*

14 ▶ Discuss the tip in the Lifelong learning box with the whole class. In pairs, Ss try the tip with some of the adjectives they have just seen from exercise 11. Ss share the sentences they have written with a partner. Get feedback from the whole class and ask different Ss to read out some of their sentences to the rest of the class.

10.3 Looking back

In this lesson, Ss listen to people describing childhood memories. They read an extract from a short story. Through this context, Ss look at the different uses of *would*. Ss then read some web extracts about childhood memories and look at different expressions to describe a childhood memory. Ss go on to talk about childhood memory of their own.

OPTIONAL WARMER

Write the following ages on the board:
4, 8, 12 and *14 years old*. With a partner, Ss discuss what they can remember about being each of these ages. Get feedback by asking different Ss to share their memories with the rest of the class.

Listening

1 ▶ Focus Ss on the situations in the box. With a partner, Ss discuss how each of the situations made them feel. Monitor conversations for errors. Get feedback by asking various Ss to tell the rest of the class what they have learned about their partners. Read out any important errors and discuss them with the whole class.

2a ▶ 🔘 2.29 Tell Ss they are going to listen to different people talking about childhood memories. Play the recording while Ss listen and mark the topics from exercise1 that each speaker mentions. Ss compare their answers with a partner. Check answers with the whole class.

Answers
Speaker 1 mentions moving house, starting/changing
    school, making friends
Speaker 2 mentions doing sport
Speaker 3 mentions summer holidays, making friends
Speaker 4 mentions summer holidays, playing/inventing
    games

OPTIONAL VARIATION

Put Ss in groups of three. Each student chooses four of the topics in the box to listen for. Play the recording. Ss listen and mark which of their four topics are mentioned. Ss then share their answers with the other Ss in the group. Check answers with the whole class.

b ▶ Ask Ss to discuss in pairs if any of the stories they have heard from the recording remind them of their own childhoods. Get feedback from the whole class.

3 ▶ Focus Ss' attention on questions 1–9. Play the recording again and ask Ss to answer the questions. Ss compare their answers with a partner. If necessary, play the recording again for Ss to check their answers. Check answers with the whole class.

Answers
1   He found it difficult to get on with other children because they knew each other and had already formed small groups of friends, and he felt 'out of it'.
2   He learnt to become very outgoing, energetic and entertaining in order to make new friends.
3   Central Manchester.
4   The weather ('the rain, and the wind and the snow'), the cars ('traffic roaring by'), the clothes ('little shorts and T-shirts ... looking like complete idiots')
5   No. She is not sporty ('not really a sporty kind of girl'), and she hates running ('I still hate sports, and running is just one of the sports I hate the most I think')
6   She talks about the hot temperatures when they got off the plane (the 'wall of heat'), the smell of the air (a 'fantastic smell'), and the colour of the pool ('I remember how blue the pool was').
7   The breakfasts took a long time ('breakfasts that went on forever')
8   He used to climb over his parents' garden fence.
9   It made him feel happy, and free. He says 'It was just a great sense of freedom, that you should really have when you're a child'.

Reading

4a ▶ Focus Ss on the picture. Ss discuss the questions in pairs. Get feedback by asking pairs to share their ideas with the rest of the class.

b ▶ Ss read the story quickly to check if their predictions from exercise 4a were correct or not. Get feedback from various Ss.

5 ▶ In pairs, Ss discuss the significance of the boxed words/ideas. Get feedback from various Ss. Ss read the story again to check their answers. Tell Ss to underline any difficult words or expressions as they read. Get feedback and check the significance of the words in the box with the whole class.

OPTIONAL EXTENSION

Ss write a paragraph describing the place they lived as a child. Encourage Ss to use imaginative vocabulary and *would* where possible. Ss read their paragraphs to the whole class.

Grammar | uses of *would*

OPTIONAL GRAMMAR LEAD-IN

Write these quotes on the board:
1 *If God did not exist, it would be necessary to invent him. (Voltaire)*
2 *Would those of you in the cheaper seats clap your hands? And the rest of you, if you'll just rattle your jewellery. (John Lennon)*
In pairs, Ss discuss the different uses of *would* in the sentences. (sentence 1: imagined situation, sentence 2: polite request)

6 ▶ Focus Ss on the Active grammar box. Ss match example sentences 1–7 to the different uses of *would* in a–g. Check answers with the whole class.

Active grammar

1 b
2 g
3 f
4 c
5 d
6 a
7 e

▶ Refer Ss to the Reference on page 145. Make sure that Ss have time to read through the notes.

7 ▶ Ss add *would* or *wouldn't* to sentences 1–8 to make them correct. Ss compare ideas with a partner. Check answers with the whole class.

Answers
1 If you would like to follow me, I'll show you to your rooms.
2 I would have much more time to do my work, if you would look after the kids a little more often.
3 When we were alone at home, we would always cook for ourselves.
4 He would never help me with my homework.
5 If only he would answer the phone, I could explain what happened.
6 She would have loved to see her grandchildren grow up.
7 We hid the parcel in the cupboard so that she wouldn't notice it.
8 Her parents wouldn't pay for her to go to university as they didn't believe in education for girls.

8a ▶ Ss complete the sentences in a way that is true for them.

b ▶ Put Ss in groups of three or four. Ss share what they have written with the other Ss in the group. Encourage Ss to ask each other follow-up questions. Monitor conversations for correct use of *would*. Get feedback. Write errors on the board and ask different Ss to correct them. Draw Ss' attention to examples of their correct use of *would* and congratulate them for using it.

Reading and speaking

9a ▶ Ss read the stories and decide on a title for each one.

b ▶ In pairs, Ss share their titles. Get feedback from the whole class and decide which are the best titles for the extracts.

OPTIONAL VARIATION

Put Ss in groups of five. Each student in the group reads one of the extracts and thinks of a title for that extract. Ss tell the others in their groups what they have read about and the title they have chosen for the extract. Ss then read all the extracts and decide if the titles chosen by the other group members were good ones. Get feedback from various groups and discuss the titles chosen.

10 ▶ In pairs, Ss cover the stories and think of different ways of completing the phrases in the How to... box. Get feedback from various pairs. Ss uncover the stories and compare their own expressions to the originals.

Answers
Introducing the story: One memory that sticks in my mind ...; I have a **vivid** recollection of ...; I'll **always** remember ...; One of my **earliest** memories is of ...
Background: We always/usually/**generally** spent ...; We were always **chasing** ...; My parents kept **telling** me ...; On Sundays we **would** often ...
Specific event: One time/But **one** night; I felt .../I was **scared** to death
Reflecting: It's **hard** to believe

11a ▶ Ss think of two or three childhood memories which they can remember clearly. If Ss need help in choosing topics, refer them to the topics given.

b ▶ Ss write notes about their memories. Monitor and help and encourage Ss to use the expressions in the How to... box.

c ▶ Ss tell the story of the memories to other Ss. Monitor for correct use of the expressions from the How to ... box. Ask various groups to tell the rest of the class about the most interesting childhood memory they have heard in their group. Write errors on the board for Ss to correct and give praise for correct use of phrases from the How to... box.

10 Vocabulary | Phrasal verbs and particles

In this lesson, Ss look at different phrasal verbs and what effect a particle can have on the verb which goes before it.

1a ▶ In pairs, Ss discuss what message the cartoon is trying to convey, who the people in the boat might be and what the boat represents.

▶ Ss read the short text and discuss the meanings of the expressions with *under*.

> **Answers**
> under pressure = in conditions that make it difficult to do a task (e.g. not enough time/resources)
> under a lot of stress = extremely worried and tired, so you can't relax
> under her thumb = controlled by someone else (usually husband controlled by wife)
> went under = closed down because of financial problems (businesses)

b ▶ Ss decide whether expressions with *under* tend to be used with positive and pleasant situations or with negative and unpleasant situations.

> **Answer**
> negative and unpleasant

2a ▶ Ss complete the sentences with a suitable particle. Ss compare answers with other Ss.

> **Answers**
> 1 down; down   3 on   5 around
> 2 back   4 off; off 6 up; up; up

b ▶ Ask Ss to discuss in pairs what each of the phrasal verbs mean. Get feedback from various pairs.

3 ▶ Ss underline the correct words in italics.

> **Answers**
> 1 up   6   back
> 2 down   7   around
> 3 out   8   on
> 4 up   9   out
> 5 on   10 around

4 ▶ In pairs, Ss explain to each other what each of the phrasal verbs in exercise 3 means.

5 ▶ Ss think about a time when they or someone they know has done the things in the box, or in which situations the Ss might do these things. Ss compare answers with a partner.

10 Communication

In this lesson, Ss listen to three people who are moaning, raving or taking a stand on something. Ss then moan about, rave about or take a stand on an issue they feel strongly about.

> **OPTIONAL WARMER**
> Tell the class about something which you moan about. In pairs, Ss share their 'top five' moans. Get feedback and try to come to an agreement about the top five moans of the whole class.

1 ▶ Check Ss understand what the three verbs mean by reading the definitions. Ss tell a partner about the last time they moaned about something, raved about something or took a stand on an issue. Monitor conversations and take note of errors for later correction. Put Ss in pairs so that they are working with a different partner. Ss tell their new partner what their previous partner has told them.

2 ▶ 🔘 2.30 Play the recording. Ss decide whether these people are moaning, raving or taking a stand on something. Ss take note of what the people are talking about and what their opinions are on the subjects. Check answers with the whole class.

> **Answers**
> Speaker 1: raving about a great restaurant
> Speaker 2: moaning about public transport
> Speaker 3: taking a stand about smoking in public

3a ▶ Focus Ss' attention on the How to... box. Ss complete the expressions.

> **Answers**
> 1 It was sensational!
> 2 I couldn't believe my eyes!
> 3 It should be banned completely.

b ▶ Play the recording again. Ss tick the expressions they hear.

4a ▶ Tell Ss that they are going to moan, rave or take a stand on something. If Ss can't think of an issue, tell them to look at the pictures to help them.

b ▶ Give Ss time to make notes. Help Ss as necessary.

5 ▶ Working in groups, Ss take turns to speak about the issue they have prepared. Ss listening take note of the topic that Ss are talking about and a question they would like to ask. When Ss have finished talking, the other Ss in the group ask them questions. Monitor carefully for errors and any interesting language the Ss use. Write errors on the board and encourage Ss to correct them. Finally, congratulate Ss on their efforts in this lesson and in the course as a whole.

10 Review and practice

1 ▶

Answers
1 The manager is likely to be angry about the situation.
2 They're bound to phone us this morning.
3 The interview is at 10.30, but I'm supposed to be there half an hour before.
4 This can't be the only way out of the building.
5 We might have time for a quick drink before the meeting.
6 They won't pay the invoice until the dispute has been resolved.
7 Should we wait for you outside the conference hall?
8 He ought to bring his own laptop.

2 ▶

Answers
1 can't have/mustn't have
2 couldn't have
3 might have been/could have been
4 must have been
5 must have/can't have/might have/should have
6 must have been
7 will have been

3 ▶

Answers
1 If I'd known, I'd have called you earlier.
2 I wish she wouldn't always tell me what to do.
3 correct
4 We left the keys in the office so you will see them when you get there./We left the keys in the office so you would see them when you got there.
5 correct
6 correct
7 I told Marcella that we'd meet her outside the cinema.
8 My parents wouldn't ever have dreamed/would never have dreamed of sending me to private school.

4 ▶

Answers
1 pleased   7 end
2 aback   8 calm
3 delighted   9 terrified
4 minds   10 worked
5 tendency   11 moon
6 upset

5 ▶

Answers
1 around   6 off/away
2 out   7 on
3 on   8 up
4 back   9 down
5 around   10 out

10 Writing bank

1 ▶ In pairs, Ss look at the photo and discuss the question. Get feedback from the whole class.

2 ▶ In pairs, Ss discuss the questions. Get feedback from the whole class.

Answers
1 The father had lost his job, and the family had no money.
2 She had wrapped up things that had gone missing earlier.
3 The best thing about Christmas is the people you share it with, not the things you receive.

3 ▶ Focus Ss' attention on the How to... box. In pairs, Ss add the sentences. Get feedback from the whole class.

Answers
Give background information: *We had been living there since 1988.*
Arouse the reader's curiosity: *Little did we know what was about to happen.*
Describe emotions: *I was over the moon!*
Add a personal reflection: *Never again would I ...*

4a ▶ Individually, Ss make notes in preparation for their story. Encourage Ss to use ideas from the How to... box.

b ▶ Ss write their anecdotes. Go round and monitor Ss who need any help.

Audioscripts

Track 1.02
M=Mark, I=Interviewer

I: Mark, you speak seven languages.

M: That's right.

I: Can you tell us a little about your level of fluency and proficiency in the languages?

M: Well, Russian is probably my best language. I speak it pretty well because I spent a lot of time in the country, but it's a little rusty. I have quite a good ear, which is a good thing and a bad thing because my accent suggests that I know more than I really do! The other languages are mainly Latin-based: Spanish, Portuguese, Italian, but also French and Polish.

I: You learned the languages through a combination of techniques.

M: That's right. In different ways, like going to classes, travel, private study …

I: Did you use any special techniques? Any magic secrets?

M: Magic secrets, no! But I did do some interesting things, like memory training. I watched films in their original language and at some point I tried sticking lists of words around the house. But I think, with me, it was more a case of being motivated, and the biggest motivator was a love of languages and pleasure in communicating with people from other countries.

I: Would you say it's easier to learn new languages if you already know languages in that family? For example, you speak Spanish and French, so maybe it was fairly easy to pick up Portuguese.

M: I wouldn't say it was easy, but yeah, I would definitely say it's a help, although occasionally it gets confusing. You might be speaking in one language and suddenly a word from another language slips out, causing complete confusion.

I: Is there any little word of encouragement you could offer those poor souls who are trying to master a language?

M: Er … that's a tricky one. What I would say is that knowing how to read and write a language doesn't mean you can speak it. You really have to get out there and try to speak at every opportunity. Take risks. Don't be afraid to look stupid, because that's the only way you're going to learn. And you know, everyone has to start somewhere. As a young man, I went to France after years of studying French to degree level, and, to my complete embarrassment, I couldn't speak the language or understand anything. All I could do was order breakfast in my hotel!

Track 1.03
P=Presenter

P: To continue our series on famous firsts … If you ask a Brazilian who first flew an aeroplane, she'll tell you it was Alberto Santos Dumont. Ask an American and he'll answer the Wright brothers. In 1906, Santos Dumont was widely believed to have flown the first plane that was heavier than air. Others say that the Americans Wilbur and Orville Wright first flew in 1903. The truth is, we don't really know who flew first, but Santos Dumont was certainly a colourful character. He's said to be the first person to have owned a flying machine for personal use. He kept his balloon tied up outside his Paris flat and regularly flew to restaurants!

Our second question … It's commonly assumed that Alexander Graham Bell invented the telephone, but now we're not so sure. Many people believe that Antonio Meucci, an Italian immigrant, got there first. And in 2003, files were discovered which suggest that a 26-year-old German science teacher, Philipp Reis, had invented the phone 15 years before Bell. Now, who was the first to the North Pole? In 1908, Dr Frederick Cook said he'd done it, but it's commonly believed that he lied, and that a man called Robert Peary made it first. There are others who claim that neither of them reached the North Pole. The light bulb. It's widely asserted that Edison invented it, but we don't really know for sure. Edison based a lot of his inventions on other people's ideas. Also, he worked with a team, and he never shared the credit.

Moving on to our football question, it's widely assumed that South America's football glory belongs to Brazil and Argentina … but it was Uruguay that hosted and won the first World Cup in 1930. They beat Argentina 4–2 in the final in front of 93,000 people in Montevideo. The cheering of the crowd is said to have been the loudest noise ever heard in Uruguay. Talking of sport, it is often thought that rugby and sheep are the main claims to fame for New Zealand. Not many people know that in 1893, New Zealand became the first country to allow women to vote. Now, talking of empowering women, one woman who has empowered herself is Ellen MacArthur. MacArthur is sometimes wrongly assumed to be the first woman to sail around the world. She wasn't. She was the fastest but not the first. That honour goes to another Englishwoman, Naomi James, who did it in 1979. Apparently, she got so seasick that soon afterwards she gave up sailing altogether. And our final question. The Ancient Olympic Games were of course first held in Greece. They were quite different from the Games today. Instead of money, the winners received a crown of leaves. They were also said to be allowed to put their statue up on Olympus.

Track 1.04
N=Newsreader

N: The headlines this lunchtime are …
A conservation institute in the United States has produced wild kittens by cross-breeding cloned adult cats. It is believed to be the first time that clones of wild animals have been bred. Researchers at the Audubon Centre for Research of Endangered Species say that the development holds enormous potential for the preservation of endangered species.
An American millionaire has succeeded in his long-held ambition to circumnavigate the world in a balloon. Fifty-eight-year-old Steve Fossett had already made five attempts on the record, but was frequently beaten back by the weather. In 1997 he was forced to land in Russia, in 1998 it was Australia, and in 2001 he found himself crash-landing on a cattle ranch in Brazil.
And finally, the story of a man who has entered the record books as the world's most renowned eater of burgers. It is estimated that Don Gorske has eaten over 15,000 Big Macs, and he even proposed to his girlfriend Mary in the car park of a McDonald's. In 15 years, he says, he has missed a Big Mac on only seven occasions, including the death of his mother, a snowstorm and a 600-mile drive without a McDonald's in sight.

Track 1.06

1

When I was at school, a friend of mine was injured in an accident while playing rugby. He was paralysed and needed to spend the rest of his life in a wheelchair. Together with some friends we decided to organise a sponsored bike ride to raise money for his family, and other people in a similar situation. So we set up a charity called 'One Step Ahead' and arranged to cycle from Scotland to Gibraltar. I'd never done anything like that before, so it was a fantastic learning experience. I'd always thought it would be great to cycle across a whole country, but this exceeded my expectations. There were about 20 or 30 of us on bikes, and the rest of the crew in vans with all the equipment, and camping gear. It was very tough cycling, especially in Spain where we had to battle against the heat. But we had a fantastic time, and at the end, when we arrived, there was a huge party for us, and the media came and took photos. We were even on the news! We felt we'd accomplished something quite important, and we raised lots of money for people with spinal injury too.

2

I've been doing volunteer work here in the rain forest, in Brazil, for a while now. Next week I'll have been here for three months, helping to teach English to the young children in the village. It's been an amazing experience, because I'd never even left Europe before, so you can imagine how different things are here. When I arrived, I really didn't know what to expect. It was a real culture shock, and I was here on my own for the first couple of months. Now my girlfriend has come out to join me, and things are a bit easier. I've been living with a small tribe of people right out in the forest, and I'd never done any teaching before either, so the whole thing has been quite a challenge, and I've learnt a lot. But some of the children are speaking quite good English with me now, and a few of them are starting to write little stories too, so I feel it's been quite an achievement.

3

I've run a marathon. In fact, I'm planning to run it again this year. I did it last year for the first time and it was great. It felt like a major achievement. I had to train really hard, getting up early in the morning to run before going to work. And as the distances got longer I had to get up earlier and earlier. And it was incredibly hard because I'd never done any training like that before. I've always run, but just for myself, to relax and to keep fit, but this was a chance to be more competitive, and really push myself to the limit. It is a fantastic run, because London is a beautiful city, and there's such a good atmosphere as you go along the route, with people cheering you on. My parents even came over from New Zealand to see me arrive at the finish. I couldn't move for about a week afterwards last time, but I was glad I'd done it and I'm looking forward to the next one.

Audioscripts

Track 1.08

E=Expert

E: If you ticked mainly 'a', then you seem to be very comfortable as you are and you're not too keen on new challenges. I think you need to make an effort to get off the sofa. Go on! Take a risk – it might have a positive effect!

Now, if your answers were mainly 'b', it means you love a challenge and you take advantage of your opportunities. You seem willing to have a go at anything and everything. So, good luck, but be careful! Those of you who ticked mainly 'c', well, you obviously make a habit of checking everything before committing yourself. You are super-cautious. Well, you may live a long, safe life, but a bit of a challenge from time to time won't do you any harm!

Track 1.09

1

I'm from South Africa. I spent two and a half years, actually more like two years, living in Vancouver, Canada. Er … my wife and I were trying to set up our own business there as packagers in the publishing industry. Unfortunately, things were not going very well economically. Canada wasn't in a depression, but it was just not a very good time to try and start your own business in publishing. What did I like about Vancouver? Well, Vancouver is one of the most beautiful cities in the world. In fact, Vancouver is regularly named as the best place in the world to live. Stunningly beautiful because of mountains, sea, forests and natural beauty and for me, combined with a large city. Vancouver is a city where you can walk to the beach. Vancouver is a city where the beaches are right in the city and you can go to the beach for your lunch break. You can take a bus and go skiing in the mountains 40 minutes later. Canadian food, of course, is not at the top of the world's list of good food, but Vancouver has got a very large Chinese population, Indian population, and of course as the rest of Canada, people from all over the world, so you can eat extraordinarily good food in Vancouver. Erm … the only food that people might consider uniquely Vancouverite is what they would call 'fusion' cuisine, which is food prepared by chefs that mix their diverse background from Asia or Europe and integrate it with the local foods and in fact you can have a very good meal that way. My best memories about Canada? Well, the open spaces, the vastness and the friendly people as well.

2

I'm from Belfast originally, but over the past ten years I've been living, erm, I've lived in Spain, Austria, France and other parts of the UK. Erm, I lived in Austria for a year when I was about 22, 23. It was a gap year from university. Er, I was studying German so I wanted to spend a year there. I was a teaching assistant there. I worked in a school four days a week, so it was really great because it meant I had long weekends. Erm, I usually went travelling with my friends at the weekends. Erm, we went to Slovenia, Prague, Italy, Germany and the best thing was I pretended I was 15 so that I could get some train discount. I got half-price train tickets which was excellent. Erm, the other great things about living there was obviously skiing and ice skating on lakes, which you can't do in Northern Ireland. Erm, obviously the scenery is beautiful. The people were lovely. The thing I didn't really like was the food, because I'm vegetarian and in Austria they tend to eat a lot of meat, but apart from that everything else was great. Erm, I think my favourite memories of Austria are the scenery, being able to go off into the mountain after school every afternoon, and go skiing or swimming in the lakes in the summer, and I'd definitely like to go back one day.

3

When I lived in Japan, actually in Tokyo, for about two years – this was about two years ago now – erm, it was, as you can imagine, a completely crazy experience for me, coming from Oxford which is a very, you know, small, provincial, very quiet kind of town. Er, I was living in Tokyo because I was working as an English-language teacher for a really tiny language school run by this lovely, lovely old lady erm, in a suburb of Tokyo. Erm, I thoroughly enjoyed Tokyo. It was such an interesting experience. It was like being, you know, dropped in the middle of a lifestyle that was completely different to my own. Erm, even going to the supermarket was a massive adventure because of course I couldn't read anything because the writing system's so different, so I'd sort of pick up a tin and think, 'Ooh that looks interesting, I'll take that take that home and, you know, I'll see what comes out' and got a few surprises of course, a few unidentifiable foods that I'd never seen before, but that's always a good thing. Erm … I think my favourite memories of the country would have to be the people. Because I was teaching English, I knew a lot of Japanese people as students, as colleagues in the school and so on, and I just found them so lovely. They were friendly, funny, really interested in what a foreigner like me was doing in Tokyo and very keen to, you know, share experiences of travelling abroad and to … to tell me all about the social customs in Japan and things like that. So it was a, it was a really rewarding experience, absolutely great.

Track 1.10

W=Woman, M=Man

M: It's made such a big difference to me. I mean, communication is miles easier than it was before. Do you remember the days when we had to go through all that hassle of writing letters?

W: Sure, I'd agree with that. But I'd still say that face-to-face communication is better. Sending an email is nowhere near as personal and meaningful as a conversation.

M: Well, it depends, doesn't it?

W: On what?

M: OK, an email is nothing like as good as seeing someone you love, or your friends or something, but I can tell you this much: rather than going to see my clients every day, or nattering on the phone, I'm much better off sending them an email. It saves time.

W: Yeah, I see what you're getting at, but I just think, the more we use email, the more we need it. It's like an addiction, with people checking their emails every five minutes even in meetings.

M: Fair enough. But I'd still rather have it than not.

W: And, well, the internet in general, there's so much rubbish on there. Do you use it to do research?

M: All the time. I think it's OK. Maybe it's not quite as good as looking in books. Well, it's not as reliable, though it's considerably faster.

W: I'd say that looking up something on the internet is marginally less reliable than shouting out of the window, 'Does anybody know the answer to this?' It's not regulated, is it? Anyone can publish anything on the internet and it may or may not be true.

M: Much the best thing about the internet is that it lets you do things more cheaply than before, like buying holidays, buying stuff on ebay.

W: I've never used eBay.

M: Or Amazon. You can get loads of cheap books.

W: Yeah, but I'd sooner go to a second-hand bookshop. I'm not into the idea of giving my bank details over the internet. No way.

M: There're lots of security measures these days …

Track 1.11

1

Erm, I'm a member of an old boys' club, erm, which is basically when when you leave school you keep in touch with your old friends and every five or ten years you have a reunion and you get together and party and remember the old days, erm … some good, some bad, obviously. Erm, we also get involved in quite a few charity events in the area where I'm from, erm … and recently we actually did some charity events to save the school that I was at, which was going to be closed. So that was something we did specially. I did it, I didn't join straight after school. Erm, I went abroad for a few years, and I found out about it through a website, er, called Friends Reunited, where you can find where your old friends are and your old school is. That was great. We probably only meet once every two years as a group. Erm, we have a big party and get to meet all the people that we remember, and some of the teachers as well, er, which is fun. What's really interesting about the group is that we've now all known each other for about 20 years, and it's so interesting to meet people every two years and see how they've changed. I'm sure that if I met some of those people in the street now after 20 years, I wouldn't recognise them, and in, in a bad sort of way, I suppose, it's, you like to measure yourself against your friends, where they've got to and how have you done in comparison. Erm, If there's something I don't like, it's that, er … it's very difficult to keep in touch when you are not meeting so regularly. Erm, and you do rely on other people to run the club and sometimes people aren't as involved as they should be, sometimes you don't hear anything for a year or two, so it is quite difficult to do. But I will definitely stick with it, because it is great to meet people and remember some of the good days.

2

Well, I'm a member of a … of a kind of society, I suppose. It's a ballroom-dancing club. Erm, it's kind of lessons, but it's also social as well. There's about … oh I suppose … it must be about 30 people in the club, and I think I'm quite unusual because I think I'm the youngest there. Erm, I go with a friend of mine, who's … who's my partner in the dancing. Erm, it's great fun, really great fun. It's kind of fun being the youngest there as well because everyone else is retired and they think we're very cool and exotic for being young. Erm, I joined about I suppose six months ago now, erm, because I just fancied giving ballroom dancing a go. I've never been terribly coordinated as a dancer and I'm not very good with choreography, but it's been absolutely great. I mean, there's quite a lot of beginners in the class so you never really feel like you know you're stuck out in the middle of all these wonderful advanced dancers. Erm, we meet once a week and sometimes we meet in a school hall, in a local suburb near to where I live. Erm, we meet in the evenings after work and sometimes it can be quite hard to get yourself out of the house again ready to do some exercise and some dancing, but it's fantastic fun. So far we've been learning … erm … the Waltz, the Foxtrot, erm … and some Latin dances like, erm, the jive and the tango. It's great fun.

Track 1.12

E=Expert

E: In 1957 a news programme called Panorama broadcast a story about spaghetti trees in Switzerland. While the reporter told the story, Swiss farmers in the background were picking spaghetti from trees. Following this, thousands of people called the show, asking how to grow spaghetti trees.

In 1998 large numbers of Americans went to Burger King asking for a new type of burger. The food company had published an ad in USA Today announcing the new 'left-handed Whopper', a burger designed for left-handed people. The following day, Burger King admitted that they had been joking all along.

Swedish technician Kjell Stensson had been working on the development of colour TV for many years when he announced in 1962 that everyone could now convert their black-and-white TV sets into colour. The procedure was simple: you had to put a nylon stocking over the TV screen. Stensson demonstrated and fooled thousands.

Pretending that it had been developing the product for some time, a British supermarket announced in 2002 that it had invented a whistling carrot. Using genetic engineering, the carrot grew with holes in it, and, when cooked, it would start whistling.

Track 1.13

1   I'd seen it before.
2   I'd prefer to go home.
3   She'd lost the opportunity.
4   Would you like to dance?
5   I didn't set the alarm.
6   What would you cook?
7   I'd have done the same.
8   Had she been there?

Track 1.14

1

My favourite fictional character has to be Philip Marlowe, the detective created by Raymond Chandler. The most famous book and movie in which he appears is, of course, *The Big Sleep*, with erm … Humphrey Bogart playing Philip Marlowe. Once you've seen Humphrey Bogart, of course it's very difficult to imagine Philip Marlowe as being anybody else other than Humphrey Bogart, because like Humphrey Bogart, Philip Marlowe is tall, good-looking, tough, very smart and a smooth talker. I suppose those are also the characteristics that I do like about Philip Marlowe. The thing about Philip Marlowe is … like … unlike most modern characters, he doesn't always say the right thing, although he always has a clever retort and he doesn't always win. Philip Marlowe is not always on top of the situation. Philip Marlowe sounds like a real guy with real problems who's very clever, very tough and likes to get to the bottom of the problem. Erm, the sort of problems that he has to overcome,

of course, as a detective in Los Angeles is generally solving murder crimes, but he's often not so much interested in who did it as to why or how. By the end of the story, you care much about, you care as much about the erm … victim as perhaps the murderer or Philip Marlowe himself. This is actually one reason why you can re-read and re-read the Raymond Chandler novels with Philip Marlowe in them, because it's not what happens in the story, it's how Philip Marlowe deals with the problems, that matters.

2

I think my favourite fictional character has to be, erm, the lead character, the heroine if you like, of, erm, Jane Austen's *Pride and Prejudice*. She's absolutely, I think, one of the best-drawn characters in, in English literature. She is of course Elizabeth Bennett. Erm, she's the heroine, she's she's sparky, she's lively, she's feisty, and when you think that this is a book that's set in the 1800s, it's really quite remarkable that you've got such a modern woman as the heroine. I mean she's, she's lippy, she talks back to all these men who are older than her and in more authority than her. Fantastic! I think it's, erm, character traits that I'd really quite like to have myself. Erm, I imagine her, and I think I'm quite influenced here by the films and so on that have been made of *Pride and Prejudice*, as being quite tall with a very lively, mobile face and possibly dark hair, as well. Erm … memorable things that she does: well, the thing that I really like about her, erm, from the story of *Pride and Prejudice* is the way that she takes control of her own life in a period of history when women really had very little power and very little control over what happened to them in the marriage market, and I think it's great that she, erm, sort of comes to a self-realisation through the events of the novel and decides to do the right thing and go for the guy that she really loves, and of course she meets lots of problems along the way: people who think she's socially unacceptable or people who, erm, have very prejudiced views about class and society and of course she succeeds and she wins the day, wins her guy in the end.

3

I think my favourite fictional character was er, the old man from *The Old Man and the Sea* by Ernest Hemingway. Er, I still have quite a strong visual image of this man. The whole story takes place in a boat off the coast of Cuba, with, with just this one character, mostly. I imagine him to be quite old. He was a lifelong fisherman. He had quite a tough life, so I imagine he had these really big strong hands that were … were cut and bruised from hauling in nets his whole life every, every night out, out in the sea. I imagine him with a little bit of grey hair, er, just old and wise, somebody who had been a fisherman his whole life, took a lot of pride in it and tried to do it as, as best he could, and he was down on his luck in the story. He hadn't caught anything for quite a long time, erm, but he still dragged himself out every night and cast his nets and hoped for, hoped that he would catch something.

In a way, he sort of reminds me of my dad, somebody who had limited opportunities in life, but found a job that he could do and did it to the best of his ability, even though there was very little glamour attached to it, and I think this in a way the fisherman was like him. He was a fisherman and he took pride in that, and did the best job he could.

Track 1.15

W=Woman

W: Groucho Marx didn't want to be a comedian at first. He loved reading and singing, and he wanted to become a doctor. But his mother had other ideas. She got the boys to start a group called the Six Mascots. During a radio show they started making jokes, and this is when they decided to become a comedy act. Their popularity grew quickly. But in 1926 the boys' mother died, and the Great Depression began. In the 1930s a man called Irving Thalberg helped the Marx Brothers to get on television. They made their most famous films, the last of which was called *A Day At the Races*. After this, Groucho became a radio host and he also made more movies, but without his brothers. In the 70s he toured with a live one-man show, but by now in his 90s he was getting weaker, and he died in 1977 on the same day as Elvis Presley.

Track 1.17

N=Newsreader

N: Resistance to antibiotics is on the increase. Research out today shows an increase in the number and strength of superbugs, resistant to normal antibiotics. Analysis of particularly resistant strains, kept in laboratory test tubes, shows that in the last 12 months …

A new virus, developed by hackers in South-East Asia has been crashing computer networks around the globe. The virus penetrates standard firewalls to affect computer software and eventually data stored in the microchip. Experts have warned that …

A breakthrough in genetic engineering technology means that human cloning can now enable scientists to re-build damaged organs in children. Cells taken from skin tissue are used to provide the necessary genes, which are then implanted …

The on-going budget crisis has been cited as the reason for the latest delay to the space mission. The new shuttle, Discover XVIII, which was originally due to launch last Thursday, is set to orbit Mars, scanning the surface for evidence of early life forms …

Track 1.18

I=Interviewer, S=Stan Lee

I: **Legendary veteran comic writer Stan Lee co-created Spider-Man and the Fantastic Four, amongst others. We asked him how he thought of Spider-Man and this was his response:**

S: **When trying to create a superhero, the first thing you have to think of, or at least the first thing I have to think of, is a super power. What super power would be different, that people hadn't seen before? I had already done the Hulk, who was the strongest character on Earth; I had done a group called the Fantastic Four: one of them could fly, one was invisible, and one's body could stretch and I was trying to think, 'What else can I do?' And I've told this story so often that for all I know it might even be true! But I was sitting and watching a fly crawling on the wall, and I thought, 'Gee – that would be great – what if a character could crawl on walls like an insect?' So I had my super power, but then I needed a name. So I**

Audioscripts

thought, 'Insect-man' ... that didn't sound good. 'Crawling-man?' And I went on and on. 'Mosquito-man?' And then somehow I said 'Spider-Man' and it just sounded dramatic and mysterious to me. So that was my name.

I: When asked why he made Spider-man a scientist, he replied:

S: I had always resented the fact that in most superhero stories, or actually in most comic books, the hero is some sort of a rugged, muscular outdoorsman, a sportsman, an adventurer. And anybody who was literate or scholarly ... they were ... he was always considered to be somewhat of a nerd. And I thought, 'My gosh, people don't have enough respect for intelligence.' So again, in trying to be different, and in trying to be realistic, I thought I would make my teenage hero a scholarship student, extra-bright; he was studying science. And just to show that there's no reason why a hero couldn't also be a kid who likes science and is good in school and is smart ... and that was the thinking behind it.

I: When asked if he was at all scientific, he replied:

S: I'm not much of a scientist. I love reading science-fiction but when it comes to actual science, I'm ... I'm a dummy. But I like to make things seem scientific!

I: Our final question asked if Stan Lee thought there would ever be real superheroes.

S: I believe that they will be able, through cloning, through genetics, they will be able to find a way to abolish most diseases. They will be able ... they will have to, see? Once these wars are finished with, if they ever are, we're going to want to go to the planets. They're going to want to go to Mars. Now it's such a long trip, and it will be so hard to get back again, they're going to have to make human beings able to adapt to Mars, adapt themselves. Or is it adopt? I never ... I always get those two mixed up! But at any rate, I believe that they will find a way to make people able to live in the atmosphere of Mars, through altering them genetically. Because of genetics, I think we can do virtually anything.

Track 1.21

Dialogue 1
K=Kevin, L=Lizzie

K: Hello?
L: Hi, Kevin. It's Lizzie.
K: Oh hi, Lizzie. How are you?
L: Yeah, great. You?
K: Yeah, fine.
L: I guess you're busy as usual this Saturday?
K: Erm ... sort of.
L: Yeah?
K: Well, I'm playing cricket.
L: Oh, I didn't know you played cricket.
K: I don't really. Well, once in a blue moon.
L: So that's all day Saturday?
K: Yeah, that'll be ... yeah ... more or less all day.
L: What are you up to in the evening?
K: Well, I might be free. Let me think. Mm, maybe about eight-ish. What have you got lined up?
L: Erm, we're thinking of going to Clancy's ...
K: Oh yeah? I used to go there from time to time when I was a student. Do you want me to pick you up?
L: Erm, or should I drive?
K: I don't mind driving. Do you want me to?

L: In a way, it's easier if I take my car. Yeah, don't worry. I think I'll drive ...

Dialogue 2
L=Lauren, A=Andy

L: Lauren James.
A: Hi, sweetheart.
L: Oh hi, darling.
A: Still working?
L: Yep.
A: Bit of a hard day?
L: Kind of. Nothing major ... just various bits and pieces.
A: Right.
L: Filling in forms, replying to emails, that kind of thing.
A: Uhuh.
L: Going over the accounts again, checking petty cash, etcetera etcetera. Actually, there were loads of mistakes.
A: Oh really?
L: Yep. But I'm nearly finished.
A: So, do you want me to get something ready?
L: Yeah, I'm a bit peckish actually.
A: Pasta maybe? Or we've got chicken in the fridge.
L: Chicken sounds good. Erm, I'll be home in an hour or so.
A: OK, I'll put the chicken in the oven ...

Track 1.22

1 How many phone calls do you make per day?
2 How many times do you check your emails per week?
3 How many close friends do you have?
4 How frequently do you write letters?
5 What do you do in the evening?
6 How long do you spend studying English at home?

Track 1.23

1 Not since Mozart has there been a greater genius.
2 Only after the age of three did she begin to show her gift.
3 Nowhere do the rules say you can't teach advanced subjects to children.
4 Only later did we understand the truth about our gifted child.
5 Not only was he able to write poetry when he was five years old, he also played the violin well.
6 No sooner had we given her a paintbrush than she produced a masterpiece.

Track 1.24

I=Interviewer, W=Woman

I: Can you tell us a little bit about the case and what made it so special?
W: The case concerned a pair of twins called John and Michael. They were, I suppose in their late teens, but they were absolutely tiny and they wore thick glasses. They used to get laughed at at school because, in a conventional sense, they weren't very bright or social.
I: They were outsiders.
W: Well, that's right. Outsiders. But they had an amazing gift. You could name any date in the past or future 40,000 years and they would be able to tell you what day of the week it was.
I: So I could say, for example, 5th June 1376 and they could tell me it was Sunday or whatever ...
W: That's right.
I: Or 10th July 2099, and ...
W: And they would say 'Monday!' But that wasn't all. During one interview, the psychologist dropped a box of matches on the floor and the twins immediately

called out 'one hundred and eleven'. The psychologist counted the matches and there were exactly 111.
I: And the twins hadn't counted them?
W: No. There was no time. As soon as the matches hit the floor, they knew there were 111. Now another thing the twins could do was remember extremely long sequences of numbers. You could say a number of up to 300 digits, and they were able to repeat it back to you perfectly.
I: So they basically have an extraordinary ability with numbers.
W: Not only with numbers. They have another talent, which is that you can name any day of their lives since they were about four years old, and they are able to tell you what the weather was like, what they did, and other events in the wider world. They can remember absolutely everything about that day.
I: Just any ordinary day?
W: Any and every ordinary day.
I: Obviously the twins, John and Michael, were studied at length by various psychologists, educators ...
W: Yes, they were.
I: What progress did these people make in coming up with explanations of their ability?
W: I think the main thing is that we realise that John and Michael's ability is actually a visual one as well as mathematical. If you ask them how they do it, they say they can 'see' the answers. When the box of matches fell, they 'saw' 111. It wasn't a calculation. Similarly, they can 'see' themselves as five-year-olds. Somehow they have an ability to record incredible numbers of things in the mind. Of course, we have no idea how it works, but it would be very interesting to learn ...

Track 1.25

1
Great discoveries of our time ... well, in the last 100 years or so, I guess medical advances, like the use of X-rays in diagnosis, or the discovery of penicillin by Fleming. I mean, he made that discovery almost by mistake, and it changed modern medicine completely. Or perhaps the elucidation of DNA by Watson and Crick in the 50s. That paved the way for the whole area of genetics and genetic engineering ...

2
I would say that sending man to the moon was one of the greatest scientific achievements, learning about space. The man who invented the liquid-fuelled rocket, Robert Goddard, was fascinated by the idea of sending a rocket into space, and he spent years researching his ideas, until he developed the first rocket, called Nell. It was 10-feet-tall, and he fired it from his aunt's farm in the US. At first nothing happened, but when the fuel finally ignited, the rocket was launched. It only reached a disappointing 14 metres into the air though and scientists were sceptical of its success. When the newspapers got hold of the story they wrote the headlines 'Moon rocket misses target by 238,799 miles.' But later, engineers in Germany and America used his ideas, and the film footage of Nell, to develop military and space-exploring rockets. The *New York Times* had to write Goddard a public apology ...

3
Computers, it has to be. Information technology and the internet. The whole way in which information is distributed and kept nowadays. It's just been revolutionised by

information technology. And things have happened so quickly. I mean, the first computer was built in 1948, I think. And was so big it took up a whole room! If you think about the latest designs now, and the capacity, it's just amazing. And it has made the world a smaller place, because it is so easy now to get information about anywhere in the world. There are no secrets …

4
I don't think we should underestimate the importance of domestic appliances, like the washing machine, dishwasher, all your electrical goods. And processes like freeze-drying food. These time-saving discoveries have allowed a whole new freedom to women, who previously had to spend their whole lives in the kitchen. It's meant that they could go out to work, and that has had a huge impact on society. Or perhaps it should be the advances in travel, with the bicycle, then the car and the aeroplane. The world must have been a very different place when the fastest way to get anywhere was on a horse!

Track 1.27
P=Presenter

1 Business partners. Why not go with friends and family?
P: While we're on the subject of choosing business partners, I cringe whenever I hear that two old friends or family members are planning to start a business together as fifty–fifty partners. It isn't that doing business with friends and family is a bad idea – many very successful businesses are family-owned. It's just that being someone's friend or relative is one of the worst reasons I can think of for making that someone your business partner. One of the problems is that once someone becomes your business partner, there is generally only one way to get rid of them (legally, of course) if things don't work out. You must buy them out for the fair value of their interest in the business. And that can be an expensive proposition.

2 What type of person makes a good business partner?
P: There are a few ways to determine if someone has what it takes to be your business partner, however. Firstly, you need to decide, are you a visionary, or an operations person? Successful partnerships combine those two kinds of people. A visionary is a strategic, 'big picture' thinker who understands the business model, the market and the overall business plan. An operations person is someone who rolls up their sleeves, wades up to their hip boots in the details and executes the strategy that the visionary comes up with. You are either one or the other – it is almost impossible to be both. Once you have determined if you are a 'visionary' or an 'operations person', look for your opposite number. That way your business is more likely to strike the right balance between strategy and tactics.

3 What skills does the company need?
P: Do you have all the skills you need on board to make the business work? Perhaps you are an inventor who is excellent at product design but clueless about selling. Perhaps you have a strong marketing background but need someone to help you crunch the numbers and make sure your products or services can be delivered within budget. Your partners should complement your set of business skills, not duplicate them. Keep in mind that you can acquire someone's skills without making them a partner. If a particular skill, such as contract negotiation or bookkeeping, is not critical to the success of your business, you may be better off hiring a lawyer, accountant or consultant to do it for you and keeping ownership of your business.

4 Will communication be a problem?
P: Can you communicate directly and honestly with this person, without pulling any punches? Communication between partners can often get rough; disagreements and arguments break out all the time. It is difficult to criticise someone harshly, yet sometimes you must be cruel with your business partners in order to do the right thing for your business. Your business may well suffer if you consistently hold back important information for fear of offending your partner or jeopardising the underlying friendship or emotional bond between you. Sometimes the most successful business partnerships are those where the partners do not socialise outside the office.

5 The long-term. Will your partner stay through good times and bad times?
P: And lastly, is your business partner willing to hang around for the long haul? This is the critical test of a business partner. Many people are happy to help out with a business during its start-up phase, only to lose interest later on when something more attractive (like a job offer from a big corporation) comes along, a life-changing event (like the birth of a new child) occurs, or the going is getting tougher and the business isn't as much 'fun' as it used to be. If you are not sure if someone is committed to the long-term success of your business, make them an employee or independent contractor, with perhaps an 'option' to acquire an interest in your business at a date two or three years down the road … provided, of course, they are still working for you at that time and you continue to be satisfied with their performance.

Track 1.29
I=Interviewer, W=Will

I: 98 percent of staff working at Piranha recruitment say they laugh a lot with their team. As many as 95 percent say that they are excited about where the company is going. So what have they all got to smile about? Last month this small London-based company won a prestigious award for being one of the best small companies in the UK to work for. With us today is Will Becks, the company director. Will, first of all, tell us a little bit more about the company and what you do.

W: Good morning. Well, Piranha is more than just a normal recruitment agency. The difference is that we actually train and then place graduates in sales jobs. That means we have a lot of young people working for us, so it's a bit like a continuation of university, but with a salary. We're only a small company, with as few as 60 employees, but there's a good atmosphere in the office. There's a great deal of energy.

I: Yes, your employees have said that there is a fun atmosphere, with outgoing, like-minded people. You have regular parties, an annual skiing holiday, a present for the most-appreciated employee of the month, and plenty of other benefits too. I'm not much of an expert on these things. Why such an emphasis on staff incentives?

W: Well, our staff are young and highly qualified. They are good at what they do, and they believe in it. We have trained sales people going into companies to try and place graduates. Quite a few of them get offered the jobs themselves. If we didn't look after our staff, they would quickly get poached by other companies. So the incentives need to be good to keep people.

I: So how are your salaries?

W: Salaries are good and there are monthly, performance-related cash bonuses. Staff also set their own targets for the coming year, and for the most part they have a say in their incentives too. Our accountant has just got the new Audi A3. He chose it, and he's delighted.

I: And how about the atmosphere in the office. How do you influence that?

W: We have a company bar, where we offer free breakfasts, and cappuccino all day long. People spend an awful lot of time in there discussing ideas over coffee, but it's very productive.

I: The vast majority of your staff say that they admire their managers, and feel that they can actively contribute to the future success of the company. How did you achieve this?

W: Well, one of the things is that we help them with finding somewhere nice to live. Rent is very expensive in London, and as lots of our employees are fresh out of university, with a lot of debts, they don't have a huge budget for accommodation. So, we've bought some properties, and quite a few staff rent them from us at reasonable rates. It makes a real difference. It means that working for the company becomes a lifestyle choice. They are involved personally. Also, we like to give people a say in the company. We have monthly meetings to discuss big issues, when we all sit around and talk about things. Initially, only a handful of people would come to the meetings. So we decided to offer free food, sandwiches and pizza, so now everyone comes, and everyone has something to say.

Track 1.31
K=Keith, B=Bridget

K: Well, I'd replace these chairs for a start. No wonder I've got backache.
B: Oh come on, we can do better than that. How about blowing it all on an all-expenses-paid jaunt to the West Indies or something?
K: Erm … would you really want to go on holiday with the rest of the staff?
B: Well, no, but … erm …
K: I think it should go on day-to-day things that'll make a difference in the long term, like renovating the office.
B: God, how boring.
K: Or maybe … what d'you mean boring?!
B: Well, it's loads of money – let's have some fun! The company could get a house by the sea that the employees could use whenever they were on holiday.
K: Yeah, but that would only be useful once every few years for each person. I mean it wouldn't make the least bit of difference really. My main priority would be to do something practical with the money …

Audioscripts

Track 2.01
E=Expert

E: The Great Pyramid is arguably the most accomplished engineering feat of the Ancient World. Built to house the body of the dead pharaoh, the base of the Great Pyramid in Egypt is 230 metres squared, large enough to cover ten football fields. According to the Greek historian Herodotus, it took 400,000 men 20 years to construct this great monument. They used 2.3 million blocks of stone, some of which weighed as much as 50 tonnes!

'La Tour Eiffel' in Paris was built in 1889 to commemorate the 100th anniversary of the French Revolution. The Industrial Revolution in Europe had brought about a new trend – the use of metal in construction. The tower, built from a lattice made from very pure iron, is light and able to withstand high wind pressures. For 40 years from the time that it was built, it stood as the tallest tower in the world, and still today it is the tallest building in Paris.

The Sydney Harbour Bridge is one of Australia's best known, and most photographed landmarks. It is the world's largest (but not the longest) steel arch bridge with the top of the bridge standing 134 metres above the harbour. Fondly known by the Australians as the 'coathanger', Sydney Harbour Bridge celebrated its 70th birthday in 2002, with its official opening in March 1932. Nowadays, a group of 12 people leave every ten minutes to climb to the top of the bridge and admire spectacular views of the city, and out to the Tasman Sea.

The Pentagon, covering 13.8 hectares, is thought to be the largest office building in the world. It takes a person 15 to 20 minutes to walk around the building once. It was built in five concentric rings, in record time during the Second World War, in order to relocate employees of the War Department from the 17 buildings they occupied within Washington D.C.

Built between 1406 and 1420 during the Ming dynasty, The Forbidden City, also called the Purple Forbidden City, or Gugong Museum in Chinese, is located in the centre of Beijing, PRC. Occupying a rectangular area of more than 720,000 square meters, the Forbidden City was the imperial home of 24 emperors of the Ming (1368–1644) and Qing (1644–1911) dynasties. It is one of the largest and best-preserved palace complexes in the world, with over a million rare and valuable objects in the Museum.

Opening on 31st December, 1999, the Millennium Dome was built to celebrate the new millennium. The massive dome is over one kilometre round and 50 metres high at its centre. It covers 20 acres of ground floor space. How big is that? Well, imagine the Eiffel Tower lying on its side. It could easily fit inside the Dome. With its 100 metre steel masts and translucent roof, the Dome was meant to paint a portrait of the nation. Unfortunately, the project became one of the most controversial in Britain, due to its enormous cost, and doubts about how to best utilise the space after 2000.

Hassan II Mosque, in Casablanca, Morocco, was built for the 60th birthday of former Moroccan king Hassan II. It is the largest religious monument in the world after Mecca. It has space for 25,000 worshippers inside and another 80,000 outside. The 210-metre minaret is the tallest in the world and is visible day and night for miles around. The mosque includes a number of modern touches: it was built to withstand earthquakes and has a heated floor, electric doors, a sliding roof, and lasers which shine at night from the top of the minaret toward Mecca.

Track 2.02
J=Jodie, I=Interviewer

J: I think, with technology, it was Microsoft that started it.

I: 'It' being the use of teenagers ...

J: Using teenagers really to find out what's in and what isn't, what the market wants next. Around the year 2000, they started observing these kids to find out what they were doing with technology.

I: And this was an American thing?

J: It was ... well, no, actually they went all over the place observing these kids: from street markets in Seattle to skating rinks in London, bars in Tokyo, anywhere they thought trends might kick off.

I: So the idea was to watch these children, or teenagers, and learn what they wanted to do with their mobile phones, with software ...

J: That's right. Because it's teenagers that really drive technology. Kids have no fear of technology. They experiment and they automatically home in on the new. One thing that became clear is that teenagers want technology they can carry around. Anything bigger than a few inches is out. That's why there was the development of these tiny mobile phones that could be attached to your arm, that type of thing. Text messaging caught on because kids wanted to pass notes to each other during class. The lights that you find on IBM's ThinkPad keyboard are there because IBM noticed that kids take notes in the dark during lectures.

I: So all of these things came about because of the needs of kids.

J: That's right.

I: And what's coming up on the horizon? Is there any big new development that has been led by teenagers?

J: Well, the next big area is collaborative computing, where you have groups of people working together online. This is really going to take off in the next few years, because it has massive potential for working environments in the sense that you may be able to work simultaneously on a project with someone who's on the other side of the world, moving data around together.

I: So is it just technology with these kids?

J: You mean where teenagers are leading the market?

I: Yes.

J: Not at all. I mean, fashion has been youth-led for years and years, but in particular, trainers. Now, if you want to keep up with the latest style of trainers, who do you ask? You don't ask anyone over 20, that's for sure. And I think it was Converse trainers who used to do lots of their market research on the streets, on the basketball courts of New York, anywhere you find teenagers. They may still do this, I don't know.

I: And, what, they just talk to these kids?

J: Talk to them, watch what they are wearing, the colours, the style, and maybe bring in a prototype, ask the kids if they'd wear these. If not, why not?

Track 2.03
A=Alison, J=Jim, M=Mark, L=Leah
Dialogue 1

A: It depends on the age.

J: Uh huh.

A: 'Cos when they're young teenagers, no I don't think so.

J: What kind of limits would you put on, say, a 15-year-old?

A: Depends. There are some places that are not for teenagers but still they want to go to these places. I wouldn't let my 15-year-old go to a bar.

Dialogue 2

A: Teenagers? I don't think so.

J: Really? Why not?

A: Because they ... they can't ... er, well, they still can't evaluate what they're seeing and how much time they're spending. They could be doing other things.

J: It's not that good for them either, is it, their eyes. And sort of, it's a bit passive, can be a bit passive.

Dialogue 3

M: Oh, definitely, yeah. They're our friends.

L: Me too. If parents can choose who they hang out with, then we should too.

M: What's the difference?

L: Exactly. It's not like we're stupid and can't judge someone's character.

Dialogue 4

L: I think if it's a school day the next day, then it makes sense to have some kind of limit.

M: Yeah, but who sets the limit? If you know you're gonna be OK on six hours' sleep or something ...

L: Yeah, you should discuss it, but if you're going to be exhausted in the morning then that's not really ...

M: I'm saying it's not up to the parents to dictate it. We know how to switch off the lights, don't we?

Track 2.06
1

Looking after rabbits is really easy. The first thing you need to do, before you even get the rabbits, is to plan where they're going to be and to make sure that you buy, erm, a hutch that's the right size for your rabbits, so that they're comfortable, and make sure that your hutch is going to be in a position where they're not exposed to anything. So you need to plan well. Once you've got your rabbits, erm, basically you feed them twice a day. Erm, you have to make sure they like the food they're given. It can be a bit tricky because they're a bit picky about what they eat, rabbits, so you need to make sure you give them the right thing. You have to clean them out once a week or more, er, so you need, er, fresh straw and hay. It's best to get it from a farmer because it's cheaper. Erm ... and you need to have them vaccinated against myxomatosis because they can come in contact with wild rabbits and then they can get ill. Erm, apart from that, that's it really.

2

It seems pretty straightforward, but actually there are lots of things that can go wrong when you choose a dog. A lot of people, for example, just go for the, erm ... the cutest dog they can find, which is understandable, but not the right way to go about it. The first thing you've got to do is er, to ask yourself a number of questions. Will you have enough time to walk the dog and give her attention? Can you afford a dog? I mean, people often forget that it isn't just food; you also have to pay a vet if the dog gets sick. Do you have enough space in the house? So, once you've answered these questions, the next thing is to think about what type of dog. If you buy a puppy, you need to consider how big and active it will be once it's grown up, and this depends on the breed. But, different breeds have different characteristics. If you have quite an active lifestyle it's OK to get a chihuahua or a doberman, but if you spend most of your time at home watching TV, get a less active dog, like a Saint Bernard. The key thing is to do your research before you buy. Talk to other dog owners and vets and maybe look in the library.

Track 2.09
D=David

D: The first thing I noticed when I entered the bureaucrat's office was that it was bright white, like a doctor's surgery or the cell of a madman. There were a few filing cabinets next to the desk and a huge photo of the king staring at us from the wall. The air was thick and a fan droned weakly, whirring overhead as a gang of flies zig-zagged across the air.
The bureaucrat behind his desk looked up to greet me.
'How can I help you?' he said. I told him I needed a visa for my trip to the Danakil Depression, and he asked me if I'd ever been in a desert. 'I've been in many,' I replied. He shifted in his chair and said, 'The Danakil Depression is the world's hottest place. It's not a tourist site. There's nothing there but hot air and salt.' I told him I knew that, and that's why I wanted to go there. 'Typical British,' he said. 'Obsessed by the weather.'
He asked me what I'd do if I got lost, and I told him I wouldn't. 'And what about the three s's?' he said. 'What three s's?' 'Snakes, spiders and scorpions. What if you get bitten?' 'I won't.' He stared at me again, glanced at my passport, and with a resounding thump, stamped it. 'One visa,' he said. 'This will get you into Danakil, but it won't get you out.'

Track 2.10
D=David

D: Going to the Danakil Depression means walking into hell on Earth. The land is sunk 100 metres below sea level and the place is a furnace. The air shakes, warped by the sun. Even the wind brings no relief from the heat. Almost everything around you is dead: stumps of trees, cracked earth, the occasional white glow of animal bones.
Along the way we saw a group of bandits on camels, brandishing their weapons. They waved and went on riding. Salt statues loomed out of the spectacular landscape, three metres high, vibrant colours and shapes from another world. An active volcano was hunched on the horizon, biding its time. We stopped to visit a ghost town, with its abandoned shacks stripped bare by the wind and the nomads and the scavenging animals. This was Danakil, where an American company had tried to set up a business in the 60s and been defeated by the heat. The ruined buildings made of salt blocks were now crumbling away, and there were

metal tracks in the ground where they had tried to build a railway but which now led nowhere.
For three days my shirt was drenched and my mouth parched. Even covered up against the sun, my skin baked and burned, and there seemed no escape from the cauldron of heat. They tell you to drink 12 litres of water a day, to remember to drink even when you're not thirsty, but it's never enough.
When we finally arrived at our destination I felt empty, as if everything had been a mistake. I didn't regret going to Danakil, but the land was so inhospitable that permanent settlement seemed impossible, and it felt wrong being there, as if we were trespassing on a place nature had intended only for itself.

Track 2.11
1 A monkey costs as little as that?
2 It's as big as an elephant.
3 We're as happy as can be.

Track 2.12
Example
A: You've got bad eyesight haven't you?
B: I'm as blind as a bat.
1 You're free now, aren't you?
2 You're strong, aren't you?
3 You're quiet, aren't you?

Track 2.13
R=Rachel, G=Graham

R: Well, it's a piece of land that's about 50 square kilometres, so there's really quite a lot you could do with it, but I mean I don't really know, I don't really have any expertise in managing the land. I don't know about you, Graham, but have you got any ideas what we could do with it?
G: Well, when I see 50 square kilometres of land, I think money. I think ...
R: Ha, that's typical!
G: Well, yeah. I think, you know, a hotel will be great here. I think there's enough room for it, and as it's in the middle of, you know, this kind of wonderful environmental area that we could really sell it.
R: Yeah, but the problem with the hotel is that you, I mean, the land's got this, these really lovely environmental features, you've got these lovely hilly bits and there's all these lovely bits, and you know it's quite a little forest down there. Perhaps it would be nicer to do something that's kind of more sympathetic with the environment, you know, like erm, you could leave it, we could leave it wild and just let the animals roam free, or you could have like a more organised animal sanctuary, erm, to really, you know, get the most out of, of the features of the land. There's a lot of wildlife.
G: What would we get out of that?
R: It's good for the environment, Graham. I mean, it's doing something good, and giving something back to, to the Earth, and making sure that they, you know, these sort of, erm, animal species are left to, to live in their own environment.
G: Mm. OK. Perhaps not a hotel then, but I think we could think of, you know, a commercial use that would fit in more with the environment. What about some kind of health resort, maybe?
R: Well, that's quite a nice idea because there's, you know, there's so much land and, you know, people could go walking in the hills, and we could do nature trails

through the forest. Erm, we could even have like a little organic garden or, you know, provide food that's really fresh and healthy because it's ... the land's really good for growing vegetables and things like that and it's a great climate in this area, so you know, maybe that's a nice idea, we could have an organic health spa. What do you think?
G: Hm ... yeah, that's a nice idea.

Track 2.14
1
That's a good question. Erm, I think I'd like some kind of gadget that means I don't have to clean the house. Like a machine or a robot that tidies everything away. Does the washing up, the ironing. Either that or get a maid.
2
A time machine. Not so I could go back and see earlier civilisations and dinosaurs (I mean, who cares about dinosaurs?) but so I could go back this morning and hit that guy who took my parking space.
3
Ooh, that's a difficult question. I'd have to think about it. Well, I wouldn't mind a weather machine, with me in control, of course. So when my friends go on holiday, I could make it rain every day and they'd stop telling me how beautiful the weather was.
4
That's tricky. How about a pill that you can substitute for food, so no one would need to starve? And so I wouldn't have to cook.
5
Let me see. You could have a pill that makes you extremely intelligent. You'd take it just before every exam or whenever the computer breaks down.
6
Well, I'd like to invent a special device that could take you to other places but only in your mind. Like a hat or glasses that give you all the sensations of being there. Then I'd use these glasses to go straight to a beach in Hawaii and spend the week there instead of in the office with all these other idiots.
7
I'd invent a clock that extends hours of the day when you need it. Like every morning when I'm lying in bed and have to get up.

Track 2.15
T=Thomas, E=Elise

T: I was on a business trip in Rome a few years ago. I'd been having dinner with a client all evening, and afterwards I discovered that the Internet connection in my hotel wasn't working. So there I was at midnight, wandering around one of the most beautiful cities in the world, and I was tearing my hair out trying to get Internet access. Anyway, I went back to the hotel, lay down on my bed and thought, do I really have to live like this? Are those emails really so important? And it just seemed as if my life in the fast lane meant I was missing out on other, more important things. So anyway I started to reappraise my life. The world is one stressed-out place. When I go to cities now, I see everyone rushing around with their mobile phones and everyone's scared they're going to miss something. You know, just before we die, no one ever says, 'Ooh, I wish I'd spent more time working in the office.' Rome was a wake-up call for me. After leaving my job, I moved to the coast. I sell surfing gear now. It doesn't make much cash, but then money isn't the be-all and end-all. To be honest, I just go with the flow and try to enjoy every day. I'm happier than ever before because I think living by the sea gives you a certain perspective on life. The waves will be rolling in every morning long after we're gone. And it makes you realise all that rushing around isn't going to make any difference.

E: I've been working in an investment company for about four years. It's a very competitive business, of course, and you have to know about every fluctuation in the market even as it's happening. So I live a very fast-paced, high-pressure lifestyle. Basically, we work around the clock. A lot of my job is done on the move, so I carry my office around with me: laptop, phone, Blackberry. I suppose you could call these my weapons of war! I don't live a particularly healthy lifestyle: I grab a sandwich when I can and drink far too much coffee. But it's not going to be like this forever. Most people in my profession burn out after three and a half years. In fact, the statistics are getting worse – I think it's under three years now. So by the time I'm 40, 45, I'll be slowing down a bit. If I get some kind of golden opportunity in another field I might change career earlier, but I don't have itchy feet. I like what I do. And I don't think I'll ever live on a farm in the middle of nowhere with my slippers on, growing vegetables. I'd hate that. I enjoy the buzz too much.

Track 2.17

M=Man, W=Woman
Dialogue 1

M: This stupid thing keeps getting jammed.
W: What, again?
M: I can't get it to make any copies.
W: It happened to me yesterday. Give it a good kick.
   Is that better?
M: Well, I feel better, yeah, but it's still not working.

Dialogue 2

W: See? It's always coming up with the same message.
M: You have performed an illegal operation. Ooh, naughty.
W: See? I don't know how to make it shut down normally.
M: Have you tried dropping it onto the floor?
W: What?
M: Or shouting at it? That works sometimes.
W: You're not funny.

Dialogue 3

M: I'm having problems switching it on.
W: Oh really?
M: This thing seems to be stuck. It won't go round.
W: Oh yes.
M: Which means I can't get any air in here. And it's so hot.
W: Right in the middle of summer as well. You can always open the windows.
M: Oh! Yeah, thanks.

Track 2.18

I=Interviewer, E=Expert

I: What can you tell us about what happens when geniuses relax?
E: Without a doubt, we can be sure that great scientists don't always make their discoveries in the lab. Archimedes's famous 'Eureka' moment came while he was having a bath. Physicist Richard Feynman saw a plate flying through the air in a college cafeteria, and was inspired to calculate electron orbits. He later won the Nobel Prize. And Alexander Fleming was making mould for his hobby, microbe painting, when he accidentally came across *Penicillium notatum*, later known as penicillin.
I: So what does this tell us?
E: Well, we're looking into the psychology of high achievers. A recent study by Robert Root-Bernstein compared the hobbies of 134 Nobel-prize winning chemists to those of other scientists. He found that the Nobel prize winners were accomplished outside the lab. Over half were artistic and almost all had a long-lasting hobby: chess or insect collecting. Twenty-five percent of the Nobel-prize winners played a musical instrument and 18 percent drew or painted regularly. Of the normal scientists, under one percent had a hobby.
I: Fascinating. So should we conclude then, that only a creative person can be a genius?
E: Well, I think that's debatable. Perhaps it's true up to a point, but I don't think it's as clear-cut as that. What we do know is that to a certain extent, creative thinking can help people to solve problems, even scientific ones. That if you are thinking about a problem all the time, often the answer eludes you. But it may come in an inspiration when you are least expecting it – perhaps when you're asleep, or thinking about other things, doing a hobby, for example. It's not 100 percent certain, but it seems that the mind has the ability to make connections from one part of your life to another, so that actually stepping back from a problem can often provide the answer. And people who are good at making these connections, people who pursue creative hobbies and interests, often excel in their particular fields.

Track 2.19

A=Abby, B=Becs, C=Chris
Dialogue 1

A: What do you think of this one?
B: Erm ... it's OK. To be honest, it's not really my taste. I'm not really into this style of portrait. And it sort of looks like a photo to me.
C: Yeah, you have to get up really close to it to see that it's a painting.
A: What do you think of it?
C: I really like it, actually.
A: Me too.
C: I like the colours, and the expression on her face is kind of intense.
A: It's a bit enigmatic, isn't it? You don't really know what she's thinking. And the details too. You can almost see the pores of her skin. Don't you think?
B: Well, as I was saying, it really does look like a photo – the detail is amazing, so as far as the skill is concerned, and the technique, I think it's great, but to tell you the truth, I still wouldn't want it hanging on my bedroom wall.

Dialogue 2

A: I love this one.
C: He's just got such an interesting face, hasn't he? He looks like one of those hippy poets from the 70s.
A: With that big beard.
C: With that big beard and the shirt.
B: Is it Hawaiian, that shirt?
C: And the medallion.
A: Oh yeah, I didn't notice that.
C: As a matter of fact, I prefer this one to the other one. At any rate, I think it's more interesting visually.
A: How about this one for your bedroom wall?

B: Nope. 'Fraid not. Mind you, I'd put it in the bathroom.

Dialogue 3

B: I think this one's great.
C: It's kind of menacing isn't it?
B: For me, what's interesting is that they are in a group, almost like a gang with this uniform.
C: The jeans and white T-shirts.
B: Exactly, except for the guy sitting in the middle. Now he's the only one sitting and looking directly at us, sort of challenging us, so maybe he's the boss.
A: Well, what I noticed is that, as you said, they're in a group, but somehow they look isolated. They're all facing in different directions and they don't seem to relate to each other at all.
C: And I wonder why it's called 'La Familia'. They obviously aren't a family in any traditional sense. At any rate, they don't look like a family, so it's kind of intriguing. I think this one should win, actually.
A: Me too.

Track 2.20

A=Abby, C=Chris

C: So which one won in the end?
A: Which do you think?
C: Well, as I said before, my favourite is 'La Familia', but ...
A: That one didn't win.
C: Oh really?
A: The winner was 'Giulietta Coates', the one that looks like a photo.
C: Right. Well, I think it's really good too, but it isn't my favourite.

Track 2.24

E=Expert

E: Clarence Birdseye was a taxidermist from New York. On a visit to the Arctic he saw how the native people preserved their food by putting it in barrels of sea water, which froze quickly. This way, the food maintained its freshness for later. So in 1923 he bought a $7 electric fan, some ice, and some buckets of salt water and experimented by putting food in them. Birdseye's experiments worked, and he went on to become the pioneer of frozen foods in the Western world. In 1929 he sold the patent for $22 million and in 1930, frozen food went on sale for the first time in the United States.

As a young man, Chester Carlson's job involved making multiple copies of patent documents by hand. Writing everything down was difficult for Carlson because he was short-sighted and had arthritis, so in 1938 he invented a machine to make copies. He tried to get funding for his idea from all sorts of well-known companies, including IBM and General Electric, but they turned him down. Eventually, the company that became Xerox bought his idea, and the first photocopier was manufactured in 1959. Now there's hardly an office in the world that doesn't contain his invention.

Track 2.25

I=Interviewer, R=Richard

I: In June 1980, Maureen Wilcox became one of the US lottery's biggest losers. She bought tickets for the Rhode Island and Massachusetts draws and chose winning numbers for both. But her Massachusetts numbers would have won the Rhode Island lottery, and vice-versa. Meanwhile, lawyer John Woods was one of many to narrowly miss death in the Twin Towers on

September 11. Not that unusual, except that he also escaped the 1993 bombing there, and the Lockerbie plane crash in a similar way.

So, are some of us just born lucky? Is there a scientific reason why some people might seem luckier than others? With us today in the studio is Professor Richard Wiseman, who has studied 'lucky' and 'unlucky' people, and thinks that the differences between them must be related to their psychology. So, Richard, how are these two groups different?

R: Lucky people are more open to opportunity, and trust their hunches. They tend to be optimistic and expect good fortune. And when things go wrong, they are robust and resilient. They won't give up. We did some research, to see if people who thought they were lucky, actually won the lottery more often, and things like that. Well, it comes as no great surprise that they didn't actually win more often.

I: No? Right.

R: But there was something interesting happening. The lucky people had much higher expectations of winning. They didn't need to win. Their optimism was still boundless. And this is important. It's what psychologists call a positive delusion. Although it's a delusion, it's actually good for you because it keeps you trying. You can't win the lottery if you don't enter, and in many areas of life, having positive expectations makes a favourable outcome more likely.

I: Is that really the case? What areas of life are you talking about?

R: In business, for example, some people seem to have the knack for making a business work, while others are bound to go from one failed venture to another. We showed in our research that you can improve your business success by learning how to be 'lucky'. Let me explain. We teamed up with a management firm, and for five months, employees took part in a specially devised programme of lectures, questionnaires, meetings and assessments designed to make them think and behave like lucky people. This was a little different from the usual business motivational training. It was more about looking for opportunities by being relaxed, open and fluid rather than developing drive and focus. The results were impressive, with 54 percent of participants believing that their personal luck had increased, and 75 percent indicating that the company's luck had increased. But perhaps more importantly, this was borne out in hard sales figures – the company's income increased by 20 percent each month.

I: Wow, that is impressive. So Richard, can I ask you, are some people just born unlucky?

R: A survey in the UK showed that 50 percent of the population thought of themselves as lucky, and 14 percent as unlucky. Presumably, these two groups differ, in their behaviour and in their psychology. So I thought we ought to look at that. And our research showed that there were big differences. So, I guess if you say that your genes affect your personality, and your behaviour, which they no doubt do, then, yes, you could be right. Some people are born lucky, or unlucky.

Lucky people are likely to create opportunities for good fortune by being extrovert, sociable, and using open body language that gets people to respond to them. They are relaxed and easy-going, and therefore, more likely to notice chance opportunities that may turn into a lucky break. They also like variety and change. One man, for instance, breaks routine by thinking of a colour when he's on his way to a party. At the party he is supposed to speak only to people wearing that colour. This takes him out of his comfort zone of chatting to those he already knows, and brings him the prospect of new friends and new opportunities. Lucky people also have positive expectations of life and things tend to go their way. A famous experiment illustrates how this can work. Psychologists told American high school teachers that certain children in their class were especially gifted. In fact, there was nothing special about these pupils. The teachers shouldn't have treated them any differently, but they began to shower the 'special children' with extra praise and encouragement. And the children responded by producing better schoolwork, doing better in tests, and generally achieving more than the other children. This study shows the power of positive expectations ...

Track 2.26

1 He's bound to cheer up soon.
2 Aren't we supposed to register at the front desk?
3 You ought to make up your mind.

Track 2.28

1

It must have been amazing to be the first modern person to see Machu Picchu, after it had been covered by jungle for so long. Erm, I think it must have been pretty hard to get there, actually, because nowadays they've built a train, there's a little village nearby, near Cuzco, and it's ... urm, easier to get to. But, the first people that went there had to climb right up the side of the huge mountain without knowing that there was anything there at the top, so they must have been really driven people to ... to make themselves climb up there. But, although they might have felt the same atmosphere when they were arriving, it couldn't have been quite as spectacular as it is today because the ruins now are all there for you to see as soon as you arrive, but it must have had more of a mysterious air when they discovered it covered in vegetation and all hidden without really knowing what it was.

2

I've often wondered what it was like to have been in the first aeroplane to take off and really fly, not just like the Kitty Hawk going for a 10-second or a 30-second hop, but really climbing into the air. It can't have been easy because you have to realise those aircraft were not very sophisticated. They must have been difficult to fly – physically and even mentally – and you would've had to do lots of calculations that no one else has done before, and then of course it would have been incredibly exhilarating as the freedom increases as you go higher and higher, and then just think of all the doubts: how's this going to work out? Are you going to control it? And then coming in for the landing. How would that have been? In a way, you would know that this is going to be a crash, but a crash that you have to control, and that too couldn't have been easy.

3

I think Yuri Gagarin must have had, I think, missed, mixed emotions about being the first person in space. I think, on the one hand, there's that sort of thrill and excitement of ... of space travel, and the absolute awe of what he's experiencing, seeing Earth from space and being the first person to see that, having never even had any concept of what it might look like from space, and sort of, erm, just the complete vastness of space and just how amazing that must be. But on the other hand, sort of being up there on your own, basically in a tin can, you know, anything could have happened up there, um, he probably didn't know if he would get back home or not. He must have felt alone and also probably quite scared as well.

Track 2.29

1

During my childhood, my parents moved quite a lot, so I was always changing schools, and starting new schools. In fact, in about six years I think we changed school three times, so it was quite often. And that was quite difficult, er, because just when you've met new friends and you've got used to the teachers and the lessons, then you're told you've got to do it all again. It's true that I got quite lonely and I found it quite difficult to relate to other children, especially because they all knew the area, they already had their small groups of friends, and I was slightly out of it. Erm, but this also made me very outgoing, because if I wasn't going to be outgoing and energetic, and entertaining, erm ... it was going to ... I was never going to have those friends. So, er, it was difficult. Sometimes I did feel quite lonely, and I did feel as if it was hard work each time, but I'm lucky that I now have a lot of friends because of it.

2

I think one of my worst memories of childhood is probably a sport-related memory because I'm not really a sporty kind of girl. Erm, I grew up in central Manchester and my school was kind of in the middle of an industrial estate, and lots of shops and ... and things like that. And they used to make us go cross-country running every week, so we'd be out there, in the rain, and the wind, and the snow in the middle of Manchester with the traffic roaring by, running around in our little shorts and T-shirts, looking like complete idiots – I absolutely hated it. I used to dread Mondays, because I knew PE lessons were coming up, and it was just going to be absolute torture. I'm still the same now. I still hate sports, and running is just one of the sports I hate the most I think. It's just something that I find so uncomfortable and so unpleasurable, so yeah that's probably my worst memory of childhood.

3

When I was a child, er, when I was a very little girl, we used to go to Majorca nearly every year. It was a real family holiday and my grandparents came as well. Erm, the last time I went we must have been about seven, I suppose. I don't remember the first few times in fact. I don't remember catching a plane. The thing I remember most vividly, um, is arriving in Majorca, and the wall of heat that used to hit us every time we got off the plane. Erm, and the smell of the air, that was so different from England. It was a fantastic smell. And I remember the things that um children remember about holidays, rather than anything too cultural. I remember the pool, I remember how blue the pool was – we used to swim every day, and the breakfasts that went on forever. Just the way the routine was completely different from what we did at home. And er the way we met people from all over the world. We made friends with a Norwegian family one year, and kept in touch with them, which was lovely. So it's just really the colours and smells that er take me back there. I haven't been there since 'cause I don't really want to spoil it. I think the magic of it might go if I was to see it now as an adult.

4
During the summer holidays, I lived in the back of a wood. Er, my parents' garden backed onto this small wood, and I used to climb over the garden fence and my friends and I used to play in the wood, literally all day. We used to climb trees, run in and out of bushes and just have a general laugh and it was just great. It was just a great sense of freedom, that you should really have when you're a child. And it was just essentially a very very good and happy time.

Track 2.30

1
Oh my goodness, I went to the most amazing restaurant last night. You would not believe it, I've never seen anything like it in my life. It was called um, it was called The Bentley and it was in South Kensington, and it was the most fascinating building 'cause it was one of those lovely old Georgian terraces that's been turned into a boutique hotel, so it was all chandeliers and really plush sofas, and incredible service. I mean, they were so polite and charming. The food was kind of French style, but it was very modern haute cuisine, and we had what's called a 'grazing' menu, which was terribly expensive but extremely exciting, because you get little plates of food. Erm, I think we had seven courses in total.

2
I just, I can't stand public transport in this country. I mean, despite the fact that it's expensive and unreliable, it's just so ridiculously complicated. Just look at trains, for example. There must be about twenty different ticket types. And it all depends on when you're travelling, what time of day, how far before you booked your ticket, it's just ridiculous. So for example, you could be sitting on a train and the person sitting opposite you could've paid ten times the amount for their ticket just because they happened to buy it on a different day. I don't understand why we don't have systems like in other countries where you just pay per kilometre and then pay perhaps an upgrade if you get on a faster train. As it is now, it's just so complicated and I, I just, personally I choose not to use it.

3
Well, I really hate smoking and I just think it should be banned completely because it's not ... people who don't smoke ... it's so unfair for us, erm, you know, you're breathing in other people's smoke and you smell of smoke at the end of the day when you've been with a smoker and you know, it's obviously not good for the smoker, but it's not good for the non-smoker either. Erm and it's really quite repulsive that you have to breathe in somebody's second-hand smoke. And, er, smokers will say, well, you know, we'll go to a part of the restaurant where it doesn't affect you or we'll go outside, but it does because even if you're outside and you're walking behind somebody who is smoking then you're breathing in their smoke. Erm, and I think they should just ban it because it's one of the few bad habits that really does affect everybody else. I mean, if you're drinking, it's only doing your body harm, but if you're smoking then you're doing harm to everybody else's body who is around you, and it's not really acceptable.

ActiveBook and ActiveTeach contents

The ActiveBook component features the Students' Book pages in digital format and includes integrated audio and video as well as interactive exercises for students to do in class or at home. The ActiveTeach component will help you get the most out of the course with its range of interactive whiteboard software tools and extra resources.

ActiveBook

Students' Book pages and interactive activities

Audio bank (Class CD material)

Video clips

Interactive video activities

Phonetic chart and dictionary

Video clips to play on a DVD player

ActiveTeach

Students' Book pages and interactive activities

Interactive whiteboard tools with save functionality

Audio bank (Class CD material)

Video clips

Interactive video activities

Phonetic chart and dictionary

Extra resources for the teacher:
- class photocopiables
- video photocopiables
- printable audio and video scripts
- editable tests

Video clips to play on a DVD player

Pearson Education Limited
Edinburgh Gate
Harlow
Essex CM20 2JE
England
and Associated Companies throughout the world.

www.pearsonELT.com

First published 2012

ISBN: New Total English Advanced Teacher's Book and Teacher's Resource Disc Pack 9781408267257

Set in Meta Plus Book-Roman
Printed in Slovakia by Neografia

Cover photo © *Front* : **Getty Images:** Mark A Paulda